I0883074

Selected Verse

ALGERNON CHARLES SWINBURNE was born in London in 1837 to an aristocratic family. As an undergraduate in Oxford, he made the acquaintance of D. G. Rossetti, William Morris and Edward Burne-Jones, all of whom would influence his work. Returning to London without having completed his degree, he continued to associate with many leading figures of the Aesthetic Movement. The dramatic poem *Atalanta in Calydon* (1865) established his literary reputation, and he followed this success with a collection, *Poems and Ballads* (1866), which made him the most controversial English poet of the day. Many other volumes followed, including *Songs Before Sunrise* (1871), two more series of *Poems and Ballads* (1878 and 1889), the Arthurian epic *Tristram of Lyonesse* (1882), and several plays. Swinburne was also an important critic of modern and early-modern literature. During his two decades in London (1860-1879), his bohemian lifestyle was infamous, and the period was marred by ill-health and alcoholism. In 1879 his friend Theodore Watts-Dunton brought him to his own home in Putney, where he could be looked after. Here Swinburne remained, still writing, until his death in 1909.

ALEX WONG studied English literature at the University of Cambridge, completing his doctoral research on Renaissance 'kissing poems'. He has published essays and articles on English and Latin poetry.

Fyfield*Books* aim to make available some of the great classics of British and European literature in clear, affordable formats, and to restore often neglected writers to their place in literary tradition.

Fyfield*Books* take their name from the Fyfield elm in Matthew Arnold's 'Scholar Gypsy' and 'Thyrsis'. The tree stood not far from the village where the series was originally devised in 1971.

Roam on! The light we sought is shining still.
Dost thou ask proof? Our tree yet crowns the hill,
Our Scholar travels yet the loved hill-side

from 'Thyrsis'

A. C. Swinburne

Selected Verse

EDITED AND INTRODUCED BY
ALEX WONG

FB
Fyfield*Books*

CARCANET

First published in Great Britain in 2015 by
Carcanet Press Limited
Alliance House
Cross Street
Manchester M2 7AQ

www.carcanet.co.uk

We welcome your comments on our publications
Write to us at info@carcanet.co.uk

Selection, introduction, and editorial matter: © Alex Wong, 2015

The right of Alex Wong to be identified as the editor of this work
has been asserted by him in accordance with the
Copyright, Designs and Patents Act of 1988
All rights reserved

A CIP catalogue record for this book is available from the British Library

ISBN 9781784100414

The publisher acknowledges financial assistance from Arts Council England

Supported by
ARTS COUNCIL
ENGLAND

Typeset by XL Publishing Services, Exmouth

Contents

Acknowledgements

I am grateful to my editors at Carcanet for making this book a possibility, and then a reality. My greatest thanks go to Michael Schmidt, who suggested the idea, having known me only a short while, and then trusted me to get it right. Helen Tookey was my first managing editor for this edition, and Luke Allan, who later took over that role, has overseen the final transformation of my drafts into a book. They have been patient, sensitive and accommodating, and I thank them both very warmly.

I am also grateful to various friends with whom I have spoken about this project. Especially I recall conversations with Alison Hennegan, Robin Holloway and (a fellow enthusiast) Laura Kilbride. And many thanks are due to Arabella Milbank, who cheerfully and expeditiously supplied the translations from Swinburne's invented French epigraphs.

Orla Polten has offered several pieces of advice that I should have been embarrassed to have gone without. I wish to give her my particular thanks, apologising, also, for having omitted 'On the Cliffs' (a favourite of hers).

Finally I would like to thank Sarah Green for her support and advice throughout the preparation of this book, and for her help in scrutinizing the proofs. Without her conversation, my introduction would have lacked a number of choice anecdotes and quotations.

If, in my introductory appreciations, I have taken some liberties such as scholars do not expect of one another, I hope to be forgiven much, *quoniam dilexi multum*. What is mine in this edition is dedicated to those friends who love Swinburne the most; and also, optimistically, to those who have hitherto liked him least. But it must also be dedicated to the Venerable Shade himself.

Introduction

ALGERNON CHARLES SWINBURNE was one of the most important poets of the nineteenth century. This is a point against which it would be hard to argue. But as one of the foremost poets of his century, he was also one of the most important poets in the whole of English literature; and for much of the last hundred years this judgement—this valuation of Swinburne not only as a major figure in his time, but as a great author of lasting significance—has met with much less broad consent.

Swinburne's significance is permanent. He had a remarkable ear for the subtleties of poetic sound, and a phenomenal facility in composition. His technical skill was kept in motion by an impulse to innovate and surprise, both in matter and in form. As one old friend of his youth said at the time of his death, 'Song was his natural voice'.[1] It did not take long for the literary world to recognise what is perhaps insufficiently minded now, that Swinburne was one of the greatest writers of lyric in the history of the language. He was also one of the most controversial authors of the Victorian age—and in that guise he has been better remembered.

His music was very much his own. Even in the wake of Tennyson, who was praised for the delicate musical judgement of his verse, Swinburne immediately stood out as a special case. Though just as discerning in matters of melody and euphony, his effects drew more attention to themselves; they were bold and often dramatic in their semblance of spontaneity. They were more exaggerated. As an experimenter with many metrical forms, he was rivalled in ambition by other poets of the age—Clough

1 George Meredith, obituary letter to *The Times*, 19 April 1909. For this and subsequent quotations see *The Letters of George Meredith*, ed. C. L. Cline, 3 vols (Oxford, 1970).

before him, for instance, and Meredith alongside him, not to mention Tennyson himself. And in its changeful fluency and songlike modulation, Swinburne's versification was at times very close to that of another great writer of lyric, Christina Rossetti, his friend. But his most characteristic effects were, in combination and certainly in sum, different from those of his peers: novel, emphatic, and yet at the same time persuasively 'natural' in movement. This musicality is more than a matter of sound alone: it has to do with the organization of the meanings of words; so that in Swinburne, to read the verse as it is designed to be read is to *understand* musically as well as to *hear* musically—more so, perhaps, than in any other poet of his age.

But his versification was not the only thing that made Swinburne a special case in the 1860s, when he first achieved fame. Since the late 1850s he had been part of the circle of Dante Gabriel Rossetti, drawing inspiration from his association with the likes of William Morris, Edward Burne-Jones and George Meredith, as well as all three of the literary Rossettis. But he had also been reading a range of French authors, including not only Victor Hugo, his lifelong hero, but also the most decadent of the moderns—Gautier, and, above all, Baudelaire. The 'divine' Marquis de Sade, too, found a place in Swinburne's personal canon, despite the disappointment and boredom of his initial reading. In the 1866 *Poems and Ballads*, Swinburne blended the late-Romantic, medievalist sensuousness of the Rossetti circle (which was itself already voluptuous) with the more explicitly sexual, sado-masochistic themes that he found in his French authors. And so he became, among other things, the most important early 'Decadent' poet in English.

Many of the pieces included in the first *Poems and Ballads* were genuinely startling in their subversions and perversions. Friends and acquaintances advised him against publication of the most extreme, but Swinburne was not persuaded. Even a few months before publication, Meredith wrote to him:

> As to the Poems—if they are not yet in the Press, do be careful of getting your reputation firmly grounded; for I have heard 'low mutterings' already from the Lion of British prudery; and I, who love your verse, would play savagely with a knife among the proofs for the sake of your fame.

When the time came, the advice having gone unheeded, he wrote to another friend:

> Swinburne's poems are out. Oh, bawdry! Oh, nakedness! Oh, naughtiness.

As Meredith predicted, and Swinburne must have expected, the Lion did roar. In *The Saturday Review* on 4 August, John Morley's unsigned notice declared Swinburne 'the libidinous laureate of a pack of satyres', and—half-quoting the poem 'Faustine'—decried his 'nameless shameless abominations'. He also found the volume 'silly'. On the same day, *The Athenaeum* ran an anonymous review by Robert Buchanan, who glanced back at the 'considerable brilliance' of Swinburne's previous book, *Atalanta in Calydon*, before denouncing the new volume. Swinburne, in his view, was 'deliberately and impertinently insincere as an artist'; he was 'unclean for the mere sake of uncleanness'. Moxon, the publisher, flew into a panic and withdrew the book. The rights were transferred almost at once to John Camden Hotten, who knew a *succès de scandale* when he saw one.[2]

The stir was justified, because Swinburne's transgressions were something truly new in main-stream English poetry. Poems such as 'Fragoletta', with its ambiguous sexuality, and 'In the Orchard', with its rather less ambiguous eroticism, were not as disturbing as those which, to many, really sounded like statements of wicked intent. In 'Anactoria' Swinburne had adopted the voice of Sappho, addressing a female beloved in terms of the most ferocious sado-masochistic eroticism, with some overt blasphemy adding yet more offence to conventional proprieties. In 'Faustine', the poet's savage beloved is addressed as a reincarnation of the Empress Faustina, whose perverse bloodthirstiness is celebrated in similarly flamboyant terms. Most notorious of all was 'Dolores', a still more blasphemous song of praise to 'Our Lady of Pain'. Its celebration of erotic torment was continued in other pieces, such as 'Satia Te Sanguine', while the antipathy to Christianity was taken further in the 'Hymn to Proserpine', 'A Lamentation', 'Félise', and many other pieces.

2 For reviews, see Clyde K. Hyder (ed.), *Swinburne: The Critical Heritage* (London, 1970).

Antitheistic sentiment had also occasioned controversy in Swinburne's previous book (and first success), the dramatic poem *Atalanta in Calydon* (1865). But in *Poems and Ballads* it could not be so easily excused, and began to emerge clearly as one of the author's personal preoccupations. Time and again, he juxtaposed 'pale' Christian morality with the vibrant sensualism and 'sin' of the pagan world, and in so doing he played a major part in the initiation of an artistic tendency that lasted well into the next century. Even so, there were other times when, taking what Rossetti would call an 'inner standing-point' in his poems, Swinburne was able to enter convincingly into Christian feeling and imagination. 'St Dorothy' is the prime, but not the sole example in the 1866 collection; and in many of the later works this Christian empathy could stand alongside blasphemy, atheism and a general hostility to ecclesial religion.

With the 1866 *Poems and Ballads*, Swinburne was establishing a deliberately inflammatory poetic persona, which teasingly underlay the many of his poems that haunted the boundary between authorial utterance and dramatic monologue. Not every poem was equally extreme in flouting the moral conventions, but most were challenging and provocative in some other way. Even when least flagrantly decadent, his early poems were laden with the kind of bold sensualism that would a few years later get Rossetti into hot water.

But Decadence, except in its very worst manifestations, is never without some element of irony, and Swinburne's verse is sophisticated in its ironic range. When he is most shocking, he is also at his most humorous; and much of his best work is characterised by a deft balancing of world-weary melancholy with mischievous wit. The masochistic instincts that motivate 'Dolores' were sincere; they emerge from authentic experince; but the extravagant images, scandalous flourishes and absurd rhymes are meant to provoke a smile as well as a saucy frisson. Even in his private correspondence, Swinburne delights in baroque fantasies of perversion (his flagellation fetish was very real); but when indulging his reveries in this vein he always has his tongue in his cheek, and feels the need to inform his confidants when he is once again talking 'in my own person'. This, it must be insisted, does not diminish the authenticity of the feeling: his irony is not an abdication of the genuine. Almost always in Swinburne, as in the 'Pre-Raphaelite' verse of his friends Rossetti and Morris, there is an element of pastiche or parody—but 'serious parody', as Jerome McGann perceptively notes.[3]

The English Decadence that reached its zenith in the 'nineties would, no doubt, have happened anyway, with or without Swinburne's example. But Swinburne helped to determine its course, and exercised an inelusible influence on the later poets, many of whom adopted aspects of his classicism, his medievalism, and the prosodic mannerisms of his stanzaic verse, even if in most cases they were not more, but rather *less* inflammatory in their own work. The combination of his novel poetic persona, with all its dark ambiguities of tone, and his novelties of form, with all those captivating cadences and compelling rhythms, not only made *Poems and Ballads* an immediate *cause célèbre* in the 1860s; it made Swinburne what he is—a major poet, *sui generis*, of enduring importance.

The press, of course, greeted the untoward matter of Swinburne's most scandalous poems with general and strong disapprobation. But even some of the sternest critics were forced to concede that the young poet possessed a rare lyrical talent. Buchanan mounts his attack on the 'prurient trash' of *Poems and Ballads* in spite of 'many pages of brilliant writing'; and Morley, who could find space in his review to talk of 'sweet and picturesque lines' and 'passages of rare vigour', was interested by 'the music of his verse', even though he found it immoderate and inconsistent with precise thinking. It says much that on 9 September 1866 John Ruskin, for all his moral sensitivity and gravity, wrote with confused feelings to Swinburne, who had sent him a copy of the volume,—

> For the matter of it—I consent to much—I regret much—I blame or reject nothing. I should as soon think of finding fault with you as with a thundercloud or a nightshade blossom. All I can say of you, or them—is that God made you, and that you are very wonderful and beautiful.

3 *Major Poems*, ed. Jerome McGann and Charles L. Sligh (Yale, 2004), p. xxvi.

Many friendly presences in Swinburne's life felt, like Ruskin, that the power of his genius was great enough to pardon the vicious material, or at least to throw a veil of dumbstruck doubt over the whole matter. And like Ruskin, many felt that Swinburne's genius ought to be turned to nobler ends; but not many of them saw any point in attempting to convince the poet himself.

After 1866, however, the nature of the shocks that Swinburne administered to the reading public was largely changed. Although the poet's masochism continued to inform his poetry throughout his life, there would be no more poems like 'Dolores', 'Faustine' or 'The Leper'. Poems of sexual perversion, calculated to astonish, gave way, on the whole, to poems of fiery, indignant republicanism and anti-clerical polemic. Even by 1871 (which saw the publication of *Songs Before Sunrise*, Swinburne's first collection since 1866), the antitheistic vociferations of the earlier volume had been replaced by a more measured, considered, constructive metaphysical system, partly inspired by his studies of William Blake. 'Hertha' and 'Genesis', which are among the best poems of this period of Swinburne's career, ceased to rail so noisily against the Christian God, and instead offered their own imaginative solutions; while the incendiary tirade 'Before a Crucifix', however deliberately offensive to Christian sensibilities, took its aim at the Church rather than the person of Christ himself. The Swinburnean sensuality remained, and continued to be richly provocative; but in later years—especially in the vivid erotic scenes in *Tristram of Lyonesse*—the frisson would come not so much from glaringly 'strange' sexualities and exquisite depravity, as simply from a commitment to be frank and graphic about sexual experience as, in his mind, it was or might be.

THE PERSONALITY

Almost everything about Swinburne encouraged people to treat him as an exception to the ordinary rules. Even his physical appearance was strange. Edmund Gosse describes it as 'a kind of fairy look'.[4] Others considered him variously boyish and girlish, and many found him 'unearthly'. He was short, slight and pale, with sloping shoulders, delicate features and a weak chin. In youth, his large head was crowned by a luxuriant mass of long, dense, bright auburn hair. We read of his odd, 'gliding' walk; of how he had to cover one eye with his hand in order to read or write; of his amazing feats of memory, being able to recite interminably from the Greek dramas at the dinner table. Throughout his life, acquaintances remarked the incessant wavering and fluttering of his hands, and his legs seem to have jerked spasmodically when he was seated. In every way he seemed prodigious: he was the ideal genius. To some, he would become the paradigmatic degenerate artist.

Swinburne's wild behaviour in the 1860s and 1870s was infamous. His life at this time took on a mythical quality for the gossips of literary London. Anecdotes collected around him, many of them canards. From 1862 to 1864 he shared with D. G. Rossetti the famous house at Cheyne Walk in Chelsea; William Michael Rossetti and George Meredith also had rooms, but were less often there. The goings-on at Cheyne Walk became legendary. The insomniac Rossetti stayed in bed till the afternoon, entertaining an array of artistic friends, and populating the premises with wombats, armadilloes and various other strange creatures—including several different kinds of owl, and a pomeranian. Some reports have Swinburne running around the house naked, and launching himself down the bannisters. At any rate, his drinking was getting out of hand. When sober, he was a model of formal politeness; when drunk, his comportment struck many as lunatic. Tempers at the Chelsea house seem to have been regularly lost: Meredith supposedly had milk thrown in his face by Rossetti when he called the latter a fool, and a poached egg pelted at him by Swinburne, in defence of Victor Hugo. Meredith voluntarily gave up his room, but in the end Rossetti had to *ask* Swinburne to leave.

The Cheyne Walk years thus came to an end in reality, though

4 Edmund Gosse, *Life of Algernon Charles Swinburne* (London, 1917), p. 284 (ch. IX).

they would continue, ever after, to provide vivid matter for raconteurs, gossips and parodists. But Swinburne did not cease to give people things to talk about. His alcoholism became steadily worse, and fame after 1865 only fuelled his immoderate ways. Although there is probably some truth in Gosse's claim (which at first sight seems incredible) that Swinburne 'strove to avoid everything like affectation or eccentricity',[5] it seems clear that he enjoyed the notoriety; and he became, to some degree, a cultivator of canards.

A whole flock of canards was unleashed in 1868, when Swinburne almost drowned off the coast of Normandy while indulging his lifelong passion for the sea. By pure chance, it appears, a young man who would soon become one of the most important writers in France just happened to be walking along the shore at the critical moment. Swinburne was rescued by a fishing boat, but not before an eighteen-year-old Guy de Maupassant had supposedly set off to offer his own assistance. To show his gratitude, Swinburne invited Maupassant to lunch the next day at the rented cottage he was sharing with George Powell, one of his closest friends of the time, and the one most dedicated to decadent living and flagellatory fantasies. They must have enjoyed the visit, because the invitation was twice repeated.

Maupassant's recollections of these three memorable lunches are found in three places, and the accounts are somewhat contradictory. The first version was preserved in the Goncourt *Journal*, and is supposed to be a transcript of the account Maupassant gave over dinner one evening in 1875, as the guest of Flaubert. In 1882 he told the tale again, in an article in *Le Gaulois* under the title *L'Anglais d'Étretat*; and from this version he later produced another, included in his introduction to the 1891 French translation of *Poems and Ballads*. He tells of strong spirits, which nearly sent him into a swoon; of copious collections of German homosexual pornography; of the flayed, severed hand of a parricide, which Swinburne used as a paperweight; and of a monkey, kept as a pet, which harassed the nervous visitor. Maupassant gradually discovers that Swinburne and Powell are sodomising their domestics, boys around fourteen or fifteen years old, as well as the

5 *Ibid*, p. 289 (ch. IX).

monkey. On a later visit, the monkey has been hanged by a jealous servant, who is later chased out of the house by Powell, and possibly shot with a revolver. Maupassant declares his suspicion that the meat he had been given to eat, which he had initially mistaken for some kind of curious fish, was in fact monkey. He is, nevertheless, impressed by Swinburne's conversation, and proclaims him pre-eminently 'artistic'.

Similar stories continued to circulate, and the Goncourts' dinner parties were at the centre of them. On one such occasion, Turgenev was present to witness an excited debate about the veracity of a story told, at second-hand, by the author Ludovic Halévy (co-author of the libretto for Bizet's *Carmen* and several operettas by Offenbach). Halévy spoke about a young man he had once met, who claimed to have had an experience markedly similar to that described by Maupassant—but this time in the Isle of Wight, not Normandy.[6] Swinburne (so the story goes) is living on the beach, in a tent, with no company besides a monkey dressed as a woman. The monkey is both lover and servant. When the young man arrives, Swinburne attempts to seduce him, meanwhile whipping the monkey, who, in a fit of jealousy, attacks the visitor with murderous intent. On a subsequent visit, Swinburne—now waited on by an Irish butler—serves up the monkey to the young man for lunch. More likely it was *canard à la presse*, for the story sounds like the purest quintessence of canard. But one cannot dismiss the suspicion that Swinburne and Powell had deliberately set such stories in motion in the first place, by having given the young Maupassant a show to remember.

Swinburne's sexuality was a subject of inexhaustible rumour, and remains a subject of speculation. His emotional life was indelibly marked by an intense early attachment to a cousin, Mary Gordon, whose marriage to another badly affected him. The failure of this love, which never seems to have been supplanted, is now generally thought to have been the inspiration for 'The Triumph of Time', and many other poems of romantic disappointment. His sexual instincts were closely involved with his

6 See Philip Henderson, *Swinburne: The Portrait of a Poet* (London, 1974), pp. 147–49.

obsession with flogging, an interest dating to his school days at Eton, and which continued to be homosocial in expression (verbally), if not necessarily in commission. He often liked to skirt around the topic of male homosexuality, and female homosexuality was a recurrent theme in his work; but there is no plain evidence of his engaging in homosexual encounters, and even the evidence for full heterosexual encounters is slight only. His professed horror of sodomy, and the ostensibly sincere distaste with which he reacted to the disgrace of his erstwhile friend, the painter Simeon Solomon, when the latter was convicted of such acts, might well seem to indicate that Swinburne was, at any rate, in no *usual* sense homosexual.

Perhaps he was not *anything* in the 'usual' sense. In the 1860s and early 1870s he regularly visited a specialist brothel in St John's Wood where he was whipped by a couple of young ladies. It seems that the flagellation was not reciprocated, and it is not quite clear whether Swinburne also indulged in the activities for which ordinary brothels are chiefly used. His only known love-affair was a six-month fling with the controversial American actress and amateur poet Adah Menken, in 1867–68; and it was said that Swinburne's friends (variously Rossetti, Richard Burton and, oddest of all, the Italian *Risorgimento* activist Giuseppe Mazzini) had set up the whole business, worried that Swinburne needed a woman's influence, or that the thirty-year-old poet, in spite of his dealings with the whipping-girls, was inexperienced. But all of these biographical anecdotes tell us less—and less important things—than the poems themselves. What is important is that we should remember that Swinburne's sexual interests were no merely fashionable caprices, but profoundly involved with the whole of his emotional life; and these erotic emotions can only have been very imperfectly answered in St John's Wood. Above all, they were also involved with the other great focus of his thought and feeling, the realm of poetry; and they found their answers, their correlatives, it would seem, in an intense fusion with the aesthetic.

It is usual to think of Swinburne's biography as a story in two volumes. The person who exercised the most profound and lasting influence over the later period of his life was the author of *Aylwin*, Theodore Watts-Dunton. 'Watts' appeared in Swinburne's life in 1872. E. F. Benson tells an amusing anecdote of that first appearance, typical of the kind of thing that was often said about meetings with the poet. Watts had been given by his friend Rossetti a letter of introduction, and went to see Swinburne at home. He knocked to no avail, and let himself into an empty living room. Hearing noise from another room, he knocked again without success, and opened the door;—

> He found Swinburne stark naked with his aureole of red hair flying round his head, performing a Dionysiac dance, all by himself in front of a large looking glass. Swinburne perceived the intruder, he rushed at him, and before Mr. Watts-Dunton could offer any explanation or deliver his letter of introduction, he was flying in panic helter-skelter down the stairs …[7]

Unfortunately, there is no reason to believe a word of Benson's delightful relation; but tales of Swinburne's startling nudity were not uncommon, and perhaps there is no smoke without fire. George Moore claimed to have visited Swinburne in the 1870s, with a letter of introduction from W. M. Rossetti. Mounting to the first floor of the building in which the poet was resident, he opened a door which did not seem likely to lead directly to private lodgings, and found an empty room containing only a truckle bed:

> Outside the sheets lay a naked man, a strange impish little body it was […]. How I knew it to be Swinburne I cannot tell. I felt that there could be nobody but Swinburne who would look like that.[8]

The young Moore was shocked, made excuses, and left. Perhaps neither story is true; it is unlikely that Moore could be have been ignorant of Swinburne's personal appearance at that time.

Moore, in any case, never encountered Swinburne again, but Watts became a fast friend. At the end of the decade he would become a guardian as well as a friend, and under his care scenes of this nature would be far less likely.

7 E. F. Benson, *As We Were: A Victorian Peep-Show* (London, 1930), p. 275 (ch. XI).

8 George Moore, letter to Gosse, 1912, printed as an appendix (App. III: 'Swinburne and Mallarmé') to Gosse's *Life of Swinburne* (*op. cit.*, 1917), pp. 327–30.

In the year following the publication of a second series of *Poems and Ballads* (1878), a collection that included such important poems as 'Ave atque Vale' and 'A Forsaken Garden', Swinburne's fragile health became worse than ever before. His alcoholism and erratic lifestyle were almost certainly to blame. Only in his early forties, he was effectively an invalid, almost completely deaf, bedridden and unable to work. Watts was alarmed, and took Swinburne in a cab from his lodgings in Guildford Street to an address in Putney, on the outskirts of London, where Watts lived with a sister. A recovery followed, and after a brief stay with his family at Holmwood, Henley-on-Thames, Swinburne agreed to move in with Watts on a more permanent basis. So began the years at number 2, The Pines, Putney, where Swinburne lived under the solicitous care of Watts for the rest of his life—thirty years, from 1879 to 1909.

In his first few years at The Pines, Swinburne completed and published his Arthurian epyllion *Tristram of Lyonesse*, which is among his most significant literary achievements. But as the years passed, though still prolific, Swinburne produced less and less *good* poetry. There is plenty of it, certainly, and the best—some of it truly remarkable—is included in this selection. It was outweighed, however, by reams of verse praising canonical English authors, or (unlikely as it may seem) celebrating the loveliness of babies. His *Sonnets on English Dramatic Poets* are almost as dull as they sound; but the bland, sincere sentimentality of the baby poems, though pleasingly humane at root, is ghastly to anyone who cares about Swinburne's poetic genius. It was an emotion which, however deeply felt, he was not able to convert into art objects worthy of himself.

'Next to love of his friends came Swinburne's love of the sea', wrote Clara Watts-Dunton—Theodore's widow—in a cosy book called *The Home Life of Algernon Charles Swinburne*. 'And next to his love of the sea ranked his love of babies'.[9] Swinburne spent mornings, in these later years, walking in Putney and Wimbledon, and he earned a reputation for admiring infants in passing peram-

9 Clara Watts-Dunton, *The Home Life of Algernon Charles Swinburne*, (London, 1922), p. 170 (ch. XV).

bulators. One of these was a very small Robert Graves, who later, in the second paragraph of *Goodbye to All That* (London, 1929), called Swinburne 'an inveterate pram-stopper and patter and kisser'. Graves claimed to remember him, presumably from days long after the pram had been left behind, as a botherer of mothers and children: 'I did not know that Swinburne was a poet, but I knew that he was a public menace'. To go by more reliable accounts, however, the Bard was positively encouraged in this peculiar devotion by 'fond parents', who, in Clara Watts-Dunton's words, 'literally pelted the poet with photographs of their respective offspring'.[10]

Now bearded and bald, and somewhat more stocky, Swinburne had achieved (or arrived at) a kind of respectability. The change from bohemian hell-raiser to the doddering suburban ward of Watts struck many as humorous, while for others it was a cautionary tale, and cause for regret. 'In my youth', wrote Max Beerbohm after Swinburne's death, 'the suburbs were rather looked down on—I never quite knew why. It was held anomalous, and a matter for merriment, that Swinburne lived in one of them'.[11] Even in suburban Putney, he continued to be a mythical figure, an old institution in the literary world, paid visits by younger writers. There was a general feeling that Watts was too controlling of the great poet, too jealous a keeper; and this side of the story was given greater emphasis after both men were in their graves. Clara Watts-Dunton, years later, addressed such grumblings and sniggers:

> I have never understood, and never expect to understand, the motive actuating those persons who, after the deaths of Swinburne and Watts-Dunton, began to belittle the famous friends. To me their intimacy is simple and beautiful.

Her defence is quite moving, both rationally and emotionally. To her, 'the Author of "Atalanta" was just a human being who wanted to be loved and taken care of'.[12]

10 *Home Life*, p. 175 (ch. XV).

11 Max Beerbohm, 'No. 2. The Pines', in *And Even Now* (London, 1920), pp. 57–88; p. 57.

12 *Home Life*, p. 73 (ch. VI).

But the domestic situation was bound to seem odd, and a little ridiculous. Watts had almost certainly saved the life of his celebrated friend, but he had also captured and domesticated a Wild Poet. 'In the suburbs', G. K. Chesterton remembered, 'Swinburne was established as Sultan and Prophet of Putney, with Watts-Dunton as a Grand Vizier'.[13] George Moore, even in the poet's lifetime, pointedly remarked that Swinburne—

> when he dodged around London, a lively young dog, wrote 'Poems and Ballads' and 'Chastelard'; since he has gone to live at Putney, he has contributed to the *Nineteenth Century* and published an interesting little volume entitled, 'A Century of Roundels', in which he continued his plaint about his mother the sea.[14]

For Moore, Swinburne's art had been spoiled by his suburban neutralization, but for others the decadence of the earlier Swinburne was still a danger, even though the poet himself was living in calm retirement. As late as 1895, the protagonist of Marie Corelli's best-selling novel *The Sorrows of Satan* can be heard vehemently decrying the viciousness of Swinburne's work of two or three decades earlier:

> At first I read the poems quickly, with a certain pleasure in the mere swing and jangle of rhythm, and without paying much attention to the subject-matter of the verse, but presently, as though a lurid blaze of lightning had stripped a fair tree of its adoring leaves, my senses suddenly perceived the cruelty and fiendish sensuality concealed under the ornate language and persuasive rhymes [...]. I concluded that Swinburne must, after all, be right in his opinions, and I followed the lazy and unthinking course of social movement, spending my days with such literature as stored my brain with a complete knowledge of things evil and pernicious.[15]

In one sense, Swinburne would forever be the poet he had been in the 'sixties and 'seventies. In another, his later work and his more mature existence would always be held up against the lingering

13 G. K. Chesterton, *Autobiography* (London, 1936, repr. 1937), p. 284 (ch. XIII).

14 George Moore, *Confessions of a Young Man* (London, 1888, rev. 1904, 1916), p. 142 (§ XI).

15 Marie Corelli, *The Sorrows of Satan* (London, 1895), pp. 406–08 (ch. XXXV).

myth of those earlier days. To Beerbohm, who must have spoken for many, 'the essential Swinburne was still the earliest. He was and would always be the flammiferous boy of the dim past'.[16]

THE PROSODIC GENIUS

No introduction to Swinburne, however brief, could do without an appreciation of his formal achievements. In all poetry, form is vital; but this is rarely, if ever, more true than it is in Swinburne. It is not that the form is everything and the content nothing, but rather that in Swinburne this troublesome but indispensible division is especially hard to make. Accounts of Swinburne that stress merely the scandalous subjects of the famous poems are always unsatisfactory, because to be scandalous is a pretty facile thing, and Swinburne is rarely facile. Similarly, the kind of critique that happily dismisses the subject and, however admiringly, looks at Swinburne as a musical arranger of words and nothing more, is just as regrettable. There is real thought, feeling and drama, real structure and subtlety in Swinburne's 'matter', so to speak. It cannot be stressed enough: the subject is therefore far from nothing. But it would be close to nothing without the form, if such a thing could be imagined. Swinburne does not translate well.

To sympathetic readers of his own age, Swinburne was above all a versifier of peculiar technical power—which meant, for the reader, aesthetic power. To say he was a brilliant or consummate prosodist is not enough, because it does not sufficiently convey this peculiarity. The following observations are intended to introduce a few aspects of Swinburne's prosodic style, and to communicate as well as I am able something of the pleasure of his effects.

Swinburne distinguished himself partly by the freedom with which he made prosodic substitutions, allowing the rhythms to alter and slide and trip, without violating the sense of the metrical limits or the repeating structures which, in him, they always entail.

16 Beerbohm, *op. cit.*, p. 58.

He was a master of many kinds of modern English metre, an experimenter with classical metres, and the inventor of stanzas and cadences that lingered in the minds of poets and readers for decades, and perhaps still do. He became known for his habitual use of careering anapaests—both in long lines and in well-tempered stanzas—and for the mixed metres and metrical inversions that give the *sense* of the galloping anapaest even where scansion reveals only disyllabic feet. Much of his most characteristic verse has a compelling rhythmic sweep, a sense of fluency enlivened by irregularities. The 'Hymn to Proserpine' illustrates his early use of long lines with a strongly anapaestic rhythm:

> All delicate days and pleasant, all spirits and sorrows are cast
> Far out with the foam of the present that sweeps to the surf of
> the past:
> Where beyond the extreme sea-wall, and between the remote
> sea-gates,
> Waste water washes, and tall ships founder, and deep death waits.

The melodic motions are produced by careful co-ordination of the internal rhymes, the caesurae, the surges of the rhythm and the lavish alliterations,—all working together and pulling against each other. His control of the rhythm is sure, and the principle is musical *variety*, achieved through enjambment and the manipulation of syntax. In the second of these two couplets, for instance, he deftly interrupts the more ordinary movement of the foregoing: first, by over-emphasising the caesura (line 3); and then by compensating for this in the next line with a strongly tripartite division of the syntax, which effectively overrides the central pause (line 4). Swinburne continued throughout his life to experiment with expansive anapaestic lines, and the habit culminated in his last great poem, 'The Lake of Gaube'.

Even more sophisticated results were attained in stanzas where the feet are mixed, apparently in caprice—but where the caprice is really an unfailing intuition for the music of the whole strophic arrangement. As in the final line of the passage quoted above, Swinburne often made skillful use of clustered stresses:

> Waste water washes, and tall ships founder, and deep death waits.

Although not all are of equal weight, there are, from a strictly metrical point of view, far too many stresses called for in this line. It is fundamentally a line of six feet, or six beats; but any sensitive reading will register more stresses than six. One *has* to place stress on 'waste', 'ships' and 'death'. It does little good to talk of spondees; these effects are not usefully described in terms of 'feet', for they are really just instinctive substitutions of emphasis which pile up over the top of the established metrical structures. This technique of *clustering* stresses was brilliantly incorporated into the stanzas of some of Swinburne's most famous poems, including 'A Forsaken Garden' (included here); but the first and best example of the particular *stanzaic* choreography of these effects was one of his very greatest poems, 'The Triumph of Time':

> Before our lives divide for ever,
>   While time is with us and hands are free,
> (Time, swift to fasten and swift to sever
>   Hand from hand, as we stand by the sea)
> I will say no word that a man might say
> Whose whole life's love goes down in a day;
> For this could never have been; and never,
>   Though the gods and the years relent, shall be.
>
> Is it worth a tear, is it worth an hour,
>   To think of things that are well outworn?
> Of fruitless husk and fugitive flower,
>   The dream foregone and the deed forborne?
> Though joy be done with and grief be vain,
> Time shall not sever us wholly in twain;
> Earth is not spoilt for a single shower;
>   But the rain has ruined the ungrown corn.

The ponderous accumulation of stresses—not a clotting but rather a kind of throbbing or thudding—occurs at moments of emotional intensity, and these are musically orchestrated. You need at least four strong stresses in the phrase '*Whose whole life's love goes down*', though ordinarily there would only be three, which is the number of metrical beats in the phrase; and it is hard to avoid stress (or prosodic 'length') in the second syllable of the word 'ungrown', while the metre calls for an accent upon the first.

The stanza pads sadly to a halt in that slow, bitter, heavy phrase with its internal half-rhymes: '*the úngrówn córn*'. Meanwhile, the shifts between basically iambic and basically anapaestic rhythms are beautifully combined with the shifts in the *feeling* and with the adjustments of all the variables, including the assonance which is so pronounced here. The speed of recital, too, is directed with wonderful sensitivity, and prosodic awkwardness is brilliantly used: look at the poignant *rubato* effect called for at the start of the third line. The essential style of this versification is based on inconsistency, the variations of slowing and quickening, taken just as far as they can go within the elastic bounds of a regularity of melody which is aesthetically unmissable and unloseable. Each stanza of the poem is a slightly different variation on the same melodic shape, plain enough to govern even the pitch and modulation of the voice. Swinburne believed that 'genuine lyric verse' determined for the reader its own proper 'singing notes'.[17]

Almost all of these idiosyncrasies were present also in Swinburne's heroic couplets, which were deliberately unconventional in motion and texture. *Tristram of Lyonesse* was his greatest work in this form, and contains passages of a lyrical velocity unmatched in kind by the same metre in any other hands. He made enjambment a matter of the utmost drama and suspense, driving forward the long climactic periods through ever-changing cadences:

And as the august great blossom of the dawn
Burst, and the full sun scarce from sea withdrawn
Seemed on the fiery water a flower afloat,
So as a fire the mighty morning *smote*
Throughout her, and incensed with the influent hour
Her whole soul's one great mystical red flower
Burst, and the bud of her sweet spirit *broke*
Rose-fashion, and the strong spring at a stroke
Thrilled, and was cloven, and from the full sheath *came*
The whole rose of the woman red as flame …

The emphasis here is mine. A series of small, connected peaks of sensuous emotion is built by the boldness with which the poet

17 So he wrote to the young poet Philip Bourke Marston. Included in Marston's *Collected Poems*, ed. Louise Chandler Moulton (Boston, 1892), p. 409.

tips the most thrilling verbs—each one monosyllabic and long—over the line-break: '*burst*' and '*thrilled*'. Counterpoint is provided by the answering verbs, also monosyllabic, which reside in the normal seat of semantic emphasis, the end of the line: '*smote*', '*broke*', '*came*'. And in this passage is found possibly the most extreme example of Swinburne's accentual agglomerations: '*Her whole soul's one great mystical red flower*'. It is amazing that a line which conveys a sense of such powerful momentum should be so very impossible to read at speed.

The lilting lyrics in slenderer stanzas, typified by 'The Garden of Proserpine', 'Ilicet', 'Before Dawn' and 'A Match', are another thing again. Metres of this kind were among those most widely and successfully imitated by the lyrical poets of the 1880s and 1890s. In was in such poems that Swinburne, whose tendency was always toward song, was closest to the traditional forms of song; and his prosodic debt in this regard to Christina Rossetti—with whom, despite significant variance of temperament and opinion, he had a warm friendship—is not often enough acknowledged.[18] Both were among the poets of the 1860s most smooth and melodic in lyrical versification. In general, Swinburne's songlike stanzaic poems show the influence of Tennyson, as well as Shelley, his natural predecessor in this respect. But the languid evolutions and repetitions of the syntax; the lavish investment in pattern and melody, and local sense even at the expense, sometimes, of total sense—building up meaning by variation as much as by successive argument: these characteristics made Swinburne's poems something new.

Yet Swinburne's best verse is not always so fluid in motion. Some of his greatest poems, especially in the first collection of *Poems and Ballads* (1866)—poems such as 'Laus Veneris', 'The Leper', 'Faustine' and 'After Death'—are characterised by a quite different prosodic manner, just as musical, if less obviously songlike. In such poems, Swinburne adapted the Pre-Raphaelite style of D. G. Rossetti's earlier poems and William Morris's *Defence*

18 But see, e.g., Dinah Roe, '"Good Satan": The unlikely poetic affinity of Swinburne and Christina Rossetti', in Catherine Manwell and Stefano Evangelista (eds), *Algernon Charles Swinburne: Unofficial Laureate* (Manchester, 2013), pp. 157–73.

of Guenevere: a style in which certain kinds of awkwardness—in syntax, metre and rhyme—were deliberately cultivated, and integrated with a highly stylized archaism. The broken, spoken rhythms of Robert Browning were combined with a lyrical primitivism, always in search of the little touches that made old verse so pleasingly strange to modern ears. Swinburne took this approach from Rossetti and Morris, together with their Keatsian sumptuousness, and added to it the stamps of his own poetic voice. One of the most obvious features of this manner, a feature shared particularly with Rossetti, is the unnatural tilting of the spoken emphasis in rhyme-words. The example which comes to mind is the first stanza of 'The Leper', which asks us to rhyme 'her' with 'well-water'. This is not a half-rhyme, of the kind we are used to from twentieth-century poets: it actually wrests the accent—not wholly, but appreciably—towards the second syllable of 'water', giving an effect that delights through calculated archaistic gawkiness. Even to the deliberately crabbed or angular metres of poems such as these, where 'natural' fluency is stemmed and redirected in various ways, Swinburne brings a continually varying music, shot through with the weird pungency of tactfully twisted syntax, the excitement of alterations in the regulated pacing, and the sharpness of his 'alliterative thunderbolts'.[19]

SWINBURNE'S LEGACY

Swinburne was a poet who needed to be *dealt with*. Watts-Dunton had to take him in hand for his own well-being; but the reading public and the literary world, too, had just as much trouble in responding to Swinburne's marvellous precedents—taking him to task, assimilating him, trying to place him suitably within the culture of the age. The succeeding age—the time of ascendant Modernism and the 'New Criticism'—was forced to deal with him over again, and did so with such efficacy that his reputation

19 The phrase comes from Robert Buchanan's disapproving essay 'The Fleshly School of Poetry', primarily aimed at Rossetti. *Contemporary Review*, vol. 18 (1871), pp. 334–50; p. 337.

at large has never quite recovered. Critics are still trying to deal with him, and his challenge remains vigorous and vital. But the challenge does not arise merely from his being shocking, in any common sense. It comes, most of all, from his being so *aesthetically* compelling in a manner so different from any other poet—even his own imitators.

Admirers of Swinburne's poetry know that its pleasures are extraordinary. But Swinburne today does not have as many admirers as he deserves. Part of the problem is that what his admirers take for his most essential merits, detractors have found grotesque or annoying. He is an extreme case. Not every reader can enjoy Swinburne, but it is necessary to acknowledge the fact that, in reality, the very same characteristics that seem irresistibly appealing to some are those that are dismissed as repugnant or ridiculous by those who do, intuitively, resist; and that, as literary history has transpired over the past century, it is the latter class of reader which has had the more decisive and enduring impact upon Swinburne's critical fortunes.

Swinburne has never really gone away; he is certainly not forgotten, and the controversy he occasioned in the 'sixties and 'seventies has kept him firmly in the background (at least) of Victorian culture, as an anecdotal presence. But some canonical authors can be little read—and even less frequently read for *pleasure*—without being in danger of losing canonical status. Swinburne is one of these. Among those who know something about him, the majority know Swinburne either as a decadent curiosity or as a scapegoat of the Modernists and New Critics—an emblem of the type of thing that the generation of Eliot and Pound supposedly disliked. It was entirely necessary for that generation to confront and overcome, for their own practice, the legacy of Swinburne; and it was right for them to do so. In truth, however, both Eliot and Pound were more moderate in their criticisms than many of their followers in the later twentieth century have been inclined to believe; and, in any case, we should no longer feel bound to observe the sides taken in a debate that is now so distant.

The younger Pound, like Yeats, was much influenced by the late-Victorian aestheticism in which Swinburne had taken a major role, and throughout his career Pound retained his interest in the literary scene on the other side of the *fin de siècle*. Swinburne turns up all over his work, a personality taken for granted, thriving in the Poundian world of cultural anecdotalism. Pound took palpable pleasure, for example, in repeating the story of George Moore's supposed encounter. But the poetry, too, is taken for granted. 'To quote his magnificant passages is but to point out familiar things in our landscape'. This is Pound in 1918, writing in defence of Swinburne against the banality (as he saw it) of Gosse's recently published biography. There remains a persistent idea that Pound hated all things Victorian, which is nonsense; and he had a place for Swinburne, so long as it was not the anodyne, respectable place being carved out for him by Victorian survivors like Gosse. Pound could not stomach the notion of a Swinburne 'coated with veneer of British officialdom and decked out for a psalm-singing audience'.[20]

Among the mixed praise and blame of that essay, Pound in 1918 remarked that 'Swinburne's art is out of fashion'.[21] It was Eliot who intervened most decisively in the history of Swinburne's reputation when, two years later, he published the essay 'Swinburne as Poet';[22] and even Eliot is suitably respectful to Swinburne's 'genius'. He takes the work seriously, and judges it not to be 'fraudulent'. But he feels able to say with confidence, entering the third decade of the twentieth century: 'we do not greatly enjoy Swinburne'.

One of the most important things to note about this statement is that it is firmly rooted in a specific moment. For although Eliot expects his reader to agree that 'we do not greatly enjoy Swinburne', it is also agreed that 'at one period in our lives we did enjoy him and now no longer enjoy him'. He talks of Swinburne

20 Ezra Pound, 'Swinburne versus Biographers', *Poetry*, 11:6 (March 1918), 322–39; respectively pp. 324, 327, 323.

21 *Ibid.*, p. 325.

22 T. S. Eliot, *Selected Essays*, 3rd edn (London, 1951), pp. 323–27 (subsequent quotations are from these pages). For more on Eliot's attitudes to Swinburne, see Catherine Maxwell, 'Atmosphere and Absorption: Swinburne, Eliot, Drinkwater', in Manwell and Evangelista (eds), *Unofficial Laureate* (*op. cit.*), pp. 212–31.

as he talks of Rossetti elsewhere: a case of 'rapture' followed by 'revolt'.[23] Both poets are relegated to the realm of adolescent thrills, soon outgrown; but it is also a matter of literary history and the supposed shift in sensibility experienced by the whole generation.

Eliot's main objection is that Swinburne is 'diffuse', though he sensibly points out the difficulty of criticism in this matter, when he acknowledges that Swinburne's diffuseness 'is one of his glories'. It is clear to Eliot that the debate is to be between those who enjoy Swinburne's characteristics and those who do not; that the characteristics are the same whether taken for merits or faults. Swinburne is 'diffuse' because he is 'general' where, in Eliot's view, he ought to be specific, concrete. The essay relies on a basic distinction between *words* and *objects*, and an assumption about their ideal relationship in poetry. For Eliot, words are there to point to meanings in the world of objects, and should be identified as fully as possible with those objects. In Swinburne, he says, 'the object has ceased to exist'. The word becomes divorced from the world, even from the world of interior feeling;—'It is, in fact, the word that gives him the thrill'. This seems to him insufficient, or at least a mistake of priorities.

A third element in poetic language is music, or sound; but owing to the peculiar way in which Eliot chooses to use the word 'music', he is able to declare, against tradition, that Swinburne is not in fact really *musical* at all: 'the beauty or effect of sound is neither that of music nor of poetry which can be set to music'. He is probably right on the latter count, though it is not clear why this should be relevant. In Campion, by contrast (and presumably Campion is chosen as an example precisely because he was a musical setter of his own lyrics), 'musical value' and 'meaning' are two distinct things, put together; but in Swinburne 'the meaning and the sound are one thing', and the result is just a muddle. Eliot appears to regard the 'music' of verse, which he considers an essential component, as something more or less extrinsic to both the 'images' and the 'ideas'; the more closely all these things are fused at their birth, the less happy he is. It is important to realise

23 'Dante', *Selected Essays*, p. 262.

that Eliot's presuppositions in this matter are rather unusual, and there is no good reason why we should continue to apply them to Swinburne, whose stylistic achievement is much better construed by reference to the famous pronouncement of his contemporary, Walter Pater, that '*All art constantly aspires to the condition of music*':—

> lyrical poetry, precisely because in it we are least able to detach the matter from the form, without a deduction of something from that matter itself, is, at least artistically, the highest and most complete form of poetry.
>
> [T]he ideal examples of poetry [are] those in which [...] form and matter, in their union or identity, present one single effect to the 'imaginative reason'.[24]

Pater shows us not only how Eliot's analysis might be countered by the use of a different, more appropriate conceptual frame, but also what Eliot himself was strenuously reacting against. He is in no way blameable in this, but it is unfortunate that his judgement has caused so much hindrance to the appreciation of Swinburne over the past hundred years.

Looking at the matter very rationally (which may be, in some ways, inappropriate), it is less than entirely clear why Eliot should object so strongly in Swinburne to the dissociation of 'words' from 'life', when elsewhere he expresses the conviction that poetry is a medium 'in which impressions and experiences combine in peculiar and unexpected ways', and that the poet should, by mingling and manipulating the emotions of real life, 'express feelings which are not in actual emotions at all'.[25] That seems a pretty fair description of what Swinburne does, in the poems to which people most often object. He creates a wholly peculiar *literary* experience, with its own *literary* emotions—related to 'actual' experience and emotions, certainly (if not always to 'reality' in the mundane sense, then to the reality of fantasy); but nevertheless *created*. That world is persuasively consistent, and quite unique; the feelings it describes are closely identified with

24 Walter Pater, 'The School of Giorgione', in the third and subsequent editions of *The Renaissance* (1877). See the edn by Adam Phillips (Oxford, 1986, repr. 1998), pp. 87–88.

25 T. S. Eliot, 'Tradition and the Individual Talent'; *Selected Essays*, pp. 20–21.

the aesthetic feelings they call out and, in turn, rely upon for conveyance. If one kind of experience, 'real life', seems less than usually solid in his work, it is because the work itself is its *own* experience, just as the literary works which inspired Swinburne count as 'experience' every bit as much as any other part of his life.

'Only a man of genius', Eliot does not grudge to admit (and without undue excess of irony), 'could dwell so exclusively and consistently among words as Swinburne'. It would be hard to disagree. Eliot did not set out to demolish Swinburne, whom he regarded as 'indestructible', and his condemnation is both measured and frankly grounded on taste. In the 1970s, the poet Veronica Forrest-Thomson wrote a detailed refutation, carefully scrutinizing Swinburne's putative 'diffuseness', and using the observations in Eliot's essay as starting points for 'a positive analysis'.[26] But it seems that she is in rather a small minority of readers since 1920 who are willing to see in Eliot the foundation for an appreciative response to Swinburne.

Forrest-Thomson's championship betokens a larger tendency. Insipid as it may be to say so, Swinburne is something of a 'poet's poet', as well as a poet's *bête noire*. For those invested in matters of poetic form, style, technique, he is the kind of figure who rouses strong feelings one way or the other. If you want to see clearly the traces of Swinburne in the work of appreciative modern poets, Wallace Stevens is a good place to begin, or George Barker. For example, read Barker's poem 'At Thurgarton Church' (1971) after Swinburne's 'By the North Sea': the mood and manner are strikingly alike, though the measure is different; and some stanzas could almost *be* Swinburne, though Barker deliberately roughens, sharpens and interrupts the familiar cadences he evokes. As for Stevens, his poem 'To the One of Fictive Music', from *Harmonium* (1923), may well be the most Swinburnean thing in the whole Modernist repertoire.[27] Or else, after immersion in Swinburne's

26 Veronica Forrest-Thomson, 'Swinburne as Poet: A Reconsideration', published from the MS. in *The Journal of Pre-Raphaelite Studies*, New Series 15 (Fall 2006), 51–71.

27 If the reader objects to this designation of Stevens as 'Modernist', I mean only to make a distinction from major poets such as Hardy or Housman,

'Faustine', 'Félise' and 'Before the Mirror', look at another poem from *Harmonium*, the 'Apostrophe to Vincentine', and it seems almost a pastiche—the regular rhythms and rhymes, which recall the Swinburnean style, broken into irregular lines, and then playfully varied in a way suggesting the bobbed final lines of the 'Dolores' stanza. It is not even that the underlying rhythms are intrinsically or specifically Swinburnean: it is a matter of the sensuous particularities of the words themselves in their repetitions and echoes and aesthetic evocations, the diction and its sounds married to the rhythm, and to the subject, in this *particular* way. And it is a matter of tone, an essential part of this 'working' of words. Modernistic as it is, the ludic, half-parodic 'Apostrophe to Vincentine' is closer to Swinburne, in a profounder way, than any of Stevens' more overtly Victorian juvenilia.

These poems by Barker and Stevens are offered simply as obvious examples, where the presence is palpable, and probably meant to be. But in each of these poets and many more, a less easily identifiable legacy of Swinburne's formal experimentation surely takes some part, even if only in the most abstract, or theoretical, or wholly unconscious way. And the surface features of his poetry, its texture, which had such an impact on the verse of the last three decades of the nineteenth century—including that of Hardy and Yeats, who mediated the influence for later poets,—lingered, sure enough, among even the most reluctant of inheritors. It has often been argued that Eliot's poetry bears Swinburnean impressions, presumably despite the author's intentions. This is the price he pays for protestation.

Many other major critics have been inclined to take a view similar to that articulated by Eliot. Leavis thought that Swinburne demanded 'a suspension, in the reader, of the critical intelligence'. The very inevitability of Swinburne's prosody, its 'tripping onrush', simply 'rushes us by all questions', but closer examination reveals imprecision of thought and illogicality of image.[28] And Leavis is *partly* right; Swinburne does sue for a peculiar kind

who may resemble Swinburne in more superficial ways, and from the many minor poets (let us remember them) who continued, until at least the 1930s, to write stanzaic verse in a diluted Rossettian-Swinburnean style.

28 F. R. Leavis, *Revaluation* (London, 1959), pp. 238–39.

of reading, a certain kind of surrender to the pleasures of being led by musical progression, and allowing words to suggest words and so pilot the thought—even while he is completely alive to the semantic subtleties of word-meaning and word-history. Hardly anyone complains of this in Hopkins, possibly because he is more stylistically forthright about that function, and because his readers often seem conscious of a very deliberate intellectual or moral intention behind his eccentricities of language. But Swinburne, despite superficial appearances, is perhaps more extreme—not least because his form is so much smoother, so much more lulling. While Hopkins draws our aesthetic attentions to the curious ways in which his words are generated, Swinburne gives them to you as though they were somehow natural or inevitable. Hence the suspicion of critics who feel they are being 'rushed by' the words themselves, as though the sound alone mattered and the semantic idiosyncrasies were more or less accidental.

But this is a large part of Swinburne's legacy to the twentieth century, even if, at the most abstract levels, it is not easy to distinguish from the legacy of Hopkins. The Swinburnean strand can be seen to advantage in Stevens especially, for what I have just been describing is almost exactly what the 'Apostrophe to Vincentine' takes further, resetting the process in a more modern form but not giving up on the idea of rhythmic smoothness. Edith Sitwell (who published her own selection of Swinburne's poems) might be another place to look; or Dylan Thomas; and in these one would find only the most obvious affinities, not necessarily the most sophisticated or significant. It follows that readers today—those who are not immediately charmed—ought to be able to get comfortable with Swinburne's manner, at least in theory. If some of his later poems, such as 'By the North Sea', seem bafflingly close to nonsense, we should turn for explanation to some of the earlier poems, such as 'A Match' and 'Rococo', which make a virtue of the practice of letting the *sensuous* sense lead the *rational* sense. They almost go out of their way to resemble mere exercises, but they show in the most conspicuous way what Swinburne is doing with language elsewhere.

On the other hand, Swinburne is never as careless or vacuous as Leavis implies, and however slight the logical premises of a given poem might be, the thoughts and images are always well considered, the syntax scrupulously correct, and the 'meaning' important. Empson was more comfortable with Swinburne's methods, and could see more clearly the 'subdued conceits and ambiguities' by which his poems build up meaning. 'People are oddly determined to regard Swinburne as an exponent of Pure Sound with no intellectual content', he wrote. They are. But there *is* an intellectual content in Swinburne, an analytic mind at work beneath the overwhelming aesthetic impressions, and the sensitive reader feels the effect of the metaphorical logic even if he or she does not necessarily reconstruct it consciously. 'When Swinburne comes off he is a very full and direct writer; it is no use saying these verses show interest in mere sound, or pattern of verbal cadence'.[29] Perhaps, however, it would also be well to entertain the possibility of *aesthetic* meanings that might be carried by the form itself, 'subdued' even further than Empson's semantic relationships, and less capable of articulation.

Empson was certainly correct to see Swinburne as much more than a prosodic virtuoso. Take for example a poem, like 'The Sundew', in which no extravagant rhythmical 'onrush' can be claimed as a distraction, and one can see how clever his poetic thinking was. It is a kind of cleverness that does not advertise its presence, or necessitate interpretative strain: it holds the poem together at each level of attention, and rewards closer enquiry. The sundew at first seems a mere symbol in the usual sense, emblematic in function and significantly anthropomorphic. Its metaphorical content becomes the more mysterious as it is extended, thought by thought. The tension builds, the mood uncertain, the flower's relevance less and less clear, as the startling, vivid images accumulate. Suddenly in the final stanza, a change of tense, lasting only two lines; and with that lightest of touches, the relevance of the whole poem, the explanation of its nervous emotion, flashes upon the reader: a specific memory, a charged moment, glints for a moment on the present. Only a great poet could do this.

29 William Empson, *Seven Types of Ambiguity*, 2nd edn (London, 1930), pp. 163–65.

And the idea that Swinburne had no talent for visual evocation is a fallacy. Ezra Pound even went as far as to say that 'A Ballad of Life', 'A Ballad of Death' and 'The Triumph of Time' were 'full of sheer imagism':[30] a forceful reminder that not every high Modernist associated Swinburne primarily with qualities of sound. He could thrust upon the reader's mind the most unexpected images, in an unexpectedly conrete way;—

> Red mouths of maidens and red feet of doves
>
> ('A Ballad of Death')

The red feet may come from Keats, but here they *seem* to come out of nowhere, a weird detail, almost grotesque. And even where the images are somewhat less than concrete—even deliberately elusive—the word-music is coloured often by word-painting of extraordinary delicacy:

> Fleet butterflies, each like a dead flower's ghost,
> White, blue, and sere leaf-coloured; but the most
> White as the sparkle of snow-flowers in the sun
>
> (*Tristram*, 2)

At other times he could appeal to all five senses at once, in a way which is not at all (as Eliot would have it) divorced from the world of objects:

> The warm smell of the fruit was good
> To feed on, and the split green wood,
> With all its bearded lips and stains
> Of mosses in the cloven veins,
> Most pleasant, if one lay or stood
> In sunshine or in happy rains.
>
> ('August')

This is certainly not 'Pure Sound'. Nor could it be called 'morbid' or 'diffuse'.

The heyday of the public literary arbiter seems to be over, and sympathetic critical work on Swinburne is now more than ever confined to the pale of scholarship. It has, consequently, relatively little effect on the reading and reputation of Swinburne generally.

30 Pound, *op. cit.*, p. 327. Pound has mistakenly written 'Triumph of Life'.

Neither has a clear positive advance been stimulated by the recent vogue for Pre-Raphaelitism in the media and popular culture. No doubt there are several reasons why it is easier to look at a picture by Millais than to read a poem by Swinburne; but he should *not* be solely an academic interest.

Why should Swinburne be read? Not only because of his eminence and influence in the history of English literature, though that is reason enough; but, more importantly, because he did such unexampled things with the music of English poetic metre just at the point when the empire of strict metre was beginning to subside—and because those things are so wonderful for their own sake. Even *that* is saying too little, because the music is not only a matter of sound. Swinburne evoked a lyrical world and created an aesthetic experience that was authentically his own, and we should read him for the pleasure of being compelled by that experience. In this sense, Swinburne was surely the most 'Aesthetic' of all the poets of the so-called 'Aesthetic Movement'. At least, his powerful idiosyncrasies of style seem the ultimate provision, from the world of poetry, to the aesthetic critic who is always asking: 'What is the peculiar sensation, what is the peculiar quality of pleasure, which his work has the property of exciting in us, and which we cannot get elsewhere?'[31] To such questioning, his work holds promise of implicit answers seemingly limitless in number (because endlessly refinable, divisible); and the force of the effects presses the reader to grasp at those answers.

And yet there is a danger in setting Swinburne too far apart from his peers; and even some of his most sophisticated critical champions in recent decades may have unwittingly contributed to his neglect by attending so enthusiastically to his uniqueness. It is a difficult problem. Academic criticism has kept Swinburne in sight, and there seems to be considerable interest in him at present; but a language of exceptionalism has grown up around Swinburne, which has not necessarily been helpful, since it has tended to imply that there is something peculiarly *difficult* about him, some complicated puzzle for which the usual critical approaches

31 Walter Pater, 'Sandro Botticelli' (1870), in *The Renaissance* (1873 and later edns). See the edn by Phillips (*op. cit.*), p. 33.

are ill-equipped. Sometimes it is even suggested that an understanding of Swinburne is reliant upon an especially large and specific arsenal of knowledge, theoretical, literary and historical. It seems to me that Swinburne, difficult though he sometimes can be, demands this kind of background no more, and perhaps even less, than many of his contemporaries. If literary scholarship at present is not so much in the habit of attending to the qualities of versification that in Swinburne call for special attention, it does not mean that those qualities are inherently problematic, or that readers cannot respond to them. Speaking in such terms may present the poetry as an exciting challenge inside the academy, but both within and without the universities it also has the undesirable effect of making Swinburne seem esoteric.

To make Swinburne esoteric on these grounds can only obscure the pleasure of reading him. The qualities that we enjoy in Swinburne are the same qualities that are, in this view, 'difficult'; but in almost no case does the sense of difficulty play any considerable part in the aesthetic enjoyment of those qualities. Swinburne *is* unique, but there is nothing arcane about his charms: they are fantastically obvious, and that is their function. His form is always lucid. The traditional complaints against Swinburne over the course of the twentieth century have usually had to do with the feeling that his intended charms, his formal blandishments, are only *too* obvious. It may be that there are now a larger number of readers and students of poetry who are not used to hearing the kinds of metrical effect that Swinburne emphasises. But Swinburne can be, in this respect, a partial solution to that problem—and thus to the problem of his own unpopularity among readers for whom the chief obstacle is form, rather than a more general distaste. A course of Swinburne would probably give a better feeling for prosody than almost any primer, because his rhythms are so hard to miss, so memorable, and so varied. However hard it may be to theorize, his form is easy to *hear*, and the question then is how to respond: with derision and scepticism, or with excitement and delight.

'Almost no one, to-day', Eliot wrote, 'will wish to read the whole of Swinburne'. If it was true then, it is likely still to be true now, although *almost* no one does not mean no one at all. For those who want the complete poems, they are easily obtainable in old copies, not much in demand. The purpose of this volume is to give readers and students of poetry a considerable anthology of only the best of Swinburne, and only the verse. There have been many earlier selections of this kind, beginning with Swinburne's own compilation of 1887. The present edition has been compiled according to the belief that it is the poetry that is of first importance, and that the prime desideratum is to get as much as possible of the good verse back into print in an accessible way, leaving out the prose and in some cases disregarding the claims of literary and critical history as criteria for inclusion. This is, therefore, a 'critical' edition in the sense that it has been assembled according to avowedly and exclusively critical principles for inclusion and omission, however subjective those principles may be. It is not a critical edition in the scholarly sense, and the notes have been limited to explication; but the text is reliable, and the contents sufficiently comprehensive to be useful to most students.

The present selection may well have struck Eliot as too generous in its amplitude, and that is as it should be; but he ought to have approved the aim, which is to give the reader a correct dose of Swinburne. One or two famous pieces are consequently missing, but they are easily found elsewhere. There has not been space to give *Atalanta* whole. *Tristram* and the two better Stuart plays have also been represented by extracts, for the same reason. All of these longer works are worth reading entire, and to that extent the present dose may need to be supplemented. But this being an edition of *Selected Verse*, rather than *Selected Poems*, I have thought it more vital to put together in one place all of the most brilliant *passages* of Swinburne, specimens of his highest attainments in various forms and moods, than to take a holistic attitude to the more voluminous works.

Under 'verse' I am including the verse dramas *Chastelard* and *Bothwell*. These have traditionally been classed, along with several others, as 'plays'. As an unfortunate consequence, they have been too often ignored in the anthologies, even though they contain some of Swinburne's very finest work. Swinburne's own collected edition of his *Poems,* issued in six volumes in 1904, includes the two 'Greek' plays, *Atalanta in Calydon* and *Erechtheus*, but all the rest of the dramatic work is lacking. Certainly the Greek plays are more like Shelleyan 'dramatic poems' than the Stuart plays, with their strong Jacobean inspiration; but the 1904 edition also neglects other dramatic poems, such as *Locrine*, which is entirely stanzaic. Subsequent editors have apparently tended to follow Swinburne's own divisions, and *Atalanta* (which is much superior to *Erechtheus* in most respects) has kept its status as a 'poem', often reprinted, while the other 'tragedies' have lapsed into obscurity. Indeed, copies of the collected plays are hard to find, and although early editions of the individual texts pop up here and there in shops, it must be fair to say that Swinburne's dramatic work, *Atalanta* excluded, is almost never read except by scholars.

About the longer works some notes have been provided, in an appendix, which should help to contextualise the extracts by which they are represented in the following pages, and which are meant also to explain the selection of those extracts. As for the rest of the poems, only a few omissions are likely to be regretted by more than a few readers. In general, the political and polemical poems have been left out. There has recently been some scholarly interest in these, but their interest is not likely to extend far beyond the academy, and so they belong in a different kind of edition.

Some readers may in fact find the inclusions more surprising than the omissions. The selections from the 1866 *Poems and Ballads* may appear disproportionately liberal, to some. Again, every poem is present on account of its merits. It is not only a matter of the apparently minor lyrics, such as 'A Ballad of Burdens', 'Before Dawn', 'Before Parting' and 'August', which are among Swinburne's best, although their attainments may seem modest beside the 'great' poems.[32] Longer poems such as the Landorian-Ten-

32 Those of the 1866 collection would be: 'The Triumph of Time', 'Laus Veneris', 'The Leper', 'Anactoria', 'Félise', 'Dolores', and perhaps the 'Hymn to Proserpine'.

nysonian monologue 'At Eleusis', and the pesudo-Chaucerian narratives of 'St Dorothy' and 'The Two Dreams', none of which anyone ever seems to talk about, contain such startling and beautiful passages that they ought not to be shuffled out of the picture through the injection, for decorum's sake, of too many less commendable pieces from later years. If the quality of Swinburne's poetry generally declined over the course of his career, we no longer need to feel bad about it. The astonishing *Tristram of Lyonesse*, and the best of the late poems—such as 'A Nympholept' and 'The Lake of Gaube'—more than adequately make up for the unnevenness of his other work after the 'seventies, and the quantity of his verse still worth reading is very considerable.

There is, therefore, no reason to be uncomfortable with the preponderance here of work from the 1860s, and especially from the first *Poems and Ballads*. It was a book which deserved its celebrity at the time of publication, and still deserves it. In his elegy for Swinburne, 'A Singer Asleep', Thomas Hardy remembered the excitement of 'that far morning of a summer day' on which he first read those early poems—dropped, as though from nowhere, into the midst of 'Victoria's formal middle time'. More than a century and a half later, they are just as exciting. It is to promote such thrills, and to do justice to the *pleasures* of Swinburne, regardless of the established repertoire, that so many of the less familiar titles have been reproduced from his greatest book.

Swinburne

Selected Verse

From ATALANTA IN CALYDON (1865)

The First Choral Song

When the hounds of spring are on winter's traces,
   The mother of months in meadow or plain
Fills the shadows and windy places
   With lisp of leaves and ripple of rain;
And the brown bright nightingale amorous
Is half assuaged for Itylus,
For the Thracian ships and the foreign faces,
   The tongueless vigil, and all the pain.

Come with bows bent and with emptying of quivers,
   Maiden most perfect, lady of light,
With a noise of winds and many rivers,
   With a clamour of waters, and with might;
Bind on thy sandals, O thou most fleet,
Over the splendour and speed of thy feet;
For the faint east quickens, the wan west shivers,
   Round the feet of the day and the feet of the night.

Where shall we find her, how shall we sing to her,
   Fold our hands round her knees, and cling?
O that man's heart were as fire and could spring to her,
   Fire, or the strength of the streams that spring!
For the stars and the winds are unto her
As raiment, as songs of the harp-player;
For the risen stars and the fallen cling to her,
   And the southwest-wind and the west-wind sing.

For winter's rains and ruins are over,
   And all the season of snows, and sins;
The days dividing lover and lover,
   The light that loses, the night that wins;
And time remembered is grief forgotten,
And frosts are slain and flowers begotten,
And in green underwood and cover
   Blossom by blossom the spring begins.

The full streams feed on flower of rushes,
   Ripe grasses trammel a travelling foot,
The faint fresh flame of the young year flushes
   From leaf to flower and flower to fruit,
And fruit and leaf are as gold and fire,
And the oat is heard above the lyre,
And the hoofèd heel of a satyr crushes
   The chestnut-husk at the chestnut-root.

And Pan by noon and Bacchus by night,
   Fleeter of foot than the fleet-foot kid,
Follows with dancing and fills with delight
   The Maenad and the Bassarid;
And soft as lips that laugh and hide
The laughing leaves of the trees divide,
And screen from seeing and leave in sight
   The god pursuing, the maiden hid.

The ivy falls with the Bacchanal's hair
   Over her eyebrows hiding her eyes;
The wild vine slipping down leaves bare
   Her bright breast shortening into sighs;
The wild vine slips with the weight of its leaves,
But the berried ivy catches and cleaves
To the limbs that glitter, the feet that scare
   The wolf that follows, the fawn that flies.

Althaea's Scorn of Prayer

Night, a black hound, follows the white fawn day,
Swifter than dreams the white flown feet of sleep;
Will ye pray back the night with any prayers?
And though the spring put back a little while
Winter, and snows that plague all men for sin,
And the iron time of cursing, yet I know
Spring shall be ruined with the rain, and storm
Eat up like fire the ashen autumn days.
I marvel what men do with prayers awake
Who dream and die with dreaming; any god,
Yea the least god of all things called divine,
Is more than sleep and waking; yet we say,
Perchance by praying a man shall match his god.
For if sleep have no mercy, and man's dreams
Bite to the blood and burn into the bone,
What shall this man do waking? By the gods,
He shall not pray to dream sweet things to-night,
Having dreamt once more bitter things than death.

The Second Choral Song

Before the beginning of years
   There came to the making of man
Time, with a gift of tears,
   Grief, with a glass that ran;
Pleasure, with pain for leaven;
   Summer, with flowers that fell;
Remembrance fallen from heaven,
   And madness risen from hell;
Strength without hands to smite,
   Love that endures for a breath,

Night, the shadow of light,
  And life, the shadow of death.

And the high gods took in hand
  Fire, and the falling of tears,
And a measure of sliding sand
  From under the feet of the years,
And froth and drift of the sea;
  And dust of the labouring earth;
And bodies of things to be
  In the houses of death and of birth;
And wrought with weeping and laughter,
  And fashioned with loathing and love,
With life before and after
  And death beneath and above,
For a day and a night and a morrow,
  That his strength might endure for a span
With travail and heavy sorrow,
  The holy spirit of man.

From the winds of the north and the south
  They gathered as unto strife;
They breathed upon his mouth,
  They filled his body with life;
Eyesight and speech they wrought
  For the veils of the soul therein,
A time for labour and thought,
  A time to serve and to sin;
They gave him light in his ways,
  And love, and a space for delight,
And beauty and length of days,
  And night, and sleep in the night.
His speech is a burning fire;
  With his lips he travaileth,
In his heart is a blind desire,
  In his eyes foreknowledge of death;
He weaves, and is clothed with derision;
  Sows, and he shall not reap,

His life is a watch or a vision
  Between a sleep and a sleep.

Meleager rejects his Mother's Counsel concerning Atalanta

O mother, I am not fain to strive in speech
Nor set my mouth against thee, who art wise
Even as they say and full of sacred words.
But one thing I know surely, and cleave to this;
That though I be not subtle of wit as thou
Nor womanlike to weave sweet words, and melt
Mutable minds of wise men as with fire,
I too, doing justly and reverencing the gods,
Shall not want wit to see what things be right.
For whom they love and whom reject, being gods,
There is no man but seeth, and in good time
Submits himself, refraining all his heart.
And I too as thou sayest have seen great things;
Seen otherwhere, but chiefly when the sail
First caught between stretched ropes the roaring west,
And all our oars smote eastward, and the wind
First flung round faces of seafaring men
White splendid snow-flakes of the sundering foam,
And the first furrow in virginal green sea
Followed the plunging ploughshare of hewn pine,
And closed, as when deep sleep subdues man's breath
Lips close and heart subsides; and closing, shone
Sunlike with many a Nereid's hair, and moved
Round many a trembling mouth of doubtful gods,
Risen out of sunless and sonorous gulfs
Through waning water and into shallow light,
That watched us; and when flying the dove was snared
As with men's hands, but we shot after and sped
Clear through the irremeable Symplegades;

And chiefliest when hoar beach and herbless cliff
Stood out ahead from Colchis, and we heard
Clefts hoarse with wind, and saw through narrowing reefs
The lightning of the intolerable wave
Flash, and the white wet flame of breakers burn
Far under a kindling south-wind, as a lamp
Burns and bends all its blowing flame one way;
Wild heights untravelled of the wind, and vales
Cloven seaward by their violent streams, and white
With bitter flowers and bright salt scurf of brine;
Heard sweep their sharp swift gales, and bowing bird-wise
Shriek with birds' voices, and with furious feet
Tread loose the long skirts of a storm; and saw
The whole white Euxine clash together and fall
Full-mouthed, and thunderous from a thousand throats;
Yet we drew thither and won the fleece and won
Medea, deadlier than the sea; but there
Seeing many a wonder and fearful things to men
I saw not one thing like this one seen here,
Most fair and fearful, feminine, a god,
Faultless; whom I that love not, being unlike,
Fear, and give honour, and choose from all the gods.

The Fourth Choral Song

Who hath given man speech? or who hath set therein
A thorn for peril and a snare for sin?
For in the word his life is and his breath,
  And in the word his death,
That madness and the infatuate heart may breed
  From the word's womb the deed
And life bring one thing forth ere all pass by,
Even one thing which is ours yet cannot die—
Death. Hast thou seen him ever anywhere,

Time's twin-born brother, imperishable as he
Is perishable and plaintive, clothed with care
　And mutable as sand,
But death is strong and full of blood and fair
And perdurable and like a lord of land?
Nay, time thou seest not, death thou wilt not see
Till life's right hand be loosened from thine hand
　And thy life-days from thee.
For the gods very subtly fashion
　Madness with sadness upon earth:
Not knowing in any wise compassion,
　Nor holding pity of any worth;
And many things they have given and taken,
　And wrought and ruined many things;
The firm land have they loosed and shaken,
　And sealed the sea with all her springs;
They have wearied time with heavy burdens
　And vexed the lips of life with breath:
Set men to labour and given them guerdons,
　Death, and great darkness after death:
Put moans into the bridal measure
　And on the bridal wools a stain,
And circled pain about with pleasure,
　And girdled pleasure about with pain;
And strewed one marriage-bed with tears and fire
For extreme loathing and supreme desire.

What shall be done with all these tears of ours?
　Shall they make watersprings in the fair heaven
To bathe the brows of morning? or like flowers
Be shed and shine before the starriest hours,
　Or made the raiment of the weeping Seven?
Or rather, O our masters, shall they be
Food for the famine of the grievous sea,
　A great well-head of lamentation
Satiating the sad gods? or fall and flow
Among the years and seasons to and fro,
　And wash their feet with tribulation

And fill them full with grieving ere they go?
Alas, our lords, and yet alas again,
Seeing all your iron heaven is gilt as gold
But all we smite thereat in vain,
Smite the gates barred with groanings manifold,
But all the floors are paven with our pain.
Yea, and with weariness of lips and eyes,
With breaking of the bosom, and with sighs,
We labour, and are clad and fed with grief
And filled with days we would not fain behold
And nights we would not hear of, we wax old,
All we wax old and wither like a leaf.
We are outcast, strayed between bright sun and moon;
Our light and darkness are as leaves of flowers,
Black flowers and white, that perish; and the noon
As midnight, and the night as daylight hours.
A little fruit a little while is ours,
And the worm finds it soon.

But up in heaven the high gods one by one
Lay hands upon the draught that quickeneth,
Fulfilled with all tears shed and all things done,
And stir with soft imperishable breath
The bubbling bitterness of life and death,
And hold it to our lips and laugh; but they
Preserve their lips from tasting night or day,
Lest they too change and sleep, the fates that spun,
The lips that made us and the hands that slay;
Lest all these change, and heaven bow down to none,
Change and be subject to the secular sway
And terrene revolution of the sun.
Therefore they thrust it from them, putting time away.

I would the wine of time, made sharp and sweet
With multitudinous days and nights and tears
And many mixing savours of strange years,
Were no more trodden of them under feet,
Cast out and spilt about their holy places:

That life were given them as a fruit to eat
And death to drink as water; that the light
Might ebb, drawn backward from their eyes, and night
  Hide for one hour the imperishable faces.
That they might rise up sad in heaven, and know
Sorrow and sleep, one paler than young snow,
  One cold as blight of dew and ruinous rain;
Rise up and rest and suffer a little, and be
Awhile as all things born with us and we,
  And grieve as men, and like slain men be slain.

For now we know not of them; but one saith
  The gods are gracious, praising God; and one,
When hast thou seen? or hast thou felt his breath
  Touch, nor consume thine eyelids as the sun,
Nor fill thee to the lips with fiery death?
  None hath beheld him, none
Seen above other gods and shapes of things,
Swift without feet and flying without wings,
Intolerable, not clad with death or life,
  Insatiable, not known of night or day,
The lord of love and loathing and of strife
  Who gives a star and takes a sun away;
Who shapes the soul, and makes her a barren wife
  To the earthly body and grievous growth of clay;
Who turns the large limbs to a little flame
  And binds the great sea with a little sand;
Who makes desire, and slays desire with shame;
  Who shakes the heaven as ashes in his hand;
Who, seeing the light and shadow for the same,
  Bids day waste night as fire devours a brand,
Smites without sword, and scourges without rod;
  The supreme evil, God.

Yea, with thine hate, O God, thou hast covered us,
  One saith, and hidden our eyes away from sight,
And made us transitory and hazardous,
  Light things and slight;

Yet have men praised thee, saying, He hath made man thus,
  And he doeth right.
Thou hast kissed us, and hast smitten; thou hast laid
Upon us with thy left hand life, and said,
Live: and again thou hast said, Yield up your breath,
And with thy right hand laid upon us death.
Thou hast sent us sleep, and stricken sleep with dreams,
  Saying, Joy is not, but love of joy shall be;
Thou hast made sweet springs for all the pleasant streams,
  In the end thou hast made them bitter with the sea.
Thou hast fed one rose with dust of many men;
  Thou hast marred one face with fire of many tears;
Thou hast taken love, and given us sorrow again;
  With pain thou hast filled us full to the eyes and ears.
Therefore because thou art strong, our father, and we
  Feeble; and thou art against us, and thine hand
Constrains us in the shallows of the sea
  And breaks us at the limits of the land;
Because thou hast bent thy lightnings as a bow,
  And loosed the hours like arrows; and let fall
Sins and wild words and many a winged woe
  And wars among us, and one end of all;
Because thou hast made the thunder, and thy feet
  Are as a rushing water when the skies
Break, but thy face as an exceeding heat
  And flames of fire the eyelids of thine eyes;
Because thou art over all who are over us;
  Because thy name is life and our name death;
Because thou art cruel and men are piteous,
  And our hands labour and thine hand scattereth;
Lo, with hearts rent and knees made tremulous,
  Lo, with ephemeral lips and casual breath,
    At least we witness of thee ere we die
That these things are not otherwise, but thus;
  That each man in his heart sigheth, and saith,
    That all men even as I,
All we are against thee, against thee, O God most high.

But ye, keep ye on earth
Your lips from over-speech,
Loud words and longing are so little worth;
And the end is hard to reach.
For silence after grievous things is good,
And reverence, and the fear that makes men whole,
And shame, and righteous governance of blood,
And lordship of the soul.
But from sharp words and wits men pluck no fruit,
And gathering thorns they shake the tree at root;
For words divide and rend;
But silence is most noble till the end.

The Herald reports the Slaying of the Boar

These having halted bade blow horns, and rode
Through woods and waste lands cleft by stormy streams,
Past yew-trees and the heavy hair of pines,
And where the dew is thickest under oaks,
This way and that; but questing up and down
They saw no trail nor scented; and one said,
Plexippus, Help, or help not, Artemis,
And we will flay thy boarskin with male hands;
But saying, he ceased and said not that he would,
Seeing where the green ooze of a sun-struck marsh
Shook with a thousand reeds untunable,
And in their moist and multitudinous flower
Slept no soft sleep, with violent visions fed,
The blind bulk of the immeasurable beast.
And seeing, he shuddered with sharp lust of praise
Through all his limbs, and launched a double dart,
And missed; for much desire divided him,
Too hot of spirit and feebler than his will,
That his hand failed, though fervent; and the shaft,

Sundering the rushes, in a tamarisk stem
Shook, and stuck fast; then all abode save one,
The Arcadian Atalanta; from her side
Sprang her hounds, labouring at the leash, and slipped,
And plashed ear-deep with plunging feet; but she
Saying, Speed it as I send it for thy sake,
Goddess, drew bow and loosed, the sudden string
Rang, and sprang inward, and the waterish air
Hissed, and the moist plumes of the songless reeds
Moved as a wave which the wind moves no more.
But the boar heaved half out of ooze and slime
His tense flank trembling round the barbed wound,
Hateful, and fiery with invasive eyes
And bristling with intolerable hair
Plunged, and the hounds clung, and green flowers and white
Reddened and broke all round them where they came.
And charging with sheer tusk he drove, and smote
Hyleus; and sharp death caught his sudden soul,
And violent sleep shed night upon his eyes.
Then Peleus, with strong strain of hand and heart,
Shot; but the sidelong arrow slid, and slew
His comrade born and loving countryman,
Under the left arm smitten, as he no less
Poised a like arrow; and bright blood brake afoam,
And falling, and weighed back by clamorous arms,
Sharp rang the dead limbs of Eurytion.
Then one shot happier; the Cadmean seer,
Amphiaraus; for his sacred shaft
Pierced the red circlet of one ravening eye
Beneath the brute brows of the sanguine boar,
Now bloodier from one slain; but he so galled
Sprang straight, and rearing cried no lesser cry
Than thunder and the roar of wintering streams
That mix their own foam with the yellower sea;
And as a tower that falls by fire in fight
With ruin of walls and all its archery,
And breaks the iron flower of war beneath,
Crushing charred limbs and molten arms of men;

So through crushed branches and the reddening brake
Clamoured and crashed the fervour of his feet,
And trampled, springing sideways from the tusk,
Too tardy a moving mould of heavy strength,
Ancaeus; and as flakes of weak-winged snow
Break, all the hard thews of his heaving limbs
Broke, and rent flesh fell every way, and blood
Flew, and fierce fragments of no more a man.
Then all the heroes drew sharp breath, and gazed,
And smote not; but Meleager, but thy son,
Right in the wild way of the coming curse
Rock-rooted, fair with fierce and fastened lips,
Clear eyes, and springing muscle and shortening limb—
With chin aslant indrawn to a tightening throat,
Grave, and with gathered sinews, like a god,—
Aimed on the left side his well-handled spear
Grasped where the ash was knottiest hewn, and smote,
And with no missile wound, the monstrous boar
Right in the hairiest hollow of his hide
Under the last rib, sheer through bulk and bone,
Deep in; and deeply smitten, and to death,
The heavy horror with his hanging shafts
Leapt, and fell furiously, and from raging lips
Foamed out the latest wrath of all his life.
And all they praised the gods with mightier heart,
Zeus and all gods, but chiefliest Artemis,
Seeing; but Meleager bade whet knives and flay,
Strip and stretch out the splendour of the spoil;
And hot and horrid from the work all these
Sat, and drew breath and drank and made great cheer
And washed the hard sweat off their calmer brows.
For much sweet grass grew higher than grew the reed,
And good for slumber, and every holier herb,
Narcissus, and the low-lying melilote,
And all of goodliest blade and bloom that springs
Where, hid by heavier hyacinth, violet buds
Blossom and burn; and fire of yellower flowers
And light of crescent lilies, and such leaves

As fear the Faun's and know the Dryad's foot;
Olive and ivy and poplar dedicate,
And many a well-spring overwatched of these.
There now they rest; but me the king bade bear
Good tidings to rejoice this town and thee.
Wherefore be glad, and all ye give much thanks,
For fallen is all the trouble of Calydon.

From *the Sixth Choral Song*

  For death is deep as the sea,
    And fate as the waves thereof.
  Shall the waves take pity on thee
    Or the southwind offer thee love?
  Wilt thou take the night for thy day
    Or the darkness for light on thy way,
  Till thou say in thine heart Enough?
Behold, thou art over fair, thou art over wise;
The sweetness of spring in thine hair, and the light in thine eyes.
The light of the spring in thine eyes, and the sound in thine ears;
Yet thine heart shall wax heavy with sighs and thine eyelids with tears.
Wilt thou cover thine hair with gold, and with silver thy feet?
Hast thou taken the purple to fold thee, and made thy mouth sweet?
Behold, when thy face is made bare, he that loved thee shall hate;
Thy face shall be no more fair at the fall of thy fate.
For thy life shall fall as a leaf and be shed as the rain;
And the veil of thine head shall be grief: and the crown shall be pain.

Althaea's Final Words, having Burnt the Brand

Girls, one thing will I say and hold my peace.
I that did this will weep not nor cry out,
Cry ye and weep: I will not call on gods,
Call ye on them; I will not pity man,
Shew ye your pity. I know not if I live;
Save that I feel the fire upon my face
And on my cheek the burning of a brand.
Yea the smoke bites me, yea I drink the steam
With nostril and with eyelid and with lip
Insatiate and intolerant; and mine hands
Burn, and fire feeds upon mine eyes; I reel
As one made drunk with living, whence he draws
Drunken delight; yet I, though mad for joy,
Loathe my long living and am waxen red
As with the shadow of shed blood; behold,
I am kindled with the flames that fade in him,
I am swollen with subsiding of his veins,
I am flooded with his ebbing; my lit eyes
Flame with the falling fire that leaves his lids
Bloodless; my cheek is luminous with blood
Because his face is ashen. Yet, O child,
Son, first-born, fairest—O sweet mouth, sweet eyes,
That drew my life out through my suckling breast,
That shone and clove mine heart through—O soft knees
Clinging, O tender treadings of soft feet,
Cheeks warm with little kissings—O child, child,
What have we made each other? Lo, I felt
Thy weight cleave to me, a burden of beauty, O son,
Thy cradled brows and loveliest loving lips,
The floral hair, the little lightening eyes,
And all thy goodly glory; with mine hands
Delicately I fed thee, with my tongue
Tenderly spake, saying, Verily in God's time,
For all the little likeness of thy limbs,
Son, I shall make thee a kingly man to fight,

A lordly leader; and hear before I die,
"She bore the goodliest sword of all the world."
Oh! oh! For all my life turns round on me;
I am severed from myself, my name is gone,
My name that was a healing, it is changed,
My name is a consuming. From this time,
Though mine eyes reach to the end of all these things,
My lips shall not unfasten till I die.

The Death of Meleager

Mother, I dying with unforgetful tongue
Hail thee as holy and worship thee as just
Who art unjust and unholy; and with my knees
Would worship, but thy fire and subtlety,
Dissundering them, devour me; for these limbs
Are as light dust and crumblings from mine urn
Before the fire has touched them; and my face
As a dead leaf or dead foot's mark on snow,
And all this body a broken barren tree
That was so strong, and all this flower of life
Disbranched and desecrated miserably,
And minished all that god-like muscle and might
And lesser than a man's: for all my veins
Fail me, and all mine ashen life burns down.
I would thou hadst let me live; but gods averse,
But fortune, and the fiery feet of change,
And time, these would not, these tread out my life,
These and not thou; me too thou hast loved, and I
Thee; but this death was mixed with all my life,
Mine end with my beginning: and this law,
This only, slays me, and not my mother at all.
And let no brother or sister grieve too sore,
Nor melt their hearts out on me with their tears,

Since extreme love and sorrowing overmuch
Vex the great gods, and overloving men
Slay and are slain for love's sake; and this house
Shall bear much better children; why should these
Weep? but in patience let them live their lives
And mine pass by forgotten: thou alone,
Mother, thou sole and only, thou not these,
Keep me in mind a little when I die
Because I was thy first-born; let thy soul
Pity me, pity even me gone hence and dead,
Though thou wert wroth, and though thou bear again
Much happier sons, and all men later born
Exceedingly excel me; yet do thou
Forget not, nor think shame; I was thy son.
Time was I did not shame thee, and time was
I thought to live and make thee honourable
With deeds as great as these men's; but they live,
These, and I die; and what thing should have been
Surely I know not; yet I charge thee, seeing
I am dead already, love me not the less,
Me, O my mother; I charge thee by these gods,
My father's, and that holier breast of thine,
By these that see me dying, and that which nursed,
Love me not less, thy first-born: though grief come,
Grief only, of me, and of all these great joy,
And shall come always to thee; for thou knowest,
O mother, O breasts that bare me, for ye know,
O sweet head of my mother, sacred eyes,
Ye know my soul albeit I sinned, ye know
Albeit I kneel not neither touch thy knees,
But with my lips I kneel, and with my heart
I fall about thy feet and worship thee.
And ye farewell now, all my friends; and ye,
Kinsmen, much younger and glorious more than I,
Sons of my mother's sister; and all farewell
That were in Colchis with me, and bare down
The waves and wars that met us: and though times
Change, and though now I be not anything,

Forget not me among you, what I did
In my good time; for even by all those days,
Those days and this, and your own living souls,
And by the light and luck of you that live,
And by this miserable spoil, and me
Dying, I beseech you, let my name not die.
But thou, dear, touch me with thy rose-like hands,
And fasten up mine eyelids with thy mouth,
A bitter kiss; and grasp me with thine arms,
Printing with heavy lips my light waste flesh,
Made light and thin by heavy-handed fate,
And with thine holy maiden eyes drop dew,
Drop tears for dew upon me who am dead,
Me who have loved thee; seeing without sin done
I am gone down to the empty weary house
Where no flesh is nor beauty nor swift eyes
Nor sound of mouth nor might of hands and feet.
But thou, dear, hide my body with thy veil,
And with thy raiment cover foot and head,
And stretch thyself upon me and touch hands
With hands and lips with lips: be pitiful
As thou art maiden perfect; let no man
Defile me to despise me, saying, This man
Died woman-wise, a woman's offering, slain
Through female fingers in his woof of life,
Dishonourable; for thou hast honoured me.
And now for God's sake kiss me once and twice
And let me go; for the night gathers me,
And in the night shall no man gather fruit.

ATALANTA.

Hail thou: but I with heavy face and feet
Turn homeward and am gone out of thine eyes.

CHORUS.

Who shall contend with his lords

Or cross them or do them wrong?
Who shall bind them as with cords?
Who shall tame them as with song?
Who shall smite them as with swords?
For the hands of their kingdom are strong.

From CHASTELARD (1865)

From Act 1, scene 3

The Queen and Chastelard (I).

QUEEN. You have a subtle riddling skill at love
Which is not like a lover. For my part,
I am resolved to be well done with love,
Though I were fairer-faced than all the world;
As there be fairer. Think you, fair my knight,
Love shall live after life in any man?
I have given you stuff for riddles.
CHASTELARD. Most sweet queen,
They say men dying remember, with sharp joy
And rapid reluctation of desire,
Some old thing, some swift breath of wind, some word,
Some sword-stroke or dead lute-strain, some lost sight,
Some sea-blossom stripped to the sun and burned
At naked ebb—some river-flower that breathes
Against the stream like a swooned swimmer's mouth—
Some tear or laugh ere lip and eye were man's—
Sweet stings that struck the blood in riding—nay,
Some garment or sky-colour or spice-smell,
And die with heart and face shut fast on it,
And know not why, and weep not; it may be
Men shall hold love fast always in such wise
In new fair lives where all are new things else,
And know not why, and weep not.

From Act 2, scene 1

The Queen and Chastelard (II).

QUEEN. You call love sweet; yea, what is bitter, then?
There's nothing broken sleep could hit upon
So bitter as the breaking down of love.
You call me sweet; I am not sweet to you,
Nor you—O, I would say not sweet to me,
And if I said so I should hardly lie.
But there have been those things between us, sir,
That men call sweet.
CHASTELARD. I know not how *There is*
Turns to *There hath been*; 'tis a heavier change
Than change of flesh to dust. Yet though years change
And good things end and evil things grow great,
The old love that was, or that was dreamed about,
That sang and kissed and wept upon itself,
Laughed and ran mad with love of its own face,
That was a sweet thing.
QUEEN. Nay, I know not well.
'Tis when the man is held fast underground
They say for sooth what manner of heart he had.
We are alive, and cannot be well sure
If we loved much or little: think you not
It were convenient one of us should die?
CHASTELARD. Madam, your speech is harsh to understand.
QUEEN. Why, there could come no change then; one of us
Would never need to fear our love might turn
To the sad thing that it may grow to be.
I would sometimes all things were dead asleep
That I have loved, all buried in soft beds
And sealed with dreams and visions, and each dawn
Sung to by sorrows, and all night assuaged
By short sweet kisses and by sweet long loves
For old life's sake, lest weeping overmuch
Should wake them in a strange new time, and arm
Memory's blind hand to kill forgetfulness.

From Act 3, scene 1

Chastelard steals into the Queen's Bedchamber.

CHASTELARD. What makes you sigh though I be found a fool?
You have no blame: and for my death, sweet friend,
I never could have lived long either way.
Why, as I live, the joy I have of this
Would make men mad that were not mad with love;
I hear my blood sing, and my lifted heart
Is like a springing water blown of wind
For pleasure of this deed. Now, in God's name,
I swear if there be danger in delight
I must die now: if joys have deadly teeth,
I'll have them bite my soul to death, and end
In the old asp's way, Egyptian-wise; be killed
In a royal purple fashion. Look, my love
Would kill me if my body were past hurt
Of any man's hand; and to die thereof,
I say, is sweeter than all sorts of life.
I would not have her love me now, for then
I should die meanlier some time. I am safe,
Sure of her face, my life's end in her sight,
My blood shed out about her feet—by God,
My heart feels drunken when I think of it.
See you, she will not rid herself of me,
Not though she slay me: her sweet lips and life
Will smell of my spilt blood.
MARY BEATON. Give me good-night.
CHASTELARD. Yea, and good thanks.
Exit MARY BEATON.
Here is the very place:
Here has her body bowed the pillows in
And here her head thrust under made the sheet
Smell soft of her mixed hair and spice: even here
Her arms pushed back the coverlet, pulled here
The golden silken curtain halfway in

It may be, and made room to lean out loose,
Fair tender fallen arms. Now, if God would,
Doubtless he might take pity on my soul
To give me three clear hours, and then red hell
Snare me forever: this were merciful:
If I were God now I should do thus much.
I must die next, and this were not so hard
For him to let me eat sweet fruit and die
With my lips sweet from it. For one shall have
This fare for common days'-bread, which to me
Should be a touch kept always on my sense
To make hell soft, yea, the keen pain of hell
Soft as the loosening of wound arms in sleep.
Ah, love is good, and the worst part of it
More than all things but death. She will be here
In some small while, and see me face to face
That am to give up life for her and go
Where a man lies with all his loves put out
And his lips full of earth. I think on her,
And the old pleasure stings and makes half-tears
Under mine eyelids. Prithee, love, come fast,
That I may die soon: yea, some kisses through,
I shall die joyfully enough, so God
Keep me alive till then. I feel her feet
Coming far off; now must I hold my heart,
Steadying my blood to see her patiently.
[...]
Enter the QUEEN.
CHASTELARD. Be not afraid.
QUEEN. Saint Mary! what a shaken wit have I!
Nay, is it you? who let you through the doors?
Where be my maidens? which way got you in?
Nay, but stand up, kiss not my hands so hard;
By God's fair body, if you but breathe on them
You are just dead and slain at once. What adder
Has bit you mirthful mad? for by this light
A man to have his head laughed off for mirth
Is no great jest. Lay not your eyes on me;

What, would you not be slain?
CHASTELARD. I pray you, madam,
Bear with me a brief space and let me speak.
I will not touch your garments even, nor speak
But in soft wise, and look some other way,
If that it like you; for I came not here
For pleasure of the eyes; yet, if you will,
Let me look on you.
QUEEN. As you will, fair sir.
Give me that coif to gather in my hair—
I thank you—and my girdle—nay, that side.
Speak, if you will; yet if you will be gone,
Why, you shall go, because I hate you not.
You know that I might slay you with my lips,
With calling out? but I will hold my peace.
CHASTELARD. Yea, do some while. I had a thing to say;
I know not wholly what thing. O my sweet,
I am come here to take farewell of love
That I have served, and life that I have lived
Made up of love, here in the sight of you
That all my life's time I loved more than God,
Who quits me thus with bitter death for it.
For you well know that I must shortly die,
My life being wound about you as it is,
Who love me not; yet do not hate me, sweet,
But tell me wherein I came short of love;
For doubtless I came short of a just love,
And fell in some fool's fault that angered you.
Now that I talk men dig my grave for me
Out in the rain, and in a little while
I shall be thrust in some sad space of earth
Out of your eyes; and you, O you my love,
A newly-wedded lady full of mirth
And a queen girt with all good people's love,
You shall be fair and merry in all your days.
Is this so much for me to have of you?
Do but speak, sweet: I know these are no words
A man should say though he were now to die,

But I am as a child for love, and have
No strength at heart; yea, I am afraid to die,
For the harsh dust will lie upon my face
Too thick to see you past. Look how I love you;
I did so love you always, that your face
Seen through my sleep has wrung mine eyes to tears
For pure delight in you. Why do you thus?
You answer not, but your lips curl in twain
And your face moves; there, I shall make you weep
And be a coward too; it were much best
I should be slain.
QUEEN. Yea, best such folk were slain;
Why should they live to cozen fools with lies?
You would swear now you have used me faithfully;
Shall I not make you swear? I am ware of you:
You will not do it; nay, for the fear of God
You will not swear. Come, I am merciful;
God made a foolish woman, making me,
And I have loved your mistress with whole heart;
Say you do love her, you shall marry her
And she give thanks: yet I could wish your love
Had not so lightly chosen forth a face;
For your fair sake, because I hate you not.
CHASTELARD. What is to say? why, you do surely know
That since my days were counted for a man's
I have loved you; yea, how past all help and sense,
Whatever thing was bitter to my love,
I have loved you; how when I rode in war
Your face went floated in among men's helms,
Your voice went through the shriek of slipping swords;
Yea, and I never have loved women well,
Seeing always in my sight I had your lips
Curled over, red and sweet; and the soft space
Of carven brows, and splendor of great throat
Swayed lily-wise; what pleasure should one have
To wind his arms about a lesser love?
I have seen you; why, this were joy enough
For God's eyes up in heaven, only to see

And to come never nearer than I am.
Why, it was in my flesh, my bone and blood,
Bound in my brain, to love you; yea, and writ
All my heart over: if I would lie to you
I doubt I could not lie. Ah, you see now,
You know now well enough; yea, there, sweet love,
Let me kiss there.
QUEEN. I love you best of them.
Clasp me quite round till your lips cleave on mine,
False mine, that did you wrong. Forgive them dearly
As you are sweet to them; for by love's love
I am not that evil woman in my heart
That laughs at a rent faith. O Chastelard,
Since this was broken to me of your new love
I have not seen the face of a sweet hour.
Nay, if there be no pardon in a man,
What shall a woman have for loving him?
Pardon me, sweet.
CHASTELARD. Yea, so I pardon you,
And this side now; the first way. Would God please
To slay me so! who knows how he might please?
Now I am thinking, if you know it not,
How I might kill you, kiss your breath clean out,
And take your soul to bring mine through to God,
That our two souls might close and be one twain
Or a twain one, and God himself want skill
To set us either severally apart.
O, you must overlive me many years,
And many years my soul be in waste hell;
But when some time God can no more refrain
To lay death like a kiss across your lips,
And great lords bear you clothed with funeral things,
And your crown girded over deadly brows,
Then after all your happy reach of life
For pity you shall touch me with your eyes,
Remembering love was fellow with my flesh
Here in sweet earth, and make me well of love
And heal my many years with piteousness.

QUEEN. You talk too sadly and too feignedly.
CHASTELARD. Too sad, but not too feigned; I am sad
That I shall die here without feigning thus;
And without feigning I were fain to live.
QUEEN. Alas, you will be taken presently
And then you are but dead. Pray you get hence.
CHASTELARD. I will not.
QUEEN. Nay, for God's love be away;
You will be slain and I get shame. God's mercy!
You were stark mad to come here; kiss me, sweet.
Oh, I do love you more than all men! yea,
Take my lips to you, close mine eyes up fast,
So you leave hold a little; there, for pity,
Abide now, and to-morrow come to me.
Nay, lest one see red kisses in my throat—
Dear God! what shall I give you to be gone?
CHASTELARD. I will not go. Look, here's full night grown up;
Why should I seek to sleep away from here?
The place is soft and the lights burn for sleep;
Be not you moved; I shall lie well enough.
QUEEN. You are utterly undone. Sweet, by my life,
You shall be saved with taking ship at once.
For if you stay this foolish love's hour out
There is not ten days' likely life in you.
This is no choice.
CHASTELARD. Nay, for I will not go.
QUEEN. O me! this is that Bayard's blood of yours
That makes you mad; yea, and you shall not stay.
I do not understand. Mind, you must die.
Alas, poor lord, you have no sense of me;
I shall be deadly to you.
CHASTELARD. Yea, I saw that;
But I saw not that when my death's day came
You could be quite so sweet to me.
QUEEN. My love!
If I could kiss my heart's root out on you
You would taste love hid at the core of me.
CHASTELARD. Kiss me twice more. This beautiful bowed head

That has such hair with kissing ripples in
And shivering soft eyelashes and brows
With fluttered blood; but laugh a little, sweetly,
That I may see your sad mouth's laughing look
I have used sweet hours in seeing. O, will you weep?
I pray you do not weep.

QUEEN. Nay, dear, I have
No tears in me; I never shall weep much,
I think, in all my life; I have wept for wrath
Sometimes and for mere pain, but for love's pity
I cannot weep at all. I would to God
You loved me less; I give you all I can
For all this love of yours, and yet I am sure
I shall live out the sorrow of your death
And be glad afterwards. You know I am sorry.
I should weep now; forgive me for your part,
God made me hard, I think. Alas, you see
I had fain been other than I am.

CHASTELARD. Yea, love.
Comfort your heart. What way am I to die?

QUEEN. Ah, will you go yet, sweet?

CHASTELARD. No, by God's body.
You will not see? how shall I make you see?
Look, it may be love was a sort of curse
Made for my plague and mixed up with my days
Somewise in their beginning; or indeed
A bitter birth begotten of sad stars
At mine own body's birth, that heaven might make
My life taste sharp where other men drank sweet;
But whether in heavy body or broken soul,
I know it must go on to be my death.
There was the matter of my fate in me
When I was fashioned first, and given such life
As goes with a sad end; no fault but God's.
Yea, and for all this I am not penitent:
You see I am perfect in these sins of mine,
I have my sins writ in a book to read;
Now I shall die and be well done with this.

But I am sure you cannot see such things,
God knows I blame you not.

QUEEN. What shall be said?
You know most well that I am sorrowful.
But you should chide me. Sweet, you have seen fair wars,
Have seen men slain and ridden red in them;
Why will you die a chamberer's death like this?
What, shall no praise be written of my knight,
For my fame's sake?

CHASTELARD. Nay, no great praise, I think;
I will no more; what should I do with death,
Though I died goodly out of sight of you?
I have gone once: here am I set now, sweet,
Till the end come. That is your husband, hark,
He knocks at the outer door. Kiss me just once.
You know now all you have to say. Nay, love,
Let him come quickly.

From POEMS AND BALLADS, FIRST SERIES (1866)

A Ballad of Life

I found in dreams a place of wind and flowers,
  Full of sweet trees and colour of glad grass,
  In midst whereof there was
A lady clothed like summer with sweet hours.
Her beauty, fervent as a fiery moon,
  Made my blood burn and swoon
    Like a flame rained upon.
Sorrow had filled her shaken eyelids' blue,
And her mouth's sad red heavy rose all through
    Seemed sad with glad things gone.

She held a little cithern by the strings,
  Shaped heartwise, strung with subtle-coloured hair
  Of some dead lute-player
That in dead years had done delicious things.
The seven strings were named accordingly;
  The first string charity,
    The second tenderness,
The rest were pleasure, sorrow, sleep, and sin,
And loving-kindness, that is pity's kin
    And is most pitiless.

There were three men with her, each garmented
  With gold and shod with gold upon the feet;
  And with plucked ears of wheat

The first man's hair was wound upon his head:
His face was red, and his mouth curled and sad;
All his gold garment had
Pale stains of dust and rust.
A riven hood was pulled across his eyes;
The token of him being upon this wise
Made for a sign of Lust.

The next was Shame, with hollow heavy face
Coloured like green wood when flame kindles it.
He hath such feeble feet
They may not well endure in any place.
His face was full of grey old miseries,
And all his blood's increase
Was even increase of pain.
The last was Fear, that is akin to Death;
He is Shame's friend, and always as Shame saith
Fear answers him again.

My soul said in me; This is marvellous,
Seeing the air's face is not so delicate
Nor the sun's grace so great,
If sin and she be kin or amorous.
And seeing where maidens served her on their knees,
I bade one crave of these
To know the cause thereof.
Then Fear said: I am Pity that was dead.
And Shame said: I am Sorrow comforted.
And Lust said: I am Love.

Thereat her hands began a lute-playing
And her sweet mouth a song in a strange tongue;
And all the while she sung
There was no sound but long tears following
Long tears upon men's faces, waxen white
With extreme sad delight.
But those three following men
Became as men raised up among the dead;

Great glad mouths open and fair cheeks made red
With child's blood come again.

Then I said: Now assuredly I see
My lady is perfect, and transfigureth
All sin and sorrow and death,
Making them fair as her own eyelids be,
Or lips wherein my whole soul's life abides;
Or as her sweet white sides
And bosom carved to kiss.
Now therefore, if her pity further me,
Doubtless for her sake all my days shall be
As righteous as she is.

Forth, ballad, and take roses in both arms,
Even till the top rose touch thee in the throat
Where the least thornprick harms;
And girdled in thy golden singing-coat,
Come thou before my lady and say this;
Borgia, thy gold hair's colour burns in me,
Thy mouth makes beat my blood in feverish rhymes;
Therefore so many as these roses be,
Kiss me so many times.
Then it may be, seeing how sweet she is,
That she will stoop herself none otherwise
Than a blown vine-branch doth,
And kiss thee with soft laughter on thine eyes,
Ballad, and on thy mouth.

A Ballad of Death

Kneel down, fair Love, and fill thyself with tears,
Girdle thyself with sighing for a girth
Upon the sides of mirth,
Cover thy lips and eyelids, let thine ears
Be filled with rumour of people sorrowing;
Make thee soft raiment out of woven sighs
Upon the flesh to cleave,
Set pains therein and many a grievous thing,
And many sorrows after each his wise
For armlet and for gorget and for sleeve.

O Love's lute heard about the lands of death,
Left hanged upon the trees that were therein;
O Love and Time and Sin,
Three singing mouths that mourn now underbreath,
Three lovers, each one evil spoken of;
O smitten lips wherethrough this voice of mine
Came softer with her praise;
Abide a little for our lady's love.
The kisses of her mouth were more than wine,
And more than peace the passage of her days.

O Love, thou knowest if she were good to see.
O Time, thou shalt not find in any land
Till, cast out of thine hand,
The sunlight and the moonlight fail from thee,
Another woman fashioned like as this.
O Sin, thou knowest that all thy shame in her
Was made a goodly thing;
Yea, she caught Shame and shamed him with her kiss,
With her fair kiss, and lips much lovelier
Than lips of amorous roses in late spring.

By night there stood over against my bed
Queen Venus with a hood striped gold and black,

Both sides drawn fully back
From brows wherein the sad blood failed of red,
And temples drained of purple and full of death.
Her curled hair had the wave of sea-water
And the sea's gold in it.
Her eyes were as a dove's that sickeneth.
Strewn dust of gold she had shed over her,
And pearl and purple and amber on her feet.

Upon her raiment of dyed sendaline
Were painted all the secret ways of love
And covered things thereof,
That hold delight as grape-flowers hold their wine;
Red mouths of maidens and red feet of doves,
And brides that kept within the bride-chamber
Their garment of soft shame,
And weeping faces of the wearied loves
That swoon in sleep and awake wearier,
With heat of lips and hair shed out like flame.

The tears that through her eyelids fell on me
Made mine own bitter where they ran between
As blood had fallen therein,
She saying; Arise, lift up thine eyes and see
If any glad thing be or any good
Now the best thing is taken forth of us;
Even she to whom all praise
Was as one flower in a great multitude,
One glorious flower of many and glorious,
One day found gracious among many days:

Even she whose handmaiden was Love—to whom
At kissing times across her stateliest bed
Kings bowed themselves and shed
Pale wine, and honey with the honeycomb,
And spikenard bruised for a burnt-offering;
Even she between whose lips the kiss became
As fire and frankincense;

Whose hair was as gold raiment on a king,
Whose eyes were as the morning purged with flame,
Whose eyelids as sweet savour issuing thence.

Then I beheld, and lo on the other side
My lady's likeness crowned and robed and dead.
Sweet still, but now not red,
Was the shut mouth whereby men lived and died.
And sweet, but emptied of the blood's blue shade,
The great curled eyelids that withheld her eyes.
And sweet, but like spoilt gold,
The weight of colour in her tresses weighed.
And sweet, but as a vesture with new dyes,
The body that was clothed with love of old.

Ah! that my tears filled all her woven hair
And all the hollow bosom of her gown—
Ah! that my tears ran down
Even to the place where many kisses were,
Even where her parted breast-flowers have place,
Even where they are cloven apart—who knows not this?
Ah! the flowers cleave apart
And their sweet fills the tender interspace;
Ah! the leaves grown thereof were things to kiss
Ere their fine gold was tarnished at the heart.

Ah! in the days when God did good to me,
Each part about her was a righteous thing;
Her mouth an almsgiving,
The glory of her garments charity,
The beauty of her bosom a good deed,
In the good days when God kept sight of us;
Love lay upon her eyes,
And on that hair whereof the world takes heed;
And all her body was more virtuous
Than souls of women fashioned otherwise.

Now, ballad, gather poppies in thine hands

And sheaves of brier and many rusted sheaves
Rain-rotten in rank lands,
Waste marigold and late unhappy leaves
And grass that fades ere any of it be mown;
And when thy bosom is filled full thereof
Seek out Death's face ere the light altereth,
And say "My master that was thrall to Love
Is become thrall to Death."
Bow down before him, ballad, sigh and groan,
But make no sojourn in thy outgoing;
For haply it may be
That when thy feet return at evening
Death shall come in with thee.

Laus Veneris

Lors dit en plourant; Hélas trop malheureux homme et mauldict pescheur, oncques ne verrai-je clémence et miséricorde de Dieu. Ores m'en irai-je d'icy et me cacherai dedans le mont Horsel, en requérant de faveur et d'amoureuse merci ma doulce dame Vénus, car pour son amour serai-je bien à tout jamais damné en enfer. Voicy la fin de tous mes faicts d'armes et de toutes mes belles chansons. Hélas, trop belle estoyt la face de ma dame et ses yeulx, et en mauvais jour je vis ces chouses-là. Lors s'en alla tout en gémissant et se retourna chez elle, et là vescut tristement en grand amour près de sa dame. Puis après advint que le pape vit un jour esclater sur son baston force belles fleurs rouges et blanches et maints boutons de feuilles, et ainsi vit-il reverdir toute l'escorce. Ce dont il eut grande crainte et moult s'en esmut, et grande pitié lui prit de ce chevalier qui s'en estoyt départi sans espoir comme un homme misérable et damné. Doncques envoya force messaigers devers luy pour le ramener, disant qu'il aurait de Dieu grace et bonne absolution de son grand pesché d'amour. Mais oncques plus ne le virent; car toujours demeura ce pauvre chevalier auprès de Vénus la haulte et forte déesse ès flancs de la montagne amoureuse.

Livre des grandes merveilles d'amour, escript en latin et en françoys par Maistre Antoine Gaget. 1530.

Asleep or waking is it? for her neck,
Kissed over close, wears yet a purple speck
  Wherein the pained blood falters and goes out;
Soft, and stung softly—fairer for a fleck.

But though my lips shut sucking on the place,
There is no vein at work upon her face;
  Her eyelids are so peaceable, no doubt
Deep sleep has warmed her blood through all its ways.

Lo, this is she that was the world's delight;
The old grey years were parcels of her might;
  The strewings of the ways wherein she trod
Were the twain seasons of the day and night.

Lo, she was thus when her clear limbs enticed
All lips that now grow sad with kissing Christ,
  Stained with blood fallen from the feet of God,
The feet and hands whereat our souls were priced.

Alas, Lord, surely thou art great and fair.
But lo her wonderfully woven hair!
  And thou didst heal us with thy piteous kiss;
But see now, Lord; her mouth is lovelier.

She is right fair; what hath she done to thee?
Nay, fair Lord Christ, lift up thine eyes and see;
  Had now thy mother such a lip—like this?
Thou knowest how sweet a thing it is to me.

Inside the Horsel here the air is hot;
Right little peace one hath for it, God wot;
  The scented dusty daylight burns the air,
And my heart chokes me till I hear it not.

Behold, my Venus, my soul's body, lies
With my love laid upon her garment-wise,
  Feeling my love in all her limbs and hair
And shed between her eyelids through her eyes.

She holds my heart in her sweet open hands
Hanging asleep; hard by her head there stands,
  Crowned with gilt thorns and clothed with flesh like fire,
Love, wan as foam blown up the salt burnt sands—

Hot as the brackish waifs of yellow spume
That shift and steam—loose clots of arid fume
   From the sea's panting mouth of dry desire;
There stands he, like one labouring at a loom.

The warp holds fast across; and every thread
That makes the woof up has dry specks of red;
   Always the shuttle cleaves clean through, and he
Weaves with the hair of many a ruined head.

Love is not glad nor sorry, as I deem;
Labouring he dreams, and labours in the dream,
   Till when the spool is finished, lo I see
His web, reeled off, curls and goes out like steam.

Night falls like fire; the heavy lights run low,
And as they drop, my blood and body so
   Shake as the flame shakes, full of days and hours
That sleep not neither weep they as they go.

Ah yet would God this flesh of mine might be
Where air might wash and long leaves cover me,
   Where tides of grass break into foam of flowers,
Or where the wind's feet shine along the sea.

Ah yet would God that stems and roots were bred
Out of my weary body and my head,
   That sleep were sealed upon me with a seal,
And I were as the least of all his dead.

Would God my blood were dew to feed the grass,
Mine ears made deaf and mine eyes blind as glass,
   My body broken as a turning wheel,
And my mouth stricken ere it saith Alas!

Ah God, that love were as a flower or flame,
That life were as the naming of a name,
   That death were not more pitiful than desire,
That these things were not one thing and the same!

Behold now, surely somewhere there is death:
For each man hath some space of years, he saith,
A little space of time ere time expire,
A little day, a little way of breath.

And lo, between the sundawn and the sun,
His day's work and his night's work are undone;
And lo, between the nightfall and the light,
He is not, and none knoweth of such an one.

Ah God, that I were as all souls that be,
As any herb or leaf of any tree,
As men that toil through hours of labouring night,
As bones of men under the deep sharp sea.

Outside it must be winter among men;
For at the gold bars of the gates again
I heard all night and all the hours of it
The wind's wet wings and fingers drip with rain.

Knights gather, riding sharp for cold; I know
The ways and woods are strangled with the snow;
And with short song the maidens spin and sit
Until Christ's birthnight, lily-like, arow.

The scent and shadow shed about me make
The very soul in all my senses ache;
The hot hard night is fed upon my breath,
And sleep beholds me from afar awake.

Alas, but surely where the hills grow deep,
Or where the wild ways of the sea are steep,
Or in strange places somewhere there is death,
And on death's face the scattered hair of sleep.

There lover-like with lips and limbs that meet
They lie, they pluck sweet fruit of life and eat;
But me the hot and hungry days devour,
And in my mouth no fruit of theirs is sweet.

No fruit of theirs, but fruit of my desire,
For her love's sake whose lips through mine respire;
   Her eyelids on her eyes like flower on flower,
Mine eyelids on mine eyes like fire on fire.

So lie we, not as sleep that lies by death,
With heavy kisses and with happy breath;
   Not as man lies by woman, when the bride
Laughs low for love's sake and the words he saith.

For she lies, laughing low with love; she lies
And turns his kisses on her lips to sighs,
   To sighing sound of lips unsatisfied,
And the sweet tears are tender with her eyes.

Ah, not as they, but as the souls that were
Slain in the old time, having found her fair;
   Who, sleeping with her lips upon their eyes,
Heard sudden serpents hiss across her hair.

Their blood runs round the roots of time like rain:
She casts them forth and gathers them again;
   With nerve and bone she weaves and multiplies
Exceeding pleasure out of extreme pain.

Her little chambers drip with flower-like red,
Her girdles, and the chaplets of her head,
   Her armlets and her anklets; with her feet
She tramples all that winepress of the dead.

Her gateways smoke with fume of flowers and fires,
With loves burnt out and unassuaged desires;
   Between her lips the steam of them is sweet,
The languor in her ears of many lyres.

Her beds are full of perfume and sad sound,
Her doors are made with music, and barred round
   With sighing and with laughter and with tears,
With tears whereby strong souls of men are bound.

There is the knight Adonis that was slain;
With flesh and blood she chains him for a chain;
   The body and the spirit in her ears
Cry, for her lips divide him vein by vein.

Yea, all she slayeth; yea, every man save me;
Me, love, thy lover that must cleave to thee
   Till the ending of the days and ways of earth,
The shaking of the sources of the sea.

Me, most forsaken of all souls that fell;
Me, satiated with things insatiable;
   Me, for whose sake the extreme hell makes mirth,
Yea, laughter kindles at the heart of hell.

Alas thy beauty! for thy mouth's sweet sake
My soul is bitter to me, my limbs quake
   As water, as the flesh of men that weep,
As their heart's vein whose heart goes nigh to break.

Ah God, that sleep with flower-sweet finger-tips
Would crush the fruit of death upon my lips;
   Ah God, that death would tread the grapes of sleep
And wring their juice upon me as it drips.

There is no change of cheer for many days,
But change of chimes high up in the air, that sways
   Rung by the running fingers of the wind;
And singing sorrows heard on hidden ways.

Day smiteth day in twain, night sundereth night,
And on mine eyes the dark sits as the light;
   Yea, Lord, thou knowest I know not, having sinned,
If heaven be clean or unclean in thy sight.

Yea, as if earth were sprinkled over me,
Such chafed harsh earth as chokes a sandy sea,
   Each pore doth yearn, and the dried blood thereof
Gasps by sick fits, my heart swims heavily,

There is a feverish famine in my veins;
Below her bosom, where a crushed grape stains
  The white and blue, there my lips caught and clove
An hour since, and what mark of me remains?

I dare not always touch her, lest the kiss
Leave my lips charred. Yea, Lord, a little bliss,
  Brief bitter bliss, one hath for a great sin;
Nathless thou knowest how sweet a thing it is.

Sin, is it sin whereby men's souls are thrust
Into the pit? yet had I a good trust
  To save my soul before it slipped therein,
Trod under by the fire-shod feet of lust.

For if mine eyes fail and my soul takes breath,
I look between the iron sides of death
  Into sad hell where all sweet love hath end,
All but the pain that never finisheth.

There are the naked faces of great kings,
The singing folk with all their lute-playings;
  There when one cometh he shall have to friend
The grave that covets and the worm that clings.

There sit the knights that were so great of hand,
The ladies that were queens of fair green land,
  Grown grey and black now, brought unto the dust,
Soiled, without raiment, clad about with sand.

There is one end for all of them; they sit
Naked and sad, they drink the dregs of it,
  Trodden as grapes in the wine-press of lust,
Trampled and trodden by the fiery feet.

I see the marvellous mouth whereby there fell
Cities and people whom the gods loved well,
  Yet for her sake on them the fire gat hold,
And for their sakes on her the fire of hell.

And softer than the Egyptian lote-leaf is,
The queen whose face was worth the world to kiss,
Wearing at breast a suckling snake of gold;
And large pale lips of strong Semiramis,

Curled like a tiger's that curl back to feed;
Red only where the last kiss made them bleed;
Her hair most thick with many a carven gem,
Deep in the mane, great-chested, like a steed.

Yea, with red sin the faces of them shine;
But in all these there was no sin like mine;
No, not in all the strange great sins of them
That made the wine-press froth and foam with wine.

For I was of Christ's choosing, I God's knight,
No blinkard heathen stumbling for scant light;
I can well see, for all the dusty days
Gone past, the clean great time of goodly fight.

I smell the breathing battle sharp with blows,
With shriek of shafts and snapping short of bows;
The fair pure sword smites out in subtle ways,
Sounds and long lights are shed between the rows

Of beautiful mailed men; the edged light slips,
Most like a snake that takes short breath and dips
Sharp from the beautifully bending head,
With all its gracious body lithe as lips

That curl in touching you; right in this wise
My sword doth, seeming fire in mine own eyes,
Leaving all colours in them brown and red
And flecked with death; then the keen breaths like sighs,

The caught-up choked dry laughters following them,
When all the fighting face is grown a flame
For pleasure, and the pulse that stuns the ears,
And the heart's gladness of the goodly game.

Let me think yet a little; I do know
These things were sweet, but sweet such years ago,
   Their savour is all turned now into tears;
Yea, ten years since, where the blue ripples blow,

The blue curled eddies of the blowing Rhine,
I felt the sharp wind shaking grass and vine
   Touch my blood too, and sting me with delight
Through all this waste and weary body of mine

That never feels clear air; right gladly then
I rode alone, a great way off my men,
   And heard the chiming bridle smite and smite,
And gave each rhyme thereof some rhyme again,

Till my song shifted to that iron one;
Seeing there rode up between me and the sun
   Some certain of my foe's men, for his three
White wolves across their painted coats did run.

The first red-bearded, with square cheeks—alack,
I made my knave's blood turn his beard to black;
   The slaying of him was a joy to see:
Perchance too, when at night he came not back,

Some woman fell a-weeping, whom this thief
Would beat when he had drunken; yet small grief
   Hath any for the ridding of such knaves;
Yea, if one wept, I doubt her teen was brief.

This bitter love is sorrow in all lands,
Draining of eyelids, wringing of drenched hands,
   Sighing of hearts and filling up of graves;
A sign across the head of the world he stands,

An one that hath a plague-mark on his brows;
Dust and spilt blood do track him to his house
   Down under earth; sweet smells of lip and cheek,
Like a sweet snake's breath made more poisonous

With chewing of some perfumed deadly grass,
Are shed all round his passage if he pass,
And their quenched savour leaves the whole soul weak,
Sick with keen guessing whence the perfume was.

As one who hidden in deep sedge and reeds
Smells the rare scent made where a panther feeds,
And tracking ever slotwise the warm smell
Is snapped upon by the sweet mouth and bleeds,

His head far down the hot sweet throat of her—
So one tracks love, whose breath is deadlier,
And lo, one springe and you are fast in hell,
Fast as the gin's grip of a wayfarer.

I think now, as the heavy hours decease
One after one, and bitter thoughts increase
One upon one, of all sweet finished things;
The breaking of the battle; the long peace

Wherein we sat clothed softly, each man's hair
Crowned with green leaves beneath white hoods of vair;
The sounds of sharp spears at great tourneyings,
And noise of singing in the late sweet air.

I sang of love too, knowing nought thereof;
"Sweeter," I said, "the little laugh of love
Than tears out of the eyes of Magdalen,
Or any fallen feather of the Dove.

"The broken little laugh that spoils a kiss,
The ache of purple pulses, and the bliss
Of blinded eyelids that expand again—
Love draws them open with those lips of his,

"Lips that cling hard till the kissed face has grown
Of one same fire and colour with their own;
Then ere one sleep, appeased with sacrifice,
Where his lips wounded, there his lips atone."

I sang these things long since and knew them not;
"Lo, here is love, or there is love, God wot,
  This man and that finds favour in his eyes,"
I said, "but I, what guerdon have I got?

"The dust of praise that is blown everywhere
In all men's faces with the common air;
  The bay-leaf that wants chafing to be sweet
Before they wind it in a singer's hair."

So that one dawn I rode forth sorrowing;
I had no hope but of some evil thing,
  And so rode slowly past the windy wheat
And past the vineyard and the water-spring,

Up to the Horsel. A great elder-tree
Held back its heaps of flowers to let me see
  The ripe tall grass, and one that walked therein,
Naked, with hair shed over to the knee.

She walked between the blossom and the grass;
I knew the beauty of her, what she was,
  The beauty of her body and her sin,
And in my flesh the sin of hers, alas!

Alas! for sorrow is all the end of this.
O sad kissed mouth, how sorrowful it is!
  O breast whereat some suckling sorrow clings,
Red with the bitter blossom of a kiss!

Ah, with blind lips I felt for you, and found
About my neck your hands and hair enwound,
  The hands that stifle and the hair that stings,
I felt them fasten sharply without sound.

Yea, for my sin I had great store of bliss:
Rise up, make answer for me, let thy kiss
  Seal my lips hard from speaking of my sin,
Lest one go mad to hear how sweet it is.

Yet I waxed faint with fume of barren bowers,
And murmuring of the heavy-headed hours;
   And let the dove's beak fret and peck within
My lips in vain, and Love shed fruitless flowers.

So that God looked upon me when your hands
Were hot about me; yea, God brake my bands
   To save my soul alive, and I came forth
Like a man blind and naked in strange lands

That hears men laugh and weep, and knows not whence
Nor wherefore, but is broken in his sense;
   Howbeit I met folk riding from the north
Towards Rome, to purge them of their souls' offence,

And rode with them, and spake to none; the day
Stunned me like lights upon some wizard way,
   And ate like fire mine eyes and mine eyesight;
So rode I, hearing all these chant and pray,

And marvelled; till before us rose and fell
White cursed hills, like outer skirts of hell
   Seen where men's eyes look through the day to night,
Like a jagged shell's lips, harsh, untunable,

Blown in between by devils' wrangling breath;
Nathless we won well past that hell and death,
   Down to the sweet land where all airs are good,
Even unto Rome where God's grace tarrieth.

Then came each man and worshipped at his knees
Who in the Lord God's likeness bears the keys
   To bind or loose, and called on Christ's shed blood,
And so the sweet-souled father gave him ease.

But when I came I fell down at his feet,
Saying, "Father, though the Lord's blood be right sweet,
   The spot it takes not off the panther's skin,
Nor shall an Ethiop's stain be bleached with it.

"Lo, I have sinned and have spat out at God,
Wherefore his hand is heavier and his rod
More sharp because of mine exceeding sin,
And all his raiment redder than bright blood

"Before mine eyes; yea, for my sake I wot
The heat of hell is waxen seven times hot
Through my great sin." Then spake he some sweet word,
Giving me cheer; which thing availed me not;

Yea, scarce I wist if such indeed were said;
For when I ceased—lo, as one newly dead
Who hears a great cry out of hell, I heard
The crying of his voice across my head.

"Until this dry shred staff, that hath no whit
Of leaf nor bark, bear blossom and smell sweet,
Seek thou not any mercy in God's sight,
For so long shalt thou be cast out from it."

Yea, what if dried-up stems wax red and green,
Shall that thing be which is not nor has been?
Yea, what if sapless bark wax green and white,
Shall any good fruit grow upon my sin?

Nay, though sweet fruit were plucked of a dry tree,
And though men drew sweet waters of the sea,
There should not grow sweet leaves on this dead stem,
This waste wan body and shaken soul of me.

Yea, though God search it warily enough,
There is not one sound thing in all thereof;
Though he search all my veins through, searching them
He shall find nothing whole therein but love.

For I came home right heavy, with small cheer,
And lo my love, mine own soul's heart, more dear
Than mine own soul, more beautiful than God,
Who hath my being between the hands of her—

Fair still, but fair for no man saving me,
As when she came out of the naked sea
   Making the foam as fire whereon she trod,
And as the inner flower of fire was she.

Yea, she laid hold upon me, and her mouth
Clove unto mine as soul to body doth,
   And, laughing, made her lips luxurious;
Her hair had smells of all the sunburnt south,

Strange spice and flower, strange savour of crushed fruit,
And perfume the swart kings tread underfoot
   For pleasure when their minds wax amorous,
Charred frankincense and grated sandal-root.

And I forgot fear and all weary things,
All ended prayers and perished thanksgivings,
   Feeling her face with all her eager hair
Cleave to me, clinging as a fire that clings

To the body and to the raiment, burning them;
As after death I know that such-like flame
   Shall cleave to me for ever; yea, what care,
Albeit I burn then, having felt the same?

Ah love, there is no better life than this;
To have known love, how bitter a thing it is,
   And afterward be cast out of God's sight;
Yea, these that know not, shall they have such bliss

High up in barren heaven before his face
As we twain in the heavy-hearted place,
   Remembering love and all the dead delight,
And all that time was sweet with for a space?

For till the thunder in the trumpet be,
Soul may divide from body, but not we
   One from another; I hold thee with my hand,
I let mine eyes have all their will of thee,

I seal myself upon thee with my might,
Abiding alway out of all men's sight
Until God loosen over sea and land
The thunder of the trumpets of the night.

EXPLICIT LAUS VENERIS

The Triumph of Time

Before our lives divide for ever,
While time is with us and hands are free,
(Time, swift to fasten and swift to sever
Hand from hand, as we stand by the sea)
I will say no word that a man might say
Whose whole life's love goes down in a day;
For this could never have been; and never,
Though the gods and the years relent, shall be.

Is it worth a tear, is it worth an hour,
To think of things that are well outworn?
Of fruitless husk and fugitive flower,
The dream foregone and the deed forborne?
Though joy be done with and grief be vain,
Time shall not sever us wholly in twain;
Earth is not spoilt for a single shower;
But the rain has ruined the ungrown corn.

It will grow not again, this fruit of my heart,
Smitten with sunbeams, ruined with rain.
The singing seasons divide and depart,
Winter and summer depart in twain.
It will grow not again, it is ruined at root,
The bloodlike blossom, the dull red fruit;
Though the heart yet sickens, the lips yet smart,
With sullen savour of poisonous pain.

I have given no man of my fruit to eat;
I trod the grapes, I have drunken the wine.
Had you eaten and drunken and found it sweet,
This wild new growth of the corn and vine,
This wine and bread without lees or leaven,
We had grown as gods, as the gods in heaven,
Souls fair to look upon, goodly to greet,
One splendid spirit, your soul and mine.

In the change of years, in the coil of things,
In the clamour and rumour of life to be,
We, drinking love at the furthest springs,
Covered with love as a covering tree,
We had grown as gods, as the gods above,
Filled from the heart to the lips with love,
Held fast in his hands, clothed warm with his wings,
O love, my love, had you loved but me!

We had stood as the sure stars stand, and moved
As the moon moves, loving the world; and seen
Grief collapse as a thing disproved,
Death consume as a thing unclean.
Twain halves of a perfect heart, made fast
Soul to soul while the years fell past;
Had you loved me once, as you have not loved;
Had the chance been with us that has not been.

I have put my days and dreams out of mind,
Days that are over, dreams that are done.
Though we seek life through, we shall surely find
There is none of them clear to us now, not one.
But clear are these things; the grass and the sand,
Where, sure as the eyes reach, ever at hand,
With lips wide open and face burnt blind,
The strong sea-daisies feast on the sun.

The low downs lean to the sea; the stream,
One loose thin pulseless tremulous vein,

Rapid and vivid and dumb as a dream,
Works downward, sick of the sun and the rain;
No wind is rough with the rank rare flowers;
The sweet sea, mother of loves and hours,
Shudders and shines as the grey winds gleam,
Turning her smile to a fugitive pain.

Mother of loves that are swift to fade,
Mother of mutable winds and hours.
A barren mother, a mother-maid,
Cold and clean as her faint salt flowers.
I would we twain were even as she,
Lost in the night and the light of the sea,
Where faint sounds falter and wan beams wade,
Break, and are broken, and shed into showers.

The loves and hours of the life of a man,
They are swift and sad, being born of the sea.
Hours that rejoice and regret for a span,
Born with a man's breath, mortal as he;
Loves that are lost ere they come to birth,
Weeds of the wave, without fruit upon earth.
I lose what I long for, save what I can,
My love, my love, and no love for me!

It is not much that a man can save
On the sands of life, in the straits of time,
Who swims in sight of the great third wave
That never a swimmer shall cross or climb.
Some waif washed up with the strays and spars
That ebb-tide shows to the shore and the stars;
Weed from the water, grass from a grave,
A broken blossom, a ruined rhyme.

There will no man do for your sake, I think,
What I would have done for the least word said.
I had wrung life dry for your lips to drink,
Broken it up for your daily bread:

Body for body and blood for blood,
As the flow of the full sea risen to flood
That yearns and trembles before it sink,
  I had given, and lain down for you, glad and dead.

Yea, hope at highest and all her fruit,
  And time at fullest and all his dower,
I had given you surely, and life to boot,
  Were we once made one for a single hour.
But now, you are twain, you are cloven apart,
Flesh of his flesh, but heart of my heart;
And deep in one is the bitter root,
  And sweet for one is the lifelong flower.

To have died if you cared I should die for you, clung
  To my life if you bade me, played my part
As it pleased you—these were the thoughts that stung,
  The dreams that smote with a keener dart
Than shafts of love or arrows of death;
These were but as fire is, dust, or breath,
Or poisonous foam on the tender tongue
  Of the little snakes that eat my heart.

I wish we were dead together to-day,
  Lost sight of, hidden away out of sight,
Clasped and clothed in the cloven clay,
  Out of the world's way, out of the light,
Out of the ages of worldly weather,
Forgotten of all men altogether,
As the world's first dead, taken wholly away,
  Made one with death, filled full of the night.

How we should slumber, how we should sleep,
  Far in the dark with the dreams and the dews!
And dreaming, grow to each other, and weep,
  Laugh low, live softly, murmur and muse;
Yea, and it may be, struck through by the dream,
Feel the dust quicken and quiver, and seem

Alive as of old to the lips, and leap
   Spirit to spirit as lovers use.

Sick dreams and sad of a dull delight;
   For what shall it profit when men are dead
To have dreamed, to have loved with the whole soul's might,
   To have looked for day when the day was fled?
Let come what will, there is one thing worth,
To have had fair love in the life upon earth:
To have held love safe till the day grew night,
   While skies had colour and lips were red.

Would I lose you now? would I take you then,
   If I lose you now that my heart has need?
And come what may after death to men,
   What thing worth this will the dead years breed?
Lose life, lose all; but at least I know,
O sweet life's love, having loved you so,
Had I reached you on earth, I should lose not again,
   In death nor life, nor in dream or deed.

Yea, I know this well: were you once sealed mine,
   Mine in the blood's beat, mine in the breath,
Mixed into me as honey in wine,
   Not time, that sayeth and gainsayeth,
Nor all strong things had severed us then;
Not wrath of gods, nor wisdom of men,
Nor all things earthly, nor all divine,
   Nor joy nor sorrow, nor life nor death.

I had grown pure as the dawn and the dew,
   You had grown strong as the sun or the sea.
But none shall triumph a whole life through:
   For death is one, and the fates are three.
At the door of life, by the gate of breath,
There are worse things waiting for men than death;
Death could not sever my soul and you,
   As these have severed your soul from me.

You have chosen and clung to the chance they sent you,
   Life sweet as perfume and pure as prayer.
But will it not one day in heaven repent you?
   Will they solace you wholly, the days that were?
Will you lift up your eyes between sadness and bliss,
Meet mine, and see where the great love is,
And tremble and turn and be changed? Content you;
   The gate is strait; I shall not be there.

But you, had you chosen, had you stretched hand,
   Had you seen good such a thing were done,
I too might have stood with the souls that stand
   In the sun's sight, clothed with the light of the sun;
But who now on earth need care how I live?
Have the high gods anything left to give,
Save dust and laurels and gold and sand?
   Which gifts are goodly; but I will none.

O all fair lovers about the world,
   There is none of you, none, that shall comfort me.
My thoughts are as dead things, wrecked and whirled
   Round and round in a gulf of the sea;
And still, through the sound and the straining stream,
Through the coil and chafe, they gleam in a dream,
The bright fine lips so cruelly curled,
   And strange swift eyes where the soul sits free.

Free, without pity, withheld from woe,
   Ignorant; fair as the eyes are fair.
Would I have you change now, change at a blow,
   Startled and stricken, awake and aware?
Yea, if I could, would I have you see
My very love of you filling me,
And know my soul to the quick, as I know
   The likeness and look of your throat and hair?

I shall not change you. Nay, though I might,
   Would I change my sweet one love with a word?

I had rather your hair should change in a night,
   Clear now as the plume of a black bright bird;
Your face fail suddenly, cease, turn grey,
Die as a leaf that dies in a day.
I will keep my soul in a place out of sight,
   Far off, where the pulse of it is not heard.

Far off it walks, in a bleak blown space,
   Full of the sound of the sorrow of years.
I have woven a veil for the weeping face,
   Whose lips have drunken the wine of tears;
I have found a way for the failing feet,
A place for slumber and sorrow to meet;
There is no rumour about the place,
   Nor light, nor any that sees or hears.

I have hidden my soul out of sight, and said
   "Let none take pity upon thee, none
Comfort thy crying: for lo, thou art dead,
   Lie still now, safe out of sight of the sun.
Have I not built thee a grave, and wrought
Thy grave-clothes on thee of grievous thought,
With soft spun verses and tears unshed,
   And sweet light visions of things undone?

"I have given thee garments and balm and myrrh,
   And gold, and beautiful burial things.
But thou, be at peace now, make no stir;
   Is not thy grave as a royal king's?
Fret not thyself though the end were sore;
Sleep, be patient, vex me no more.
Sleep; what hast thou to do with her?
   The eyes that weep, with the mouth that sings?"

Where the dead red leaves of the years lie rotten,
   The cold old crimes and the deeds thrown by,
The misconceived and the misbegotten,
   I would find a sin to do ere I die,

Sure to dissolve and destroy me all through,
That would set you higher in heaven, serve you
And leave you happy, when clean forgotten,
  As a dead man out of mind, am I.

Your lithe hands draw me, your face burns through me,
  I am swift to follow you, keen to see;
But love lacks might to redeem or undo me;
  As I have been, I know I shall surely be;
"What should such fellows as I do?" Nay,
My part were worse if I chose to play;
For the worst is this after all; if they knew me,
  Not a soul upon earth would pity me.

And I play not for pity of these; but you,
  If you saw with your soul what man am I,
You would praise me at least that my soul all through
  Clove to you, loathing the lives that lie;
The souls and lips that are bought and sold,
The smiles of silver and kisses of gold,
The lapdog loves that whine as they chew,
  The little lovers that curse and cry.

There are fairer women, I hear; that may be;
  But I, that I love you and find you fair,
Who are more than fair in my eyes if they be,
  Do the high gods know or the great gods care?
Though the swords in my heart for one were seven,
Would the iron hollow of doubtful heaven,
That knows not itself whether night-time or day be,
  Reverberate words and a foolish prayer?

I will go back to the great sweet mother,
  Mother and lover of men, the sea.
I will go down to her, I and none other,
  Close with her, kiss her and mix her with me;
Cling to her, strive with her, hold her fast:
O fair white mother, in days long past

Born without sister, born without brother,
  Set free my soul as thy soul is free.

O fair green-girdled mother of mine,
  Sea, that art clothed with the sun and the rain,
Thy sweet hard kisses are strong like wine,
  Thy large embraces are keen like pain.
Save me and hide me with all thy waves,
Find me one grave of thy thousand graves,
Those pure cold populous graves of thine
  Wrought without hand in a world without stain.

I shall sleep, and move with the moving ships,
  Change as the winds change, veer in the tide;
My lips will feast on the foam of thy lips,
  I shall rise with thy rising, with thee subside;
Sleep, and not know if she be, if she were,
Filled full with life to the eyes and hair,
As a rose is fulfilled to the roseleaf tips
  With splendid summer and perfume and pride.

This woven raiment of nights and days,
  Were it once cast off and unwound from me,
Naked and glad would I walk in thy ways,
  Alive and aware of thy ways and thee;
Clear of the whole world, hidden at home,
Clothed with the green and crowned with the foam,
A pulse of the life of thy straits and bays,
  A vein in the heart of the streams of the sea.

Fair mother, fed with the lives of men,
  Thou art subtle and cruel of heart, men say.
Thou hast taken, and shalt not render again;
  Thou art full of thy dead, and cold as they.
But death is the worst that comes of thee;
Thou art fed with our dead, O mother, O sea,
But when hast thou fed on our hearts? or when,
  Having given us love, hast thou taken away?

O tender-hearted, O perfect lover,
  Thy lips are bitter, and sweet thine heart.
The hopes that hurt and the dreams that hover,
  Shall they not vanish away and apart?
But thou, thou art sure, thou art older than earth;
Thou art strong for death and fruitful of birth;
Thy depths conceal and thy gulfs discover;
  From the first thou wert; in the end thou art.

And grief shall endure not for ever, I know.
  As things that are not shall these things be;
We shall live through seasons of sun and of snow,
  And none be grievous as this to me.
We shall hear, as one in a trance that hears,
The sound of time, the rhyme of the years;
Wrecked hope and passionate pain will grow
  As tender things of a spring-tide sea.

Sea-fruit that swings in the waves that hiss,
  Drowned gold and purple and royal rings.
And all time past, was it all for this?
  Times unforgotten, and treasures of things?
Swift years of liking and sweet long laughter,
That wist not well of the years thereafter
Till love woke, smitten at heart by a kiss,
  With lips that trembled and trailing wings?

There lived a singer in France of old
  By the tideless dolorous midland sea.
In a land of sand and ruin and gold
  There shone one woman, and none but she.
And finding life for her love's sake fail,
Being fain to see her, he bade set sail,
Touched land, and saw her as life grew cold,
  And praised God, seeing; and so died he.

Died, praising God for his gift and grace:
  For she bowed down to him weeping, and said

"Live;" and her tears were shed on his face
  Or ever the life in his face was shed.
The sharp tears fell through her hair, and stung
Once, and her close lips touched him and clung
Once, and grew one with his lips for a space;
  And so drew back, and the man was dead.

O brother, the gods were good to you.
  Sleep, and be glad while the world endures.
Be well content as the years wear through;
  Give thanks for life, and the loves and lures;
Give thanks for life, O brother, and death,
For the sweet last sound of her feet, her breath,
For gifts she gave you, gracious and few,
  Tears and kisses, that lady of yours.

Rest, and be glad of the gods; but I,
  How shall I praise them, or how take rest?
There is not room under all the sky
  For me that know not of worst or best,
Dream or desire of the days before,
Sweet things or bitterness, any more.
Love will not come to me now though I die,
  As love came close to you, breast to breast.

I shall never be friends again with roses;
  I shall loathe sweet tunes, where a note grown strong
Relents and recoils, and climbs and closes,
  As a wave of the sea turned back by song.
There are sounds where the soul's delight takes fire,
Face to face with its own desire;
A delight that rebels, a desire that reposes;
  I shall hate sweet music my whole life long.

The pulse of war and passion of wonder,
  The heavens that murmur, the sounds that shine,
The stars that sing and the loves that thunder,
  The music burning at heart like wine,

An armed archangel whose hands raise up
All senses mixed in the spirit's cup
Till flesh and spirit are molten in sunder—
   These things are over, and no more mine.

These were a part of the playing I heard
   Once, ere my love and my heart were at strife;
Love that sings and hath wings as a bird,
   Balm of the wound and heft of the knife.
Fairer than earth is the sea, and sleep
Than overwatching of eyes that weep,
Now time has done with his one sweet word,
   The wine and leaven of lovely life.

I shall go my ways, tread out my measure,
   Fill the days of my daily breath
With fugitive things not good to treasure,
   Do as the world doth, say as it saith;
But if we had loved each other—O sweet,
Had you felt, lying under the palms of your feet,
The heart of my heart, beating harder with pleasure
   To feel you tread it to dust and death—

Ah, had I not taken my life up and given
   All that life gives and the years let go,
The wine and honey, the balm and leaven,
   The dreams reared high and the hopes brought low?
Come life, come death, not a word be said;
Should I lose you living, and vex you dead?
I never shall tell you on earth; and in heaven,
   If I cry to you then, will you hear or know?

Les Noyades

Whatever a man of the sons of men
 Shall say to his heart of the lords above,
They have shown man verily, once and again,
 Marvellous mercies and infinite love.

In the wild fifth year of the change of things,
 When France was glorious and blood-red, fair
With dust of battle and deaths of kings,
 A queen of men, with helmeted hair,

Carrier came down to the Loire and slew,
 Till all the ways and the waves waxed red:
Bound and drowned, slaying two by two,
 Maidens and young men, naked and wed.

They brought on a day to his judgment-place
 One rough with labour and red with fight,
And a lady noble by name and face,
 Faultless, a maiden, wonderful, white.

She knew not, being for shame's sake blind,
 If his eyes were hot on her face hard by.
And the judge bade strip and ship them, and bind
 Bosom to bosom, to drown and die.

The white girl winced and whitened; but he
 Caught fire, waxed bright as a great bright flame
Seen with thunder far out on the sea,
 Laughed hard as the glad blood went and came.

Twice his lips quailed with delight, then said,
 "I have but a word to you all, one word;
Bear with me; surely I am but dead;"
 And all they laughed and mocked him and heard.

"Judge, when they open the judgment-roll,
I will stand upright before God and pray:
'Lord God, have mercy on one man's soul,
For his mercy was great upon earth, I say.

" 'Lord, if I loved thee—Lord, if I served—
If these who darkened thy fair Son's face
I fought with, sparing not one, nor swerved
A hand's-breadth, Lord, in the perilous place—

" 'I pray thee say to this man, O Lord,
Sit thou for him at my feet on a throne.
I will face thy wrath, though it bite as a sword,
And my soul shall burn for his soul, and atone.

" 'For, Lord, thou knowest, O God most wise,
How gracious on earth were his deeds towards me.
Shall this be a small thing in thine eyes,
That is greater in mine than the whole great sea?'

"I have loved this woman my whole life long,
And even for love's sake when have I said
'I love you'? when have I done you wrong,
Living? but now I shall have you dead.

"Yea, now, do I bid you love me, love?
Love me or loathe, we are one not twain.
But God be praised in his heaven above
For this my pleasure and that my pain!

"For never a man, being mean like me,
Shall die like me till the whole world dies.
I shall drown with her, laughing for love; and she
Mix with me, touching me, lips and eyes.

"Shall she not know me and see me all through,
Me, on whose heart as a worm she trod?
You have given me, God requite it you,
What man yet never was given of God."

O sweet one love, O my life's delight,
   Dear, though the days have divided us,
Lost beyond hope, taken far out of sight,
   Not twice in the world shall the gods do thus.

Had it been so hard for my love? but I,
   Though the gods gave all that a god can give,
I had chosen rather the gift to die,
   Cease, and be glad above all that live.

For the Loire would have driven us down to the sea,
   And the sea would have pitched us from shoal to shoal;
And I should have held you, and you held me,
   As flesh holds flesh, and the soul the soul.

Could I change you, help you to love me, sweet,
   Could I give you the love that would sweeten death,
We should yield, go down, locked hands and feet,
   Die, drown together, and breath catch breath;

But you would have felt my soul in a kiss,
   And known that once if I loved you well;
And I would have given my soul for this
   To burn for ever in burning hell.

A Leave-Taking

Let us go hence, my songs; she will not hear.
Let us go hence together without fear;
Keep silence now, for singing-time is over,
And over all old things and all things dear.
She loves not you nor me as all we love her.
Yea, though we sang as angels in her ear,
     She would not hear.

Let us rise up and part; she will not know.
Let us go seaward as the great winds go,
Full of blown sand and foam; what help is here?
There is no help, for all these things are so,
And all the world is bitter as a tear.
And how these things are, though ye strove to show,
She would not know.

Let us go home and hence; she will not weep.
We gave love many dreams and days to keep,
Flowers without scent, and fruits that would not grow,
Saying "If thou wilt, thrust in thy sickle and reap."
All is reaped now; no grass is left to mow;
And we that sowed, though all we fell on sleep,
She would not weep.

Let us go hence and rest; she will not love.
She shall not hear us if we sing hereof,
Nor see love's ways, how sore they are and steep.
Come hence, let be, lie still; it is enough.
Love is a barren sea, bitter and deep;
And though she saw all heaven in flower above,
She would not love.

Let us give up, go down; she will not care.
Though all the stars made gold of all the air,
And the sea moving saw before it move
One moon-flower making all the foam-flowers fair;
Though all those waves went over us, and drove
Deep down the stifling lips and drowning hair,
She would not care.

Let us go hence, go hence; she will not see.
Sing all once more together; surely she,
She too, remembering days and words that were,
Will turn a little toward us, sighing; but we,
We are hence, we are gone, as though we had not been there.
Nay, and though all men seeing had pity on me,
She would not see.

Anactoria

τίνος αὖ τὺ πειθοῖ
μὰψ σαγηνεύσας φιλότατα;

SAPPHO.

My life is bitter with thy love; thine eyes
Blind me, thy tresses burn me, thy sharp sighs
Divide my flesh and spirit with soft sound,
And my blood strengthens, and my veins abound.
I pray thee sigh not, speak not, draw not breath;
Let life burn down, and dream it is not death.
I would the sea had hidden us, the fire
(Wilt thou fear that, and fear not my desire?)
Severed the bones that bleach, the flesh that cleaves,
And let our sifted ashes drop like leaves.
I feel thy blood against my blood: my pain
Pains thee, and lips bruise lips, and vein stings vein.
Let fruit be crushed on fruit, let flower on flower,
Breast kindle breast, and either burn one hour.
Why wilt thou follow lesser loves? are thine
Too weak to bear these hands and lips of mine?
I charge thee for my life's sake, O too sweet
To crush love with thy cruel faultless feet,
I charge thee keep thy lips from hers or his,
Sweetest, till theirs be sweeter than my kiss:
Lest I too lure, a swallow for a dove,
Erotion or Erinna to my love.
I would my love could kill thee; I am satiated
With seeing thee live, and fain would have thee dead.
I would earth had thy body as fruit to eat,
And no mouth but some serpent's found thee sweet.
I would find grievous ways to have thee slain,
Intense device, and superflux of pain;
Vex thee with amorous agonies, and shake
Life at thy lips, and leave it there to ache;
Strain out thy soul with pangs too soft to kill,

Intolerable interludes, and infinite ill;
Relapse and reluctation of the breath,
Dumb tunes and shuddering semitones of death.
I am weary of all thy words and soft strange ways,
Of all love's fiery nights and all his days,
And all the broken kisses salt as brine
That shuddering lips make moist with waterish wine,
And eyes the bluer for all those hidden hours
That pleasure fills with tears and feeds from flowers,
Fierce at the heart with fire that half comes through,
But all the flowerlike white stained round with blue;
The fervent underlid, and that above
Lifted with laughter or abashed with love;
Thine amorous girdle, full of thee and fair,
And leavings of the lilies in thine hair.
Yea, all sweet words of thine and all thy ways,
And all the fruit of nights and flower of days,
And stinging lips wherein the hot sweet brine
That Love was born of burns and foams like wine,
And eyes insatiable of amorous hours,
Fervent as fire and delicate as flowers,
Coloured like night at heart, but cloven through
Like night with flame, dyed round like night with blue,
Clothed with deep eyelids under and above—
Yea, all thy beauty sickens me with love;
Thy girdle empty of thee and now not fair,
And ruinous lilies in thy languid hair.
Ah, take no thought for Love's sake; shall this be,
And she who loves thy lover not love thee?
Sweet soul, sweet mouth of all that laughs and lives,
Mine is she, very mine; and she forgives.
For I beheld in sleep the light that is
In her high place in Paphos, heard the kiss
Of body and soul that mix with eager tears
And laughter stinging through the eyes and ears;
Saw Love, as burning flame from crown to feet,
Imperishable, upon her storied seat;
Clear eyelids lifted toward the north and south,

A mind of many colours, and a mouth
Of many tunes and kisses; and she bowed,
With all her subtle face laughing aloud,
Bowed down upon me, saying, "Who doth thee wrong,
Sappho?" but thou—thy body is the song,
Thy mouth the music; thou art more than I,
Though my voice die not till the whole world die;
Though men that hear it madden; though love weep,
Though nature change, though shame be charmed to sleep.
Ah, wilt thou slay me lest I kiss thee dead?
Yet the queen laughed from her sweet heart and said:
"Even she that flies shall follow for thy sake,
And she shall give thee gifts that would not take,
Shall kiss that would not kiss thee" (yea, kiss me)
"When thou wouldst not"—when I would not kiss thee!
Ah, more to me than all men as thou art,
Shall not my songs assuage her at the heart?
Ah, sweet to me as life seems sweet to death,
Why should her wrath fill thee with fearful breath?
Nay, sweet, for is she God alone? hath she
Made earth and all the centuries of the sea,
Taught the sun ways to travel, woven most fine
The moonbeams, shed the starbeams forth as wine,
Bound with her myrtles, beaten with her rods,
The young men and the maidens and the gods?
Have we not lips to love with, eyes for tears,
And summer and flower of women and of years?
Stars for the foot of morning, and for noon
Sunlight, and exaltation of the moon;
Waters that answer waters, fields that wear
Lilies, and languor of the Lesbian air?
Beyond those flying feet of fluttered doves,
Are there not other gods for other loves?
Yea, though she scourge thee, sweetest, for my sake,
Blossom not thorns and flowers not blood should break.
Ah that my lips were tuneless lips, but pressed
To the bruised blossom of thy scourged white breast!
Ah that my mouth for Muses' milk were fed

On the sweet blood thy sweet small wounds had bled!
That with my tongue I felt them, and could taste
The faint flakes from thy bosom to the waist!
That I could drink thy veins as wine, and eat
Thy breasts like honey! that from face to feet
Thy body were abolished and consumed,
And in my flesh thy very flesh entombed!
Ah, ah, thy beauty! like a beast it bites,
Stings like an adder, like an arrow smites.
Ah sweet, and sweet again, and seven times sweet,
The paces and the pauses of thy feet!
Ah sweeter than all sleep or summer air
The fallen fillets fragrant from thine hair!
Yea, though their alien kisses do me wrong,
Sweeter thy lips than mine with all their song;
Thy shoulders whiter than a fleece of white,
And flower-sweet fingers, good to bruise or bite
As honeycomb of the inmost honey-cells,
With almond-shaped and roseleaf-coloured shells
And blood like purple blossom at the tips
Quivering; and pain made perfect in thy lips
For my sake when I hurt thee; O that I
Durst crush thee out of life with love, and die,
Die of thy pain and my delight, and be
Mixed with thy blood and molten into thee!
Would I not plague thee dying overmuch?
Would I not hurt thee perfectly? not touch
Thy pores of sense with torture, and make bright
Thine eyes with bloodlike tears and grievous light?
Strike pang from pang as note is struck from note,
Catch the sob's middle music in thy throat,
Take thy limbs living, and new-mould with these
A lyre of many faultless agonies?
Feed thee with fever and famine and fine drouth,
With perfect pangs convulse thy perfect mouth,
Make thy life shudder in thee and burn afresh,
And wring thy very spirit through the flesh?
Cruel? but love makes all that love him well

As wise as heaven and crueller than hell.
Me hath love made more bitter toward thee
Than death toward man; but were I made as he
Who hath made all things to break them one by one,
If my feet trod upon the stars and sun
And souls of men as his have alway trod,
God knows I might be crueller than God.
For who shall change with prayers or thanksgivings
The mystery of the cruelty of things?
Or say what God above all gods and years
With offering and blood-sacrifice of tears,
With lamentation from strange lands, from graves
Where the snake pastures, from scarred mouths of slaves,
From prison, and from plunging prows of ships
Through flamelike foam of the sea's closing lips—
With thwartings of strange signs, and wind-blown hair
Of comets, desolating the dim air,
When darkness is made fast with seals and bars,
And fierce reluctance of disastrous stars,
Eclipse, and sound of shaken hills, and wings
Darkening, and blind inexpiable things—
With sorrow of labouring moons, and altering light
And travail of the planets of the night,
And weeping of the weary Pleiads seven,
Feeds the mute melancholy lust of heaven?
Is not his incense bitterness, his meat
Murder? his hidden face and iron feet
Hath not man known, and felt them on their way
Threaten and trample all things and every day?
Hath he not sent us hunger? who hath cursed
Spirit and flesh with longing? filled with thirst
Their lips who cried unto him? who bade exceed
The fervid will, fall short the feeble deed,
Bade sink the spirit and the flesh aspire,
Pain animate the dust of dead desire,
And life yield up her flower to violent fate?
Him would I reach, him smite, him desecrate,
Pierce the cold lips of God with human breath,

And mix his immortality with death.
Why hath he made us? what had all we done
That we should live and loathe the sterile sun,
And with the moon wax paler as she wanes,
And pulse by pulse feel time grow through our veins?
Thee too the years shall cover; thou shalt be
As the rose born of one same blood with thee,
As a song sung, as a word said, and fall
Flower-wise, and be not any more at all,
Nor any memory of thee anywhere;
For never Muse has bound above thine hair
The high Pierian flower whose graft outgrows
All summer kinship of the mortal rose
And colour of deciduous days, nor shed
Reflex and flush of heaven about thine head,
Nor reddened brows made pale by floral grief
With splendid shadow from that lordlier leaf.
Yea, thou shalt be forgotten like spilt wine,
Except these kisses of my lips on thine
Brand them with immortality; but me—
Men shall not see bright fire nor hear the sea,
Nor mix their hearts with music, nor behold
Cast forth of heaven, with feet of awful gold
And plumeless wings that make the bright air blind,
Lightning, with thunder for a hound behind
Hunting through fields unfurrowed and unsown,
But in the light and laughter, in the moan
And music, and in grasp of lip and hand
And shudder of water that makes felt on land
The immeasurable tremor of all the sea,
Memories shall mix and metaphors of me.
Like me shall be the shuddering calm of night,
When all the winds of the world for pure delight
Close lips that quiver and fold up wings that ache;
When nightingales are louder for love's sake,
And leaves tremble like lute-strings or like fire;
Like me the one star swooning with desire
Even at the cold lips of the sleepless moon,

As I at thine; like me the waste white noon,
Burnt through with barren sunlight; and like me
The land-stream and the tide-stream in the sea.
I am sick with time as these with ebb and flow,
And by the yearning in my veins I know
The yearning sound of waters; and mine eyes
Burn as that beamless fire which fills the skies
With troubled stars and travailing things of flame;
And in my heart the grief consuming them
Labours, and in my veins the thirst of these,
And all the summer travail of the trees
And all the winter sickness; and the earth,
Filled full with deadly works of death and birth,
Sore spent with hungry lusts of birth and death,
Has pain like mine in her divided breath;
Her spring of leaves is barren, and her fruit
Ashes; her boughs are burdened, and her root
Fibrous and gnarled with poison; underneath
Serpents have gnawn it through with tortuous teeth
Made sharp upon the bones of all the dead,
And wild birds rend her branches overhead.
These, woven as raiment for his word and thought,
These hath God made, and me as these, and wrought
Song, and hath lit it at my lips; and me
Earth shall not gather though she feed on thee.
As a shed tear shalt thou be shed; but I—
Lo, earth may labour, men live long and die,
Years change and stars, and the high God devise
New things, and old things wane before his eyes
Who wields and wrecks them, being more strong than they—
But, having made me, me he shall not slay.
Nor slay nor satiate, like those herds of his
Who laugh and live a little, and their kiss
Contents them, and their loves are swift and sweet,
And sure death grasps and gains them with slow feet,
Love they or hate they, strive or bow their knees—
And all these end; he hath his will of these.
Yea, but albeit he slay me, hating me—

Albeit he hide me in the deep dear sea
And cover me with cool wan foam, and ease
This soul of mine as any soul of these,
And give me water and great sweet waves, and make
The very sea's name lordlier for my sake,
The whole sea sweeter—albeit I die indeed
And hide myself and sleep and no man heed,
Of me the high God hath not all his will.
Blossom of branches, and on each high hill
Clear air and wind, and under in clamorous vales
Fierce noises of the fiery nightingales,
Buds burning in the sudden spring like fire,
The wan washed sand and the waves' vain desire,
Sails seen like blown white flowers at sea, and words
That bring tears swiftest, and long notes of birds
Violently singing till the whole world sings—
I Sappho shall be one with all these things,
With all high things for ever; and my face
Seen once, my songs once heard in a strange place,
Cleave to men's lives, and waste the days thereof
With gladness and much sadness and long love.
Yea, they shall say, earth's womb has borne in vain
New things, and never this best thing again;
Borne days and men, borne fruits and wars and wine,
Seasons and songs, but no song more like mine.
And they shall know me as ye who have known me here,
Last year when I loved Atthis, and this year
When I love thee; and they shall praise me, and say
"She hath all time as all we have our day,
Shall she not live and have her will"—even I?
Yea, though thou diest, I say I shall not die.
For these shall give me of their souls, shall give
Life, and the days and loves wherewith I live,
Shall quicken me with loving, fill with breath,
Save me and serve me, strive for me with death.
Alas, that neither moon nor snow nor dew
Nor all cold things can purge me wholly through,
Assuage me nor allay me nor appease,

Till supreme sleep shall bring me bloodless ease;
Till time wax faint in all his periods;
Till fate undo the bondage of the gods,
And lay, to slake and satiate me all through,
Lotus and Lethe on my lips like dew,
And shed around and over and under me
Thick darkness and the insuperable sea.

Hymn to Proserpine

(AFTER THE PROCLAMATION IN ROME OF THE CHRISTIAN FAITH)

Vicisti, Galilæe.

I have lived long enough, having seen one thing, that love hath an end;
Goddess and maiden and queen, be near me now and befriend.
Thou art more than the day or the morrow, the seasons that laugh or that weep;
For these give joy and sorrow; but thou, Proserpina, sleep.
Sweet is the treading of wine, and sweet the feet of the dove;
But a goodlier gift is thine than foam of the grapes or love.
Yea, is not even Apollo, with hair and harpstring of gold,
A bitter God to follow, a beautiful God to behold?
I am sick of singing: the bays burn deep and chafe: I am fain
To rest a little from praise and grievous pleasure and pain.
For the Gods we know not of, who give us our daily breath,
We know they are cruel as love or life, and lovely as death.
O Gods dethroned and deceased, cast forth, wiped out in a day!
From your wrath is the world released, redeemed from your chains, men say.
New Gods are crowned in the city; their flowers have broken your rods;
They are merciful, clothed with pity, the young compassionate Gods.
But for me their new device is barren, the days are bare;

Things long past over suffice, and men forgotten that were.
Time and the Gods are at strife; ye dwell in the midst thereof,
Draining a little life from the barren breasts of love.
I say to you, cease, take rest; yea, I say to you all, be at peace,
Till the bitter milk of her breast and the barren bosom shall cease.
Wilt thou yet take all, Galilean? but these thou shalt not take,
The laurel, the palms and the pæan, the breasts of the nymphs in the brake;
Breasts more soft than a dove's, that tremble with tenderer breath;
And all the wings of the Loves, and all the joy before death;
All the feet of the hours that sound as a single lyre,
Dropped and deep in the flowers, with strings that flicker like fire.
More than these wilt thou give, things fairer than all these things?
Nay, for a little we live, and life hath mutable wings.
A little while and we die; shall life not thrive as it may?
For no man under the sky lives twice, outliving his day.
And grief is a grievous thing, and a man hath enough of his tears:
Why should he labour, and bring fresh grief to blacken his years?
Thou hast conquered, O pale Galilean; the world has grown grey from thy breath;
We have drunken of things Lethean, and fed on the fullness of death.
Laurel is green for a season, and love is sweet for a day;
But love grows bitter with treason, and laurel outlives not May.
Sleep, shall we sleep after all? for the world is not sweet in the end;
For the old faiths loosen and fall, the new years ruin and rend.
Fate is a sea without shore, and the soul is a rock that abides;
But her ears are vexed with the roar and her face with the foam of the tides.
O lips that the live blood faints in, the leavings of racks and rods!
O ghastly glories of saints, dead limbs of gibbeted Gods!
Though all men abase them before you in spirit, and all knees bend,
I kneel not neither adore you, but standing, look to the end.
All delicate days and pleasant, all spirits and sorrows are cast

Far out with the foam of the present that sweeps to the surf of the past:
Where beyond the extreme sea-wall, and between the remote sea-gates,
Waste water washes, and tall ships founder, and deep death waits:
Where, mighty with deepening sides, clad about with the seas as with wings,
And impelled of invisible tides, and fulfilled of unspeakable things,
White-eyed and poisonous-finned, shark-toothed and serpentine-curled,
Rolls, under the whitening wind of the future, the wave of the world.
The depths stand naked in sunder behind it, the storms flee away;
In the hollow before it the thunder is taken and snared as a prey;
In its sides is the north-wind bound; and its salt is of all men's tears;
With light of ruin, and sound of changes, and pulse of years:
With travail of day after day, and with trouble of hour upon hour;
And bitter as blood is the spray; and the crests are as fangs that devour:
And its vapour and storm of its steam as the sighing of spirits to be;
And its noise as the noise in a dream; and its depth as the roots of the sea:
And the height of its heads as the height of the utmost stars of the air:
And the ends of the earth at the might thereof tremble, and time is made bare.
Will ye bridle the deep sea with reins, will ye chasten the high sea with rods?
Will ye take her to chain her with chains, who is older than all ye Gods?
All ye as a wind shall go by, as a fire shall ye pass and be past;
Ye are Gods, and behold, ye shall die, and the waves be upon you at last.
In the darkness of time, in the deeps of the years, in the changes of things,

Ye shall sleep as a slain man sleeps, and the world shall forget
you for kings.
Though the feet of thine high priests tread where thy lords and
our forefathers trod,
Though these that were Gods are dead, and thou being dead art
a God,
Though before thee the throned Cytherean be fallen, and hidden
her head,
Yet thy kingdom shall pass, Galilean, thy dead shall go down to
thee dead.
Of the maiden thy mother men sing as a goddess with grace
clad around;
Thou art throned where another was king; where another was
queen she is crowned.
Yea, once we had sight of another: but now she is queen, say these.
Not as thine, not as thine was our mother, a blossom of
flowering seas,
Clothed round with the world's desire as with raiment, and fair
as the foam,
And fleeter than kindled fire, and a goddess, and mother of
Rome.
For thine came pale and a maiden, and sister to sorrow; but ours,
Her deep hair heavily laden with odour and colour of flowers,
White rose of the rose-white water, a silver splendour, a flame,
Bent down unto us that besought her, and earth grew sweet with
her name.
For thine came weeping, a slave among slaves, and rejected;
but she
Came flushed from the full-flushed wave, and imperial, her foot
on the sea.
And the wonderful waters knew her, the winds and the viewless
ways,
And the roses grew rosier, and bluer the sea-blue stream of the
bays.
Ye are fallen, our lords, by what token? we wist that ye should
not fall.
Ye were all so fair that are broken; and one more fair than
ye all.

But I turn to her still, having seen she shall surely abide in the end;
Goddess and maiden and queen, be near me now and befriend.
O daughter of earth, of my mother, her crown and blossom of birth,
I am also, I also, thy brother; I go as I came unto earth.
In the night where thine eyes are as moons are in heaven, the night where thou art,
Where the silence is more than all tunes, where sleep overflows from the heart,
Where the poppies are sweet as the rose in our world, and the red rose is white,
And the wind falls faint as it blows with the fume of the flowers of the night,
And the murmur of spirits that sleep in the shadow of Gods from afar
Grows dim in thine ears and deep as the deep dim soul of a star,
In the sweet low light of thy face, under heavens untrod by the sun,
Let my soul with their souls find place, and forget what is done and undone.
Thou art more than the Gods who number the days of our temporal breath:
For these give labour and slumber; but thou, Proserpina, death.
Therefore now at thy feet I abide for a season in silence. I know
I shall die as my fathers died, and sleep as they sleep; even so.
For the glass of the years is brittle wherein we gaze for a span;
A little soul for a little bears up this corpse which is man.*
So long I endure, no longer; and laugh not again, neither weep.
For there is no God found stronger than death; and death is a sleep.

* ψυχάριον εἶ βαστάζον νεκρόν.

EPICTETUS.

Ilicet

There is an end of joy and sorrow;
Peace all day long, all night, all morrow,
  But never a time to laugh or weep.
The end is come of pleasant places,
The end of tender words and faces,
  The end of all, the poppied sleep.

No place for sound within their hearing,
No room to hope, no time for fearing,
  No lips to laugh, no lids for tears.
The old years have run out all their measure;
No chance of pain, no chance of pleasure,
  No fragment of the broken years.

Outside of all the worlds and ages,
There where the fool is as the sage is,
  There where the slayer is clean of blood,
No end, no passage, no beginning,
There where the sinner leaves off sinning,
  There where the good man is not good.

There is not one thing with another,
But Evil saith to Good: My brother,
  My brother, I am one with thee:
They shall not strive nor cry for ever:
No man shall choose between them: never
  Shall this thing end and that thing be.

Wind wherein seas and stars are shaken
Shall shake them, and they shall not waken;
  None that has lain down shall arise;
The stones are sealed across their places;
One shadow is shed on all their faces,
  One blindness cast on all their eyes.

Sleep, is it sleep perchance that covers
Each face, as each face were his lover's?
   Farewell; as men that sleep fare well.
The grave's mouth laughs unto derision
Desire and dread and dream and vision,
   Delight of heaven and sorrow of hell.

No soul shall tell nor lip shall number
The names and tribes of you that slumber;
   No memory, no memorial.
"Thou knowest"—who shall say thou knowest?
There is none highest and none lowest:
   An end, an end, an end of all.

Good night, good sleep, good rest from sorrow
To these that shall not have good morrow;
   The gods be gentle to all these.
Nay, if death be not, how shall they be?
Nay, is there help in heaven? it may be
   All things and lords of things shall cease.

The stooped urn, filling, dips and flashes;
The bronzèd brims are deep in ashes;
   The pale old lips of death are fed.
Shall this dust gather flesh hereafter?
Shall one shed tears or fall to laughter,
   At sight of all these poor old dead?

Nay, as thou wilt; these know not of it;
Thine eyes' strong weeping shall not profit,
   Thy laughter shall not give thee ease;
Cry aloud, spare not, cease not crying,
Sigh, till thou cleave thy sides with sighing,
   Thou shalt not raise up one of these.

Burnt spices flash, and burnt wine hisses,
The breathing flame's mouth curls and kisses
   The small dried rows of frankincense;

All round the sad red blossoms smoulder,
Flowers coloured like the fire, but colder,
  In sign of sweet things taken hence;

Yea, for their sake and in death's favour
Things of sweet shape and of sweet savour
  We yield them, spice and flower and wine;
Yea, costlier things than wine or spices,
Whereof none knoweth how great the price is,
  And fruit that comes not of the vine.

From boy's pierced throat and girl's pierced bosom
Drips, reddening round the blood-red blossom,
  The slow delicious bright soft blood,
Bathing the spices and the pyre,
Bathing the flowers and fallen fire,
  Bathing the blossom by the bud.

Roses whose lips the flame has deadened
Drink till the lapping leaves are reddened
  And warm wet inner petals weep;
The flower whereof sick sleep gets leisure,
Barren of balm and purple pleasure,
  Fumes with no native steam of sleep.

Why will ye weep? what do ye weeping?
For waking folk and people sleeping,
  And sands that fill and sands that fall,
The days rose-red, the poppied hours,
Blood, wine, and spice and fire and flowers,
  There is one end of one and all.

Shall such an one lend love or borrow?
Shall these be sorry for thy sorrow?
  Shall these give thanks for words or breath?
Their hate is as their loving-kindness;
The frontlet of their brows is blindness,
  The armlet of their arms is death.

Lo, for no noise or light of thunder
Shall these grave-clothes be rent in sunder;
   He that hath taken, shall he give?
He hath rent them: shall he bind together?
He hath bound them: shall he break the tether?
   He hath slain them: shall he bid them live?

A little sorrow, a little pleasure,
Fate metes us from the dusty measure
   That holds the date of all of us;
We are born with travail and strong crying,
And from the birth-day to the dying
   The likeness of our life is thus.

One girds himself to serve another,
Whose father was the dust, whose mother
   The little dead red worm therein;
They find no fruit of things they cherish;
The goodness of a man shall perish,
   It shall be one thing with his sin.

In deep wet ways by grey old gardens
Fed with sharp spring the sweet fruit hardens;
   They know not what fruits wane or grow;
Red summer burns to the utmost ember;
They know not, neither can remember,
   The old years and flowers they used to know.

Ah, for their sakes, so trapped and taken,
For theirs, forgotten and forsaken,
   Watch, sleep not, gird thyself with prayer.
Nay, where the heart of wrath is broken,
Where long love ends as a thing spoken,
   How shall thy crying enter there?

Though the iron sides of the old world falter,
The likeness of them shall not alter
   For all the rumour of periods,

The stars and seasons that come after,
The tears of latter men, the laughter
  Of the old unalterable gods.

Far up above the years and nations,
The high gods, clothed and crowned with patience,
  Endure through days of deathlike date;
They bear the witness of things hidden;
Before their eyes all life stands chidden,
  As they before the eyes of Fate.

Not for their love shall Fate retire,
Nor they relent for our desire,
  Nor the graves open for their call.
The end is more than joy and anguish,
Than lives that laugh and lives that languish,
  The poppied sleep, the end of all.

Hermaphroditus

I

Lift up thy lips, turn round, look back for love,
  Blind love that comes by night and casts out rest;
  Of all things tired thy lips look weariest,
Save the long smile that they are wearied of.
Ah sweet, albeit no love be sweet enough,
  Choose of two loves and cleave unto the best;
  Two loves at either blossom of thy breast
Strive until one be under and one above.
Their breath is fire upon the amorous air,
  Fire in thine eyes and where thy lips suspire:
And whosoever hath seen thee, being so fair,
  Two things turn all his life and blood to fire;

A strong desire begot on great despair,
  A great despair cast out by strong desire.

II

Where between sleep and life some brief space is,
  With love like gold bound round about the head,
  Sex to sweet sex with lips and limbs is wed,
Turning the fruitful feud of hers and his
To the waste wedlock of a sterile kiss;
  Yet from them something like as fire is shed
  That shall not be assuaged till death be dead,
Though neither life nor sleep can find out this.
Love made himself of flesh that perisheth
  A pleasure-house for all the loves his kin;
But on the one side sat a man like death,
  And on the other a woman sat like sin.
So with veiled eyes and sobs between his breath
  Love turned himself and would not enter in.

III

Love, is it love or sleep or shadow or light
  That lies between thine eyelids and thine eyes?
  Like a flower laid upon a flower it lies,
Or like the night's dew laid upon the night.
Love stands upon thy left hand and thy right,
  Yet by no sunset and by no moonrise
  Shall make thee man and ease a woman's sighs,
Or make thee woman for a man's delight.
To what strange end hath some strange god made fair
  The double blossom of two fruitless flowers?
Hid love in all the folds of all thy hair,
  Fed thee on summers, watered thee with showers,
Given all the gold that all the seasons wear
  To thee that art a thing of barren hours?

IV

Yea, love, I see; it is not love but fear.
  Nay, sweet, it is not fear but love, I know;
  Or wherefore should thy body's blossom blow
So sweetly, or thine eyelids leave so clear
Thy gracious eyes that never made a tear—
  Though for their love our tears like blood should flow,
  Though love and life and death should come and go,
So dreadful, so desirable, so dear?
Yea, sweet, I know; I saw in what swift wise
  Beneath the woman's and the water's kiss
  Thy moist limbs melted into Salmacis,
And the large light turned tender in thine eyes,
And all thy boy's breath softened into sighs;
  But Love being blind, how should he know of this?

Au Musée du Louvre, Mars 1863.

Fragoletta

O Love! what shall be said of thee?
The son of grief begot by joy?
Being sightless, wilt thou see?
Being sexless, wilt thou be
Maiden or boy?

I dreamed of strange lips yesterday
And cheeks wherein the ambiguous blood
Was like a rose's—yea,
A rose's when it lay
Within the bud.

What fields have bred thee, or what groves
Concealed thee, O mysterious flower,
O double rose of Love's,
With leaves that lure the doves
From bud to bower?

I dare not kiss it, lest my lip
Press harder than an indrawn breath,
And all the sweet life slip
Forth, and the sweet leaves drip,
Bloodlike, in death.

O sole desire of my delight!
O sole delight of my desire!
Mine eyelids and eyesight
Feed on thee day and night
Like lips of fire.

Lean back thy throat of carven pearl,
Let thy mouth murmur like the dove's;
Say, Venus hath no girl,
No front of female curl,
Among her Loves.

Thy sweet low bosom, thy close hair,
Thy strait soft flanks and slenderer feet,
Thy virginal strange air,
Are these not over fair
For Love to greet?

How should he greet thee? what new name,
Fit to move all men's hearts, could move
Thee, deaf to love or shame,
Love's sister, by the same
Mother as Love?

Ah sweet, the maiden's mouth is cold,
Her breast-blossoms are simply red,
Her hair mere brown or gold,
Fold over simple fold
Binding her head.

Thy mouth is made of fire and wine,
Thy barren bosom takes my kiss
And turns my soul to thine
And turns thy lip to mine,
And mine it is.

Thou hast a serpent in thine hair,
In all the curls that close and cling;
And ah, thy breast-flower!
Ah love, thy mouth too fair
To kiss and sting!

Cleave to me, love me, kiss mine eyes,
Satiate thy lips with loving me;
Nay, for thou shalt not rise;
Lie still as Love that dies
For love of thee.

Mine arms are close about thine head,
My lips are fervent on thy face,
And where my kiss hath fed
Thy flower-like blood leaps red
To the kissed place.

O bitterness of things too sweet!
O broken singing of the dove!
Love's wings are over fleet,
And like the panther's feet
The feet of Love.

Rondel

These many years since we began to be,
What have the gods done with us? what with me,
What with my love? they have shown me fates and fears,
Harsh springs, and fountains bitterer than the sea,
Grief a fixed star, and joy a vane that veers,
    These many years.

With her, my love, with her have they done well?
But who shall answer for her? who shall tell
Sweet things or sad, such things as no man hears?
May no tears fall, if no tears ever fell,
From eyes more dear to me than starriest spheres
    These many years!

But if tears ever touched, for any grief,
Those eyelids folded like a white-rose leaf,
Deep double shells wherethrough the eye-flower peers,
Let them weep once more only, sweet and brief,
Brief tears and bright, for one who gave her tears
    These many years.

Satia Te Sanguine

If you loved me ever so little,
  I could bear the bonds that gall,
I could dream the bonds were brittle;
  You do not love me at all.

O beautiful lips, O bosom
  More white than the moon's and warm,
A sterile, a ruinous blossom
  Is blown your way in a storm.

As the lost white feverish limbs
  Of the Lesbian Sappho, adrift
In foam where the sea-weed swims,
  Swam loose for the streams to lift,

My heart swims blind in a sea
  That stuns me; swims to and fro,
And gathers to windward and lee
  Lamentation, and mourning, and woe.

A broken, an emptied boat,
  Sea saps it, winds blow apart,
Sick and adrift and afloat,
  The barren waif of a heart.

Where, when the gods would be cruel,
  Do they go for a torture? where
Plant thorns, set pain like a jewel?
  Ah, not in the flesh, not there!

The racks of earth and the rods
  Are weak as foam on the sands;
In the heart is the prey for gods,
  Who crucify hearts, not hands.

Mere pangs corrode and consume,
  Dead when life dies in the brain;
In the infinite spirit is room
  For the pulse of an infinite pain.

I wish you were dead, my dear;
  I would give you, had I to give,
Some death too bitter to fear;
  It is better to die than live.

I wish you were stricken of thunder
  And burnt with a bright flame through,
Consumed and cloven in sunder,
  I dead at your feet like you.

If I could but know after all,
  I might cease to hunger and ache,
Though your heart were ever so small,
  If it were not a stone or a snake.

You are crueller, you that we love,
  Than hatred, hunger, or death;
You have eyes and breasts like a dove,
  And you kill men's hearts with a breath.

As plague in a poisonous city
  Insults and exults on her dead,
So you, when pallid for pity
  Comes love, and fawns to be fed.

As a tame beast writhes and wheedles,
  He fawns to be fed with wiles;
You carve him a cross of needles,
  And whet them sharp as your smiles.

He is patient of thorn and whip,
  He is dumb under axe or dart;
You suck with a sleepy red lip
  The wet red wounds in his heart.

You thrill as his pulses dwindle,
  You brighten and warm as he bleeds,
With insatiable eyes that kindle
  And insatiable mouth that feeds.

Your hands nailed love to the tree,
  You stript him, scourged him with rods,
And drowned him deep in the sea
  That hides the dead and their gods.

And for all this, die will he not;
  There is no man sees him but I;
You came and went and forgot;
  I hope he will some day die.

A Lamentation

I

Who hath known the ways of time
  Or trodden behind his feet?
    There is no such man among men.
For chance overcomes him, or crime
  Changes; for all things sweet
    In time wax bitter again.
Who shall give sorrow enough,
  Or who the abundance of tears?
Mine eyes are heavy with love
  And a sword gone thorough mine ears,
    A sound like a sword and fire,
    For pity, for great desire;
Who shall ensure me thereof,
  Lest I die, being full of my fears?

Who hath known the ways and the wrath,
  The sleepless spirit, the root
    And blossom of evil will,
      The divine device of a god?
Who shall behold it or hath?
  The twice-tongued prophets are mute,
    The many speakers are still;
      No foot has travelled or trod,
No hand has meted, his path.
  Man's fate is a blood-red fruit,
    And the mighty gods have their fill
      And relax not the rein, or the rod.

Ye were mighty in heart from of old,
  Ye slew with the spear, and are slain.
Keen after heat is the cold,
  Sore after summer is rain,
And melteth man to the bone.

  As water he weareth away,
  As a flower, as an hour in a day,
Fallen from laughter to moan.
But my spirit is shaken with fear
  Lest an evil thing begin,
New-born, a spear for a spear,
  And one for another sin.
Or ever our tears began,
  It was known from of old and said;
One law for a living man,
  And another law for the dead.
For these are fearful and sad,
  Vain, and things without breath;
    While he lives let a man be glad,
      For none hath joy of his death.

II

Who hath known the pain, the old pain of earth,
  Or all the travail of the sea,
The many ways and waves, the birth
Fruitless, the labour nothing worth?
  Who hath known, who knoweth, O gods? not we.
There is none shall say he hath seen,
  There is none he hath known.
Though he saith, Lo, a lord have I been,
  I have reaped and sown;
I have seen the desire of mine eyes,
  The beginning of love,
The season of kisses and sighs
  And the end thereof.
I have known the ways of the sea,
  All the perilous ways,
Strange winds have spoken with me,
  And the tongues of strange days.
I have hewn the pine for ships;
  Where steeds run arow,

I have seen from their bridled lips
  Foam blown as the snow.
With snapping of chariot-poles
  And with straining of oars
I have grazed in the race the goals,
  In the storm the shores;
As a greave is cleft with an arrow
  At the joint of the knee,
I have cleft through the sea-straits narrow
  To the heart of the sea.
When air was smitten in sunder
  I have watched on high
The ways of the stars and the thunder
  In the night of the sky;
Where the dark brings forth light as a flower,
  As from lips that dissever;
One abideth the space of an hour,
  One endureth for ever.
Lo, what hath he seen or known,
  Of the way and the wave
Unbeholden, unsailed on, unsown,
  From the breast to the grave?

Or ever the stars were made, or skies,
  Grief was born, and the kinless night,
    Mother of gods without form or name.
And light is born out of heaven and dies,
  And one day knows not another's light,
    But night is one, and her shape the same.

But dumb the goddesses underground
  Wait, and we hear not on earth if their feet
    Rise, and the night wax loud with their wings;
Dumb, without word or shadow of sound;
  And sift in scales and winnow as wheat
    Men's souls, and sorrow of manifold things.

III

Nor less of grief than ours
  The gods wrought long ago
    To bruise men one by one;
But with the incessant hours
  Fresh grief and greener woe
    Spring, as the sudden sun
Year after year makes flowers;
  And these die down and grow,
    And the next year lacks none.

As these men sleep, have slept
  The old heroes in time fled,
    No dream-divided sleep;
And holier eyes have wept
  Than ours, when on her dead
    Gods have seen Thetis weep,
With heavenly hair far-swept
  Back, heavenly hands outspread
    Round what she could not keep,

Could not one day withhold,
  One night; and like as these
    White ashes of no weight,
Held not his urn the cold
  Ashes of Heracles?
    For all things born one gate
Opens, no gate of gold;
  Opens; and no man sees
    Beyond the gods and fate.

Anima Anceps

Till death have broken
Sweet life's love-token,
Till all be spoken
    That shall be said,
What dost thou praying,
O soul, and playing
With song and saying,
    Things flown and fled?
For this we know not—
That fresh springs flow not
And fresh griefs grow not
    When men are dead;
When strange years cover
Lover and lover,
And joys are over
    And tears are shed.

If one day's sorrow
Mar the day's morrow—
If man's life borrow
    And man's death pay—
If souls once taken,
If lives once shaken,
Arise, awaken,
    By night, by day—
Why with strong crying
And years of sighing,
Living and dying,
    Fast ye and pray?
For all your weeping,
Waking and sleeping,
Death comes to reaping
    And takes away.

Though time rend after
Roof-tree from rafter,
A little laughter
    Is much more worth
Than thus to measure
The hour, the treasure,
The pain, the pleasure,
    The death, the birth;
Grief, when days alter,
Like joy shall falter;
Song-book and psalter,
    Mourning and mirth.
Live like the swallow;
Seek not to follow
Where earth is hollow
    Under the earth.

In the Orchard

(Provençal Burden)

Leave go my hands, let me catch breath and see;
Let the dew-fall drench either side of me;
    Clear apple-leaves are soft upon that moon
Seen sidelong like a blossom in the tree;
    Ah God, ah God, that day should be so soon.

The grass is thick and cool, it lets us lie.
Kissed upon either cheek and either eye,
    I turn to thee as some green afternoon
Turns toward sunset, and is loth to die;
    Ah God, ah God, that day should be so soon.

Lie closer, lean your face upon my side,
Feel where the dew fell that has hardly dried,
    Hear how the blood beats that went nigh to swoon;
The pleasure lives there when the sense has died;
    Ah God, ah God, that day should be so soon.

O my fair lord, I charge you leave me this:
Is it not sweeter than a foolish kiss?
    Nay take it then, my flower, my first in June,
My rose, so like a tender mouth it is:
    Ah God, ah God, that day should be so soon.

Love, till dawn sunder night from day with fire,
Dividing my delight and my desire,
    The crescent life and love the plenilune,
Love me though dusk begin and dark retire;
    Ah God, ah God, that day should be so soon.

Ah, my heart fails, my blood draws back; I know,
When life runs over, life is near to go;
    And with the slain of love love's ways are strewn,
And with their blood, if love will have it so;
    Ah God, ah God, that day should be so soon.

Ah, do thy will now; slay me if thou wilt;
There is no building now the walls are built,
    No quarrying now the corner-stone is hewn,
No drinking now the vine's whole blood is spilt;
    Ah God, ah God, that day should be so soon.

Nay, slay me now; nay, for I will be slain;
Pluck thy red pleasure from the teeth of pain,
    Break down thy vine ere yet grape-gatherers prune,
Slay me ere day can slay desire again;
    Ah God, ah God, that day should be so soon.

Yea, with thy sweet lips, with thy sweet sword; yea,
Take life and all, for I will die, I say;
    Love, I gave love, is life a better boon?
For sweet night's sake I will not live till day;
    Ah God, ah God, that day should be so soon.

Nay, I will sleep then only; nay, but go.
Ah sweet, too sweet to me, my sweet, I know
    Love, sleep, and death go to the sweet same tune;
Hold my hair fast, and kiss me through it so.
    Ah God, ah God, that day should be so soon.

A Match

If love were what the rose is,
  And I were like the leaf,
Our lives would grow together
In sad or singing weather,
Blown fields or flowerful closes,
  Green pleasure or grey grief;
If love were what the rose is,
  And I were like the leaf.

If I were what the words are,
  And love were like the tune,
With double sound and single
Delight our lips would mingle,
With kisses glad as birds are
  That get sweet rain at noon;
If I were what the words are,
  And love were like the tune.

If you were life, my darling,
  And I your love were death,
We'd shine and snow together
Ere March made sweet the weather
With daffodil and starling
  And hours of fruitful breath;
If you were life, my darling,
  And I your love were death.

If you were thrall to sorrow,
  And I were page to joy,
We'd play for lives and seasons
With loving looks and treasons
And tears of night and morrow
  And laughs of maid and boy;
If you were thrall to sorrow,
  And I were page to joy.

If you were April's lady,
  And I were lord in May,
We'd throw with leaves for hours
And draw for days with flowers,
Till day like night were shady
  And night were bright like day;
If you were April's lady,
  And I were lord in May.

If you were queen of pleasure,
  And I were king of pain,
We'd hunt down love together,
Pluck out his flying-feather,
And teach his feet a measure,
  And find his mouth a rein;
If you were queen of pleasure,
  And I were king of pain.

Faustine

Ave Faustina Imperatrix, morituri te salutant.

Lean back, and get some minutes' peace;
 Let your head lean
Back to the shoulder with its fleece
 Of locks, Faustine.

The shapely silver shoulder stoops,
 Weighed over clean
With state of splendid hair that droops
 Each side, Faustine.

Let me go over your good gifts
 That crown you queen;
A queen whose kingdom ebbs and shifts
 Each week, Faustine.

Bright heavy brows well gathered up:
 White gloss and sheen;
Carved lips that make my lips a cup
 To drink, Faustine,

Wine and rank poison, milk and blood,
 Being mixed therein
Since first the devil threw dice with God
 For you, Faustine.

Your naked new-born soul, their stake,
 Stood blind between;
God said "let him that wins her take
 And keep Faustine."

But this time Satan throve, no doubt;
 Long since, I ween,
God's part in you was battered out;
 Long since, Faustine.

The die rang sideways as it fell,
Rang cracked and thin,
Like a man's laughter heard in hell
Far down, Faustine,

A shadow of laughter like a sigh,
Dead sorrow's kin;
So rang, thrown down, the devil's die
That won Faustine.

A suckling of his breed you were,
One hard to wean;
But God, who lost you, left you fair,
We see, Faustine.

You have the face that suits a woman
For her soul's screen—
The sort of beauty that's called human
In hell, Faustine.

You could do all things but be good
Or chaste of mien;
And that you would not if you could,
We know, Faustine.

Even he who cast seven devils out
Of Magdalene
Could hardly do as much, I doubt,
For you, Faustine.

Did Satan make you to spite God?
Or did God mean
To scourge with scorpions for a rod
Our sins, Faustine?

I know what queen at first you were,
As though I had seen
Red gold and black imperious hair
Twice crown Faustine.

As if your fed sarcophagus
  Spared flesh and skin,
You come back face to face with us,
  The same Faustine.

She loved the games men played with death,
  Where death must win;
As though the slain man's blood and breath
  Revived Faustine.

Nets caught the pike, pikes tore the net;
  Lithe limbs and lean
From drained-out pores dripped thick red sweat
  To soothe Faustine.

She drank the steaming drift and dust
  Blown off the scene;
Blood could not ease the bitter lust
  That galled Faustine.

All round the foul fat furrows reeked,
  Where blood sank in;
The circus splashed and seethed and shrieked
  All round Faustine.

But these are gone now: years entomb
  The dust and din;
Yea, even the bath's fierce reek and fume
  That slew Faustine.

Was life worth living then? and now
  Is life worth sin?
Where are the imperial years? and how
  Are you Faustine?

Your soul forgot her joys, forgot
  Her times of teen;
Yea, this life likewise will you not
  Forget, Faustine?

For in the time we know not of
  Did fate begin
Weaving the web of days that wove
  Your doom, Faustine.

The threads were wet with wine, and all
  Were smooth to spin;
They wove you like a Bacchanal,
  The first Faustine.

And Bacchus cast your mates and you
  Wild grapes to glean;
Your flower-like lips were dashed with dew
  From his, Faustine.

Your drenched loose hands were stretched to hold
  The vine's wet green,
Long ere they coined in Roman gold
  Your face, Faustine.

Then after change of soaring feather
  And winnowing fin,
You woke in weeks of feverish weather,
  A new Faustine.

A star upon your birthday burned,
  Whose fierce serene
Red pulseless planet never yearned
  In heaven, Faustine.

Stray breaths of Sapphic song that blew
  Through Mitylene
Shook the fierce quivering blood in you
  By night, Faustine.

The shameless nameless love that makes
  Hell's iron gin
Shut on you like a trap that breaks
  The soul, Faustine.

And when your veins were void and dead,
What ghosts unclean
Swarmed round the straitened barren bed
That hid Faustine?

What sterile growths of sexless root
Or epicene?
What flower of kisses without fruit
Of love, Faustine?

What adders came to shed their coats?
What coiled obscene
Small serpents with soft stretching throats
Caressed Faustine?

But the time came of famished hours,
Maimed loves and mean,
This ghastly thin-faced time of ours,
To spoil Faustine.

You seem a thing that hinges hold,
A love-machine
With clockwork joints of supple gold—
No more, Faustine.

Not godless, for you serve one God,
The Lampsacene,
Who metes the gardens with his rod;
Your lord, Faustine.

If one should love you with real love
(Such things have been,
Things your fair face knows nothing of,
It seems, Faustine);

That clear hair heavily bound back,
The lights wherein
Shift from dead blue to burnt-up black;
Your throat, Faustine,

Strong, heavy, throwing out the face
  And hard bright chin
And shameful scornful lips that grace
  Their shame, Faustine,

Curled lips, long-since half kissed away,
  Still sweet and keen;
You'd give him—poison shall we say?
  Or what, Faustine?

Rococo

Take hands and part with laughter;
  Touch lips and part with tears;
Once more and no more after,
  Whatever comes with years.
We twain shall not remeasure
  The ways that left us twain;
Nor crush the lees of pleasure
  From sanguine grapes of pain.

We twain once well in sunder,
  What will the mad gods do
For hate with me, I wonder,
  Or what for love with you?
Forget them till November,
  And dream there's April yet;
Forget that I remember,
  And dream that I forget.

Time found our tired love sleeping,
  And kissed away his breath;
But what should we do weeping,
  Though light love sleep to death?

We have drained his lips at leisure,
   Till there's not left to drain
A single sob of pleasure,
   A single pulse of pain.

Dream that the lips once breathless
   Might quicken if they would;
Say that the soul is deathless;
   Dream that the gods are good;
Say March may wed September,
   And time divorce regret;
But not that you remember,
   And not that I forget.

We have heard from hidden places
   What love scarce lives and hears:
We have seen on fervent faces
   The pallor of strange tears:
We have trod the wine-vat's treasure,
   Whence, ripe to steam and stain,
Foams round the feet of pleasure
   The blood-red must of pain.

Remembrance may recover
   And time bring back to time
The name of your first lover,
   The ring of my first rhyme;
But rose-leaves of December
   The frosts of June shall fret,
The day that you remember,
   The day that I forget.

The snake that hides and hisses
   In heaven we twain have known;
The grief of cruel kisses,
   The joy whose mouth makes moan;
The pulse's pause and measure,
   Where in one furtive vein

Throbs through the heart of pleasure
  The purpler blood of pain.

We have done with tears and treasons
  And love for treason's sake;
Room for the swift new seasons,
  The years that burn and break,
Dismantle and dismember
  Men's days and dreams, Juliette;
For love may not remember,
  But time will not forget.

Life treads down love in flying,
  Time withers him at root;
Bring all dead things and dying,
  Reaped sheaf and ruined fruit,
Where, crushed by three days' pressure,
  Our three days' love lies slain;
And earlier leaf of pleasure,
  And latter flower of pain.

Breathe close upon the ashes,
  It may be flame will leap;
Unclose the soft close lashes,
  Lift up the lids, and weep.
Light love's extinguished ember,
  Let one tear leave it wet
For one that you remember
  And ten that you forget.

Stage Love

When the game began between them for a jest,
He played king and she played queen to match the best;
Laughter soft as tears, and tears that turned to laughter,
These were things she sought for years and sorrowed after.

Pleasure with dry lips, and pain that walks by night;
All the sting and all the stain of long delight;
These were things she knew not of, that knew not of her,
When she played at half a love with half a lover.

Time was chorus, gave them cues to laugh or cry;
They would kill, befool, amuse him, let him die;
Set him webs to weave to-day and break to-morrow,
Till he died for good in play, and rose in sorrow.

What the years mean; how time dies and is not slain;
How love grows and laughs and cries and wanes again;
These were things she came to know, and take their measure,
When the play was played out so for one man's pleasure.

The Leper

Nothing is better, I well think,
  Than love; the hidden well-water
Is not so delicate to drink:
  This was well seen of me and her.

I served her in a royal house;
  I served her wine and curious meat.
For will to kiss between her brows,
  I had no heart to sleep or eat.

Mere scorn God knows she had of me,
A poor scribe, nowise great or fair,
Who plucked his clerk's hood back to see
Her curled-up lips and amorous hair.

I vex my head with thinking this.
Yea, though God always hated me,
And hates me now that I can kiss
Her eyes, plait up her hair to see

How she then wore it on the brows,
Yet am I glad to have her dead
Here in this wretched wattled house
Where I can kiss her eyes and head.

Nothing is better, I well know,
Than love; no amber in cold sea
Or gathered berries under snow:
That is well seen of her and me.

Three thoughts I make my pleasure of:
First I take heart and think of this:
That knight's gold hair she chose to love,
His mouth she had such will to kiss.

Then I remember that sundawn
I brought him by a privy way
Out at her lattice, and thereon
What gracious words she found to say.

(Cold rushes for such little feet—
Both feet could lie into my hand.
A marvel was it of my sweet
Her upright body could so stand.)

"Sweet friend, God give you thank and grace;
Now am I clean and whole of shame,
Nor shall men burn me in the face
For my sweet fault that scandals them."

I tell you over word by word.
  She, sitting edgewise on her bed,
Holding her feet, said thus. The third,
  A sweeter thing than these, I said.

God, that makes time and ruins it
  And alters not, abiding God,
Changed with disease her body sweet,
  The body of love wherein she abode.

Love is more sweet and comelier
  Than a dove's throat strained out to sing.
All they spat out and cursed at her
  And cast her forth for a base thing.

They cursed her, seeing how God had wrought
  This curse to plague her, a curse of his.
Fools were they surely, seeing not
  How sweeter than all sweet she is.

He that had held her by the hair,
  With kissing lips blinding her eyes,
Felt her bright bosom, strained and bare,
  Sigh under him, with short mad cries

Out of her throat and sobbing mouth
  And body broken up with love,
With sweet hot tears his lips were loth
  Her own should taste the savour of,

Yea, he inside whose grasp all night
  Her fervent body leapt or lay,
Stained with sharp kisses red and white,
  Found her a plague to spurn away.

I hid her in this wattled house,
  I served her water and poor bread.
For joy to kiss between her brows
  Time upon time I was nigh dead.

Bread failed; we got but well-water
  And gathered grass with dropping seed.
I had such joy of kissing her,
  I had small care to sleep or feed.

Sometimes when service made me glad
  The sharp tears leapt between my lids,
Falling on her, such joy I had
  To do the service God forbids.

"I pray you let me be at peace,
  Get hence, make room for me to die."
She said that: her poor lip would cease,
  Put up to mine, and turn to cry.

I said, "Bethink yourself how love
  Fared in us twain, what either did;
Shall I unclothe my soul thereof?
  That I should do this, God forbid."

Yea, though God hateth us, he knows
  That hardly in a little thing
Love faileth of the work it does
  Till it grow ripe for gathering.

Six months, and now my sweet is dead
  A trouble takes me; I know not
If all were done well, all well said,
  No word or tender deed forgot.

Too sweet, for the least part in her,
  To have shed life out by fragments; yet,
Could the close mouth catch breath and stir,
  I might see something I forget.

Six months, and I sit still and hold
  In two cold palms her cold two feet.
Her hair, half grey half ruined gold,
  Thrills me and burns me in kissing it.

Love bites and stings me through, to see
  Her keen face made of sunken bones.
Her worn-off eyelids madden me,
  That were shot through with purple once.

She said, "Be good with me; I grow
  So tired for shame's sake, I shall die
If you say nothing:" even so.
  And she is dead now, and shame put by.

Yea, and the scorn she had of me
  In the old time, doubtless vexed her then.
I never should have kissed her. See
  What fools God's anger makes of men!

She might have loved me a little too,
  Had I been humbler for her sake.
But that new shame could make love new
  She saw not—yet her shame did make.

I took too much upon my love,
  Having for such mean service done
Her beauty and all the ways thereof,
  Her face and all the sweet thereon.

Yea, all this while I tended her,
  I know the old love held fast his part:
I know the old scorn waxed heavier,
  Mixed with sad wonder, in her heart.

It may be all my love went wrong—
  A scribe's work writ awry and blurred,
Scrawled after the blind evensong—
  Spoilt music with no perfect word.

But surely I would fain have done
  All things the best I could. Perchance
Because I failed, came short of one,
  She kept at heart that other man's.

I am grown blind with all these things:
It may be now she hath in sight
Some better knowledge; still there clings
The old question. Will not God do right?

En ce temps-là estoyt dans ce pays grand nombre de ladres et de meseaulx, ce dont le roy eut grand desplaisir, veu que Dieu dust en estre moult griefvement courroucé. Ores il advint qu'une noble damoyselle appelée Yolande de Sallières estant atteincte et touste guastée de ce vilain mal, tous ses amys et ses parens ayant devant leurs yeux la paour de Dieu la firent issir fors de leurs maisons et oncques ne voulurent recepvoir ni reconforter chose mauldicte de Dieu et à tous les hommes puante et abhominable. Ceste dame avoyt esté moult belle et gracieuse de formes, et de son corps elle estoyt large et de vie lascive. Pourtant nul des amans qui l'avoyent souventesfois accollée et baisée moult tendrement ne voulust plus héberger si laide femme et si détestable pescheresse. Ung seul clerc qui feut premièrement son lacquays et son entremetteur en matière d'amour la reçut chez luy et la récéla dans une petite cabane. Là mourut la meschinette de grande misère et de male mort: et après elle décéda ledist clerc qui pour grand amour l'avoyt six mois durant soignée, lavée, habillée et deshabillée tous les jours de ses mains propres. Mesme dist-on que ce meschant homme et mauldict clerc se remémourant de la grande beauté passée et guastée de ceste femme se délectoyt maintesfois à la baiser sur sa bouche orde et lépreuse et l'accoller doulcement de ses mains amoureuses. Aussy est-il mort de ceste mesme maladie abhominable. Cecy advint près Fontainebellant en Gastinois. Et quand ouyt le roy Philippe ceste adventure moult en estoyt esmerveillé.

Grandes Chroniques de France, 1505.

A Ballad of Burdens

The burden of fair women. Vain delight,
And love self-slain in some sweet shameful way,
And sorrowful old age that comes by night
As a thief comes that has no heart by day,
And change that finds fair cheeks and leaves them grey,
And weariness that keeps awake for hire,
And grief that says what pleasure used to say;
This is the end of every man's desire.

The burden of bought kisses. This is sore,
  A burden without fruit in childbearing;
Between the nightfall and the dawn threescore,
  Threescore between the dawn and evening.
  The shuddering in thy lips, the shuddering
In thy sad eyelids tremulous like fire,
  Makes love seem shameful and a wretched thing.
This is the end of every man's desire.

The burden of sweet speeches. Nay, kneel down,
  Cover thy head, and weep; for verily
These market-men that buy thy white and brown
  In the last days shall take no thought for thee.
  In the last days like earth thy face shall be,
Yea, like sea-marsh made thick with brine and mire,
  Sad with sick leavings of the sterile sea.
This is the end of every man's desire.

The burden of long living. Thou shalt fear
  Waking, and sleeping mourn upon thy bed;
And say at night "Would God the day were here,"
  And say at dawn "Would God the day were dead."
  With weary days thou shalt be clothed and fed,
And wear remorse of heart for thine attire,
  Pain for thy girdle and sorrow upon thine head;
This is the end of every man's desire.

The burden of bright colours. Thou shalt see
  Gold tarnished, and the grey above the green;
And as the thing thou seest thy face shall be,
  And no more as the thing beforetime seen.
  And thou shalt say of mercy "It hath been,"
And living, watch the old lips and loves expire,
  And talking, tears shall take thy breath between;
This is the end of every man's desire.

The burden of sad sayings. In that day
  Thou shalt tell all thy days and hours, and tell

Thy times and ways and words of love, and say
  How one was dear and one desirable,
  And sweet was life to hear and sweet to smell,
But now with lights reverse the old hours retire
  And the last hour is shod with fire from hell;
This is the end of every man's desire.

The burden of four seasons. Rain in spring,
  White rain and wind among the tender trees;
A summer of green sorrows gathering,
  Rank autumn in a mist of miseries,
  With sad face set towards the year, that sees
The charred ash drop out of the dropping pyre,
  And winter wan with many maladies;
This is the end of every man's desire.

The burden of dead faces. Out of sight
  And out of love, beyond the reach of hands,
Changed in the changing of the dark and light,
  They walk and weep about the barren lands
  Where no seed is nor any garner stands,
Where in short breaths the doubtful days respire,
  And time's turned glass lets through the sighing sands;
This is the end of every man's desire.

The burden of much gladness. Life and lust
  Forsake thee, and the face of thy delight;
And underfoot the heavy hour strews dust,
  And overhead strange weathers burn and bite;
  And where the red was, lo the bloodless white,
And where truth was, the likeness of a liar,
  And where day was, the likeness of the night;
This is the end of every man's desire.

L'ENVOY

Princes, and ye whom pleasure quickeneth,
  Heed well this rhyme before your pleasure tire;

For life is sweet, but after life is death.
  This is the end of every man's desire.

Rondel

Kissing her hair I sat against her feet,
Wove and unwove it, wound and found it sweet;
Made fast therewith her hands, drew down her eyes,
Deep as deep flowers and dreamy like dim skies;
With her own tresses bound and found her fair,
    Kissing her hair.

Sleep were no sweeter than her face to me,
Sleep of cold sea-bloom under the cold sea;
What pain could get between my face and hers?
What new sweet thing would love not relish worse?
Unless, perhaps, white death had kissed me there,
    Kissing her hair?

Before the Mirror

(VERSES WRITTEN UNDER A PICTURE)

INSCRIBED TO J. A. WHISTLER

I

White rose in red rose-garden
  Is not so white;
Snowdrops that plead for pardon
  And pine for fright
Because the hard East blows

Over their maiden rows
  Grow not as this face grows from pale to bright.

Behind the veil, forbidden,
  Shut up from sight,
Love, is there sorrow hidden,
  Is there delight?
Is joy thy dower or grief,
White rose of weary leaf,
  Late rose whose life is brief, whose loves are light?

Soft snows that hard winds harden
  Till each flake bite
Fill all the flowerless garden
  Whose flowers took flight
Long since when summer ceased,
And men rose up from feast,
  And warm west wind grew east, and warm day night.

II

"Come snow, come wind or thunder
  High up in air,
I watch my face, and wonder
  At my bright hair;
Nought else exalts or grieves
The rose at heart, that heaves
  With love of her own leaves and lips that pair.

"She knows not loves that kissed her
  She knows not where.
Art thou the ghost, my sister,
  White sister there,
Am I the ghost, who knows?
My hand, a fallen rose,
  Lies snow-white on white snows, and takes no care.

"I cannot see what pleasures
  Or what pains were;
What pale new loves and treasures
  New years will bear;
What beam will fall, what shower,
What grief or joy for dower;
  But one thing knows the flower; the flower is fair."

III

Glad, but not flushed with gladness,
  Since joys go by;
Sad, but not bent with sadness,
  Since sorrows die;
Deep in the gleaming glass
She sees all past things pass,
  And all sweet life that was lie down and lie.

There glowing ghosts of flowers
  Draw down, draw nigh;
And wings of swift spent hours
  Take flight and fly;
She sees by formless gleams,
She hears across cold streams,
  Dead mouths of many dreams that sing and sigh.

Face fallen and white throat lifted,
  With sleepless eye
She sees old loves that drifted,
  She knew not why,
Old loves and faded fears
Float down a stream that hears
  The flowing of all men's tears beneath the sky.

Before Dawn

Sweet life, if life were stronger,
Earth clear of years that wrong her,
Then two things might live longer,
  Two sweeter things than they;
Delight, the rootless flower,
And love, the bloomless bower;
Delight that lives an hour,
  And love that lives a day.

From evensong to daytime,
When April melts in Maytime,
Love lengthens out his playtime,
  Love lessens breath by breath,
And kiss by kiss grows older
On listless throat or shoulder
Turned sideways now, turned colder
  Than life that dreams of death.

This one thing once worth giving
Life gave, and seemed worth living;
Sin sweet beyond forgiving
  And brief beyond regret:
To laugh and love together
And weave with foam and feather
And wind and words the tether
  Our memories play with yet.

Ah, one thing worth beginning,
One thread in life worth spinning,
Ah sweet, one sin worth sinning
  With all the whole soul's will;
To lull you till one stilled you,
To kiss you till one killed you,
To feed you till one filled you,
  Sweet lips, if love could fill;

To hunt sweet Love and lose him
Between white arms and bosom,
Between the bud and blossom,
   Between your throat and chin;
To say of shame—what is it?
Of virtue—we can miss it,
Of sin—we can but kiss it,
   And it's no longer sin:

To feel the strong soul, stricken
Through fleshly pulses, quicken
Beneath swift sighs that thicken,
   Soft hands and lips that smite;
Lips that no love can tire,
With hands that sting like fire,
Weaving the web Desire
   To snare the bird Delight.

But love so lightly plighted,
Our love with torch unlighted,
Paused near us unaffrighted,
   Who found and left him free;
None, seeing us cloven in sunder,
Will weep or laugh or wonder;
Light love stands clear of thunder,
   And safe from winds at sea.

As, when late larks give warning
Of dying lights and dawning,
Night murmurs to the morning,
   "Lie still, O love, lie still;"
And half her dark limbs cover
The white limbs of her lover,
With amorous plumes that hover
   And fervent lips that chill;

As scornful day represses
Night's void and vain caresses,

And from her cloudier tresses
  Unwinds the gold of his,
With limbs from limbs dividing
And breath by breath subsiding;
For love has no abiding,
  But dies before the kiss;

So hath it been, so be it;
For who shall live and flee it?
But look that no man see it
  Or hear it unaware;
Lest all who love and choose him
See Love, and so refuse him;
For all who find him lose him,
  But all have found him fair.

Dolores

(NOTRE-DAME DES SEPT DOULEURS)

Cold eyelids that hide like a jewel
  Hard eyes that grow soft for an hour;
The heavy white limbs, and the cruel
  Red mouth like a venomous flower;
When these are gone by with their glories,
  What shall rest of thee then, what remain,
O mystic and sombre Dolores,
  Our Lady of Pain?

Seven sorrows the priests give their Virgin;
  But thy sins, which are seventy times seven,
Seven ages would fail thee to purge in,
  And then they would haunt thee in heaven:
Fierce midnights and famishing morrows,
  And the loves that complete and control

All the joys of the flesh, all the sorrows
That wear out the soul.

O garment not golden but gilded,
O garden where all men may dwell,
O tower not of ivory, but builded
By hands that reach heaven from hell;
O mystical rose of the mire,
O house not of gold but of gain,
O house of unquenchable fire,
Our Lady of Pain!

O lips full of lust and of laughter,
Curled snakes that are fed from my breast,
Bite hard, lest remembrance come after
And press with new lips where you pressed.
For my heart too springs up at the pressure,
Mine eyelids too moisten and burn;
Ah, feed me and fill me with pleasure,
Ere pain come in turn.

In yesterday's reach and to-morrow's,
Out of sight though they lie of to-day,
There have been and there yet shall be sorrows
That smite not and bite not in play.
The life and the love thou despisest,
These hurt us indeed, and in vain,
O wise among women, and wisest,
Our Lady of Pain.

Who gave thee thy wisdom? what stories
That stung thee, what visions that smote?
Wert thou pure and a maiden, Dolores,
When desire took thee first by the throat?
What bud was the shell of a blossom
That all men may smell to and pluck?
What milk fed thee first at what bosom?
What sins gave thee suck?

We shift and bedeck and bedrape us,
  Thou art noble and nude and antique;
Libitina thy mother, Priapus
  Thy father, a Tuscan and Greek.
We play with light loves in the portal,
  And wince and relent and refrain;
Loves die, and we know thee immortal,
  Our Lady of Pain.

Fruits fail and love dies and time ranges;
  Thou art fed with perpetual breath,
And alive after infinite changes,
  And fresh from the kisses of death;
Of languors rekindled and rallied,
  Of barren delights and unclean,
Things monstrous and fruitless, a pallid
  And poisonous queen.

Could you hurt me, sweet lips, though I hurt you?
  Men touch them, and change in a trice
The lilies and languors of virtue
  For the raptures and roses of vice;
Those lie where thy foot on the floor is,
  These crown and caress thee and chain,
O splendid and sterile Dolores,
  Our Lady of Pain.

There are sins it may be to discover,
  There are deeds it may be to delight.
What new work wilt thou find for thy lover,
  What new passions for daytime or night?
What spells that they know not a word of
  Whose lives are as leaves overblown?
What tortures undreamt of, unheard of,
  Unwritten, unknown?

Ah beautiful passionate body
  That never has ached with a heart!

On thy mouth though the kisses are bloody,
   Though they sting till it shudder and smart,
More kind than the love we adore is,
   They hurt not the heart or the brain,
O bitter and tender Dolores,
   Our Lady of Pain.

As our kisses relax and redouble,
   From the lips and the foam and the fangs
Shall no new sin be born for men's trouble,
   No dream of impossible pangs?
With the sweet of the sins of old ages
   Wilt thou satiate thy soul as of yore?
Too sweet is the rind, say the sages,
   Too bitter the core.

Hast thou told all thy secrets the last time,
   And bared all thy beauties to one?
Ah, where shall we go then for pastime,
   If the worst that can be has been done?
But sweet as the rind was the core is;
   We are fain of thee still, we are fain,
O sanguine and subtle Dolores,
   Our Lady of Pain.

By the hunger of change and emotion,
   By the thirst of unbearable things,
By despair, the twin-born of devotion,
   By the pleasure that winces and stings,
The delight that consumes the desire,
   The desire that outruns the delight,
By the cruelty deaf as a fire
   And blind as the night,

By the ravenous teeth that have smitten
   Through the kisses that blossom and bud,
By the lips intertwisted and bitten
   Till the foam has a savour of blood,

By the pulse as it rises and falters,
  By the hands as they slacken and strain,
I adjure thee, respond from thine altars,
  Our Lady of Pain.

Wilt thou smile as a woman disdaining
  The light fire in the veins of a boy?
But he comes to thee sad, without feigning,
  Who has wearied of sorrow and joy;
Less careful of labour and glory
  Than the elders whose hair has uncurled;
And young, but with fancies as hoary
  And grey as the world.

I have passed from the outermost portal
  To the shrine where a sin is a prayer;
What care though the service be mortal?
  O our Lady of Torture, what care?
All thine the last wine that I pour is,
  The last in the chalice we drain,
O fierce and luxurious Dolores,
  Our Lady of Pain.

All thine the new wine of desire,
  The fruit of four lips as they clung
Till the hair and the eyelids took fire,
  The foam of a serpentine tongue,
The froth of the serpents of pleasure,
  More salt than the foam of the sea,
Now felt as a flame, now at leisure
  As wine shed for me.

Ah thy people, thy children, thy chosen,
  Marked cross from the womb and perverse!
They have found out the secret to cozen
  The gods that constrain us and curse;
They alone, they are wise, and none other;
  Give me place, even me, in their train,

O my sister, my spouse, and my mother,
Our Lady of Pain.

For the crown of our life as it closes
Is darkness, the fruit thereof dust;
No thorns go as deep as a rose's,
And love is more cruel than lust.
Time turns the old days to derision,
Our loves into corpses or wives;
And marriage and death and division
Make barren our lives.

And pale from the past we draw nigh thee,
And satiate with comfortless hours;
And we know thee, how all men belie thee,
And we gather the fruit of thy flowers;
The passion that slays and recovers,
The pangs and the kisses that rain
On the lips and the limbs of thy lovers,
Our Lady of Pain.

The desire of thy furious embraces
Is more than the wisdom of years,
On the blossom though blood lie in traces,
Though the foliage be sodden with tears.
For the lords in whose keeping the door is
That opens on all who draw breath
Gave the cypress to love, my Dolores,
The myrtle to death.

And they laughed, changing hands in the measure,
And they mixed and made peace after strife;
Pain melted in tears, and was pleasure;
Death tingled with blood, and was life.
Like lovers they melted and tingled,
In the dusk of thine innermost fane;
In the darkness they murmured and mingled,
Our Lady of Pain.

In a twilight where virtues are vices,
  In thy chapels, unknown of the sun,
To a tune that enthralls and entices,
  They were wed, and the twain were as one.
For the tune from thine altar hath sounded
  Since God bade the world's work begin,
And the fume of thine incense abounded,
  To sweeten the sin.

Love listens, and paler than ashes,
  Through his curls as the crown on them slips,
Lifts languid wet eyelids and lashes,
  And laughs with insatiable lips.
Thou shalt hush him with heavy caresses,
  With music that scares the profane;
Thou shalt darken his eyes with thy tresses,
  Our Lady of Pain.

Thou shalt blind his bright eyes though he wrestle,
  Thou shalt chain his light limbs though he strive;
In his lips all thy serpents shall nestle,
  In his hands all thy cruelties thrive.
In the daytime thy voice shall go through him,
  In his dreams he shall feel thee and ache;
Thou shalt kindle by night and subdue him
  Asleep and awake.

Thou shalt touch and make redder his roses
  With juice not of fruit nor of bud;
When the sense in the spirit reposes,
  Thou shalt quicken the soul through the blood.
Thine, thine the one grace we implore is,
  Who would live and not languish or feign,
O sleepless and deadly Dolores,
  Our Lady of Pain.

Dost thou dream, in a respite of slumber,
  In a lull of the fires of thy life,

Of the days without name, without number,
  When thy will stung the world into strife;
When, a goddess, the pulse of thy passion
  Smote kings as they revelled in Rome;
And they hailed thee re-risen, O Thalassian,
  Foam-white, from the foam?

When thy lips had such lovers to flatter;
  When the city lay red from thy rods,
And thine hands were as arrows to scatter
  The children of change and their gods;
When the blood of thy foemen made fervent
  A sand never moist from the main,
As one smote them, their lord and thy servant,
  Our Lady of Pain.

On sands by the storm never shaken,
  Nor wet from the washing of tides;
Nor by foam of the waves overtaken,
  Nor winds that the thunder bestrides;
But red from the print of thy paces,
  Made smooth for the world and its lords,
Ringed round with a flame of fair faces,
  And splendid with swords.

There the gladiator, pale for thy pleasure,
  Drew bitter and perilous breath;
There torments laid hold on the treasure
  Of limbs too delicious for death;
When thy gardens were lit with live torches;
  When the world was a steed for thy rein;
When the nations lay prone in thy porches,
  Our Lady of Pain.

When, with flame all around him aspirant,
  Stood flushed, as a harp-player stands,
The implacable beautiful tyrant,
  Rose-crowned, having death in his hands;

And a sound as the sound of loud water
  Smote far through the flight of the fires,
And mixed with the lightning of slaughter
  A thunder of lyres.

Dost thou dream of what was and no more is,
  The old kingdoms of earth and the kings?
Dost thou hunger for these things, Dolores,
  For these, in a world of new things?
But thy bosom no fasts could emaciate,
  No hunger compel to complain
Those lips that no bloodshed could satiate,
  Our Lady of Pain.

As of old when the world's heart was lighter,
  Through thy garments the grace of thee glows,
The white wealth of thy body made whiter
  By the blushes of amorous blows,
And seamed with sharp lips and fierce fingers,
  And branded by kisses that bruise;
When all shall be gone that now lingers,
  Ah, what shall we lose?

Thou wert fair in the fearless old fashion,
  And thy limbs are as melodies yet,
And move to the music of passion
  With lithe and lascivious regret.
What ailed us, O gods, to desert you
  For creeds that refuse and restrain?
Come down and redeem us from virtue,
  Our Lady of Pain.

All shrines that were Vestal are flameless,
  But the flame has not fallen from this;
Though obscure be the god, and though nameless
  The eyes and the hair that we kiss;
Low fires that love sits by and forges
  Fresh heads for his arrows and thine;

Hair loosened and soiled in mid orgies
With kisses and wine.

Thy skin changes country and colour,
And shrivels or swells to a snake's.
Let it brighten and bloat and grow duller,
We know it, the flames and the flakes,
Red brands on it smitten and bitten,
Round skies where a star is a stain,
And the leaves with thy litanies written,
Our Lady of Pain.

On thy bosom though many a kiss be,
There are none such as knew it of old.
Was it Alciphron once or Arisbe,
Male ringlets or feminine gold,
That thy lips met with under the statue,
Whence a look shot out sharp after thieves
From the eyes of the garden-god at you
Across the fig-leaves?

Then still, through dry seasons and moister,
One god had a wreath to his shrine;
Then love was the pearl of his oyster,*
And Venus rose red out of wine.
We have all done amiss, choosing rather
Such loves as the wise gods disdain;
Intercede for us thou with thy father,
Our Lady of Pain.

In spring he had crowns of his garden,
Red corn in the heat of the year,
Then hoary green olives that harden
When the grape-blossom freezes with fear;
And milk-budded myrtles with Venus
And vine-leaves with Bacchus he trod;
And ye said, "We have seen, he hath seen us,
A visible God."

What broke off the garlands that girt you?
  What sundered you spirit and clay?
Weak sins yet alive are as virtue
  To the strength of the sins of that day.
For dried is the blood of thy lover,
  Ipsithilla, contracted the vein;
Cry aloud, "Will he rise and recover,
  Our Lady of Pain?"

Cry aloud; for the old world is broken:
  Cry out; for the Phrygian is priest,
And rears not the bountiful token
  And spreads not the fatherly feast.
From the midmost of Ida, from shady
  Recesses that murmur at morn,
They have brought and baptized her, Our Lady,
  A goddess new-born.

And the chaplets of old are above us,
  And the oyster-bed teems out of reach;
Old poets outsing and outlove us,
  And Catullus makes mouths at our speech.
Who shall kiss, in thy father's own city,
  With such lips as he sang with, again?
Intercede for us all of thy pity,
  Our Lady of Pain.

Out of Dindymus heavily laden
  Her lions draw bound and unfed
A mother, a mortal, a maiden,
  A queen over death and the dead.
She is cold, and her habit is lowly,
  Her temple of branches and sods;
Most fruitful and virginal, holy,
  A mother of gods.

She hath wasted with fire thine high places,
  She hath hidden and marred and made sad

The fair limbs of the Loves, the fair faces
   Of gods that were goodly and glad.
She slays, and her hands are not bloody;
   She moves as a moon in the wane,
White-robed, and thy raiment is ruddy,
   Our Lady of Pain.

They shall pass and their places be taken,
   The gods and the priests that are pure.
They shall pass, and shalt thou not be shaken?
   They shall perish, and shalt thou endure?
Death laughs, breathing close and relentless
   In the nostrils and eyelids of lust,
With a pinch in his fingers of scentless
   And delicate dust.

But the worm shall revive thee with kisses;
   Thou shalt change and transmute as a god,
As the rod to a serpent that hisses,
   As the serpent again to a rod.
Thy life shall not cease though thou doff it;
   Thou shalt live until evil be slain,
And good shall die first, said thy prophet,
   Our Lady of Pain.

Did he lie? did he laugh? does he know it,
   Now he lies out of reach, out of breath,
Thy prophet, thy preacher, thy poet,
   Sin's child by incestuous Death?
Did he find out in fire at his waking,
   Or discern as his eyelids lost light,
When the bands of the body were breaking
   And all came in sight?

Who has known all the evil before us,
   Or the tyrannous secrets of time?
Though we match not the dead men that bore us
   At a song, at a kiss, at a crime—

Though the heathen outface and outlive us,
  And our lives and our longings are twain—
Ah, forgive us our virtues, forgive us,
  Our Lady of Pain.

Who are we that embalm and embrace thee
  With spices and savours of song?
What is time, that his children should face thee?
  What am I, that my lips do thee wrong?
I could hurt thee—but pain would delight thee;
  Or caress thee—but love would repel;
And the lovers whose lips would excite thee
  Are serpents in hell.

Who now shall content thee as they did,
  Thy lovers, when temples were built
And the hair of the sacrifice braided
  And the blood of the sacrifice spilt,
In Lampsacus fervent with faces,
  In Aphaca red from thy reign,
Who embraced thee with awful embraces,
  Our Lady of Pain?

Where are they, Cotytto or Venus,
  Astarte or Ashtaroth, where?
Do their hands as we touch come between us?
  Is the breath of them hot in thy hair?
From their lips have thy lips taken fever,
  With the blood of their bodies grown red?
Hast thou left upon earth a believer
  If these men are dead?

They were purple of raiment and golden,
  Filled full of thee, fiery with wine,
Thy lovers, in haunts unbeholden,
  In marvellous chambers of thine.
They are fled, and their footprints escape us,
  Who appraise thee, adore, and abstain,

O daughter of Death and Priapus,
  Our Lady of Pain.

What ails us to fear overmeasure,
  To praise thee with timorous breath,
O mistress and mother of pleasure,
  The one thing as certain as death?
We shall change as the things that we cherish,
  Shall fade as they faded before,
As foam upon water shall perish,
  As sand upon shore.

We shall know what the darkness discovers,
  If the grave-pit be shallow or deep;
And our fathers of old, and our lovers,
  We shall know if they sleep not or sleep.
We shall see whether hell be not heaven,
  Find out whether tares be not grain,
And the joys of thee seventy times seven,
  Our Lady of Pain.

* *Nam te præcipuè in suis urbibus colit ora*
Hellespontia, cæteris ostreosior oris.
CATULL. *Carm.* xviii.

The Garden of Proserpine

Here, where the world is quiet;
  Here, where all trouble seems
Dead winds' and spent waves' riot
  In doubtful dreams of dreams;
I watch the green field growing
  For reaping folk and sowing,
For harvest-time and mowing,
  A sleepy world of streams.

I am tired of tears and laughter,
   And men that laugh and weep;
Of what may come hereafter
   For men that sow to reap:
I am weary of days and hours,
   Blown buds of barren flowers,
Desires and dreams and powers
   And everything but sleep.

Here life has death for neighbour,
   And far from eye or ear
Wan waves and wet winds labour,
   Weak ships and spirits steer;
They drive adrift, and whither
   They wot not who make thither;
But no such winds blow hither,
   And no such things grow here.

No growth of moor or coppice,
   No heather-flower or vine,
But bloomless buds of poppies,
   Green grapes of Proserpine,
Pale beds of blowing rushes
Where no leaf blooms or blushes
Save this whereout she crushes
   For dead men deadly wine.

Pale, without name or number,
   In fruitless fields of corn,
They bow themselves and slumber
   All night till light is born;
And like a soul belated,
In hell and heaven unmated,
By cloud and mist abated
   Comes out of darkness morn.

Though one were strong as seven,
   He too with death shall dwell,

Nor wake with wings in heaven,
   Nor weep for pains in hell;
Though one were fair as roses,
His beauty clouds and closes;
And well though love reposes,
   In the end it is not well.

Pale, beyond porch and portal,
   Crowned with calm leaves, she stands
Who gathers all things mortal
   With cold immortal hands;
Her languid lips are sweeter
Than love's who fears to greet her
To men that mix and meet her
   From many times and lands.

She waits for each and other,
   She waits for all men born;
Forgets the earth her mother,
   The life of fruits and corn;
And spring and seed and swallow
Take wing for her and follow
Where summer song rings hollow
   And flowers are put to scorn.

There go the loves that wither,
   The old loves with wearier wings;
And all dead years draw thither,
   And all disastrous things;
Dead dreams of days forsaken,
Blind buds that snows have shaken,
Wild leaves that winds have taken,
   Red strays of ruined springs.

We are not sure of sorrow,
   And joy was never sure;
To-day will die to-morrow;
   Time stoops to no man's lure;

And love, grown faint and fretful,
With lips but half regretful
Sighs, and with eyes forgetful
Weeps that no loves endure.

From too much love of living,
From hope and fear set free,
We thank with brief thanksgiving
Whatever gods may be
That no life lives for ever;
That dead men rise up never;
That even the weariest river
Winds somewhere safe to sea.

Then star nor sun shall waken,
Nor any change of light:
Nor sound of waters shaken,
Nor any sound or sight:
Nor wintry leaves nor vernal,
Nor days nor things diurnal;
Only the sleep eternal
In an eternal night.

Before Parting

A month or twain to live on honeycomb
Is pleasant; but one tires of scented time,
Cold sweet recurrence of accepted rhyme,
And that strong purple under juice and foam
Where the wine's heart has burst;
Nor feel the latter kisses like the first.

Once yet, this poor one time; I will not pray
Even to change the bitterness of it,

The bitter taste ensuing on the sweet,
To make your tears fall where your soft hair lay
All blurred and heavy in some perfumed wise
Over my face and eyes.

And yet who knows what end the scythèd wheat
Makes of its foolish poppies' mouths of red?
These were not sown, these are not harvested,
They grow a month and are cast under feet
And none has care thereof,
As none has care of a divided love.

I know each shadow of your lips by rote,
Each change of love in eyelids and eyebrows;
The fashion of fair temples tremulous
With tender blood, and colour of your throat;
I know not how love is gone out of this,
Seeing that all was his.

Love's likeness there endures upon all these:
But out of these one shall not gather love.
Day hath not strength nor the night shade enough
To make love whole and fill his lips with ease,
As some bee-builded cell
Feels at filled lips the heavy honey swell.

I know not how this last month leaves your hair
Less full of purple colour and hid spice,
And that luxurious trouble of closed eyes
Is mixed with meaner shadow and waste care;
And love, kissed out by pleasure, seems not yet
Worth patience to regret.

The Sundew

A little marsh-plant, yellow green,
And pricked at lip with tender red.
Tread close, and either way you tread
Some faint black water jets between
Lest you should bruise the curious head.

A live thing maybe; who shall know?
The summer knows and suffers it;
For the cool moss is thick and sweet
Each side, and saves the blossom so
That it lives out the long June heat.

The deep scent of the heather burns
About it; breathless though it be,
Bow down and worship; more than we
Is the least flower whose life returns,
Least weed renascent in the sea.

We are vexed and cumbered in earth's sight
With wants, with many memories;
These see their mother what she is,
Glad-growing, till August leave more bright
The apple-coloured cranberries.

Wind blows and bleaches the strong grass,
Blown all one way to shelter it
From trample of strayed kine, with feet
Felt heavier than the moorhen was,
Strayed up past patches of wild wheat.

You call it sundew: how it grows,
If with its colour it have breath,
If life taste sweet to it, if death
Pain its soft petal, no man knows:
Man has no sight or sense that saith.

My sundew, grown of gentle days,
In these green miles the spring begun
Thy growth ere April had half done
With the soft secret of her ways
Or June made ready for the sun.

O red-lipped mouth of marsh-flower,
I have a secret halved with thee.
The name that is love's name to me
Thou knowest, and the face of her
Who is my festival to see.

The hard sun, as thy petals knew,
Coloured the heavy moss-water:
Thou wert not worth green midsummer
Nor fit to live to August blue,
O sundew, not remembering her.

Félise

Mais où sont les neiges d'antan?

What shall be said between us here
  Among the downs, between the trees,
In fields that knew our feet last year,
  In sight of quiet sands and seas,
  This year, Félise?

Who knows what word were best to say?
  For last year's leaves lie dead and red
On this sweet day, in this green May,
  And barren corn makes bitter bread.
  What shall be said?

Here as last year the fields begin,
  A fire of flowers and glowing grass;
The old fields we laughed and lingered in,
  Seeing each our souls in last year's glass,
  Félise, alas!

Shall we not laugh, shall we not weep,
  Not we, though this be as it is?
For love awake or love asleep
  Ends in a laugh, a dream, a kiss,
  A song like this.

I that have slept awake, and you
  Sleep, who last year were well awake.
Though love do all that love can do,
  My heart will never ache or break
  For your heart's sake.

The great sea, faultless as a flower,
  Throbs, trembling under beam and breeze,
And laughs with love of the amorous hour.
  I found you fairer once, Félise,
  Than flowers or seas.

We played at bondsman and at queen;
  But as the days change men change too;
I find the grey sea's notes of green,
  The green sea's fervent flakes of blue,
  More fair than you.

Your beauty is not over fair
  Now in mine eyes, who am grown up wise.
The smell of flowers in all your hair
  Allures not now; no sigh replies
  If your heart sighs.

But you sigh seldom, you sleep sound,
  You find love's new name good enough.

Less sweet I find it than I found
  The sweetest name that ever love
  Grew weary of.

My snake with bright bland eyes, my snake
  Grown tame and glad to be caressed,
With lips athirst for mine to slake
  Their tender fever! who had guessed
  You loved me best?

I had died for this last year, to know
  You loved me. Who shall turn on fate?
I care not if love come or go
  Now, though your love seek mine for mate.
  It is too late.

The dust of many strange desires
  Lies deep between us; in our eyes
Dead smoke of perishable fires
  Flickers, a fume in air and skies,
  A steam of sighs.

You loved me and you loved me not;
  A little, much, and overmuch.
Will you forget as I forgot?
  Let all dead things lie dead; none such
  Are soft to touch.

I love you and I do not love,
  Too much, a little, not at all;
Too much, and never yet enough.
  Birds quick to fledge and fly at call
  Are quick to fall.

And these love longer now than men,
  And larger loves than ours are these.
No diver brings up love again
  Dropped once, my beautiful Félise,
  In such cold seas.

Gone deeper than all plummets sound,
  Where in the dim green dayless day
The life of such dead things lies bound
  As the sea feeds on, wreck and stray
  And castaway.

Can I forget? yea, that can I,
  And that can all men; so will you,
Alive, or later, when you die.
  Ah, but the love you plead was true?
  Was mine not too?

I loved you for that name of yours
  Long ere we met, and long enough.
Now that one thing of all endures—
  The sweetest name that ever love
  Waxed weary of.

Like colours in the sea, like flowers,
  Like a cat's splendid circled eyes
That wax and wane with love for hours,
  Green as green flame, blue-grey like skies,
  And soft like sighs—

And all these only like your name,
  And your name full of all of these.
I say it, and it sounds the same—
  Save that I say it now at ease,
  Your name, Félise.

I said "she must be swift and white,
  And subtly warm, and half perverse,
And sweet like sharp soft fruit to bite,
  And like a snake's love lithe and fierce."
  Men have guessed worse.

What was the song I made of you
  Here where the grass forgets our feet

As afternoon forgets the dew?
  Ah that such sweet things should be fleet,
  Such fleet things sweet!

As afternoon forgets the dew,
  As time in time forgets all men,
As our old place forgets us two,
  Who might have turned to one thing then
  But not again.

    O lips that mine have grown into
      Like April's kissing May,
    O fervent eyelids letting through
    Those eyes the greenest of things blue,
      The bluest of things grey,

    If you were I and I were you,
      How could I love you, say?
    How could the roseleaf love the rue,
    The day love nightfall and her dew,
      Though night may love the day?

You loved it may be more than I;
  We know not; love is hard to seize.
And all things are not good to try;
  And lifelong loves the worst of these
  For us, Félise.

Ah, take the season and have done,
  Love well the hour and let it go:
Two souls may sleep and wake up one,
  Or dream they wake and find it so,
  And then—you know.

Kiss me once hard as though a flame
  Lay on my lips and made them fire;
The same lips now, and not the same;
  What breath shall fill and re-inspire
  A dead desire?

The old song sounds hollower in mine ear
Than thin keen sounds of dead men's speech—
A noise one hears and would not hear;
Too strong to die, too weak to reach
From wave to beach.

We stand on either side the sea,
Stretch hands, blow kisses, laugh and lean
I toward you, you toward me;
But what hears either save the keen
Grey sea between?

A year divides us, love from love,
Though you love now, though I loved then.
The gulf is strait, but deep enough;
Who shall recross, who among men
Shall cross again?

Love was a jest last year, you said,
And what lives surely, surely dies.
Even so; but now that love is dead,
Shall love rekindle from wet eyes,
From subtle sighs?

For many loves are good to see;
Mutable loves, and loves perverse;
But there is nothing, nor shall be,
So sweet, so wicked, but my verse
Can dream of worse.

For we that sing and you that love
Know that which man may, only we.
The rest live under us; above,
Live the great gods in heaven, and see
What things shall be.

So this thing is and must be so;
For man dies, and love also dies.

Though yet love's ghost moves to and fro
  The sea-green mirrors of your eyes,
  And laughs, and lies.

Eyes coloured like a water-flower,
  And deeper than the green sea's glass;
Eyes that remember one sweet hour—
  In vain we swore it should not pass;
  In vain, alas!

Ah my Félise, if love or sin,
  If shame or fear could hold it fast,
Should we not hold it? Love wears thin,
  And they laugh well who laugh the last.
  Is it not past?

The gods, the gods are stronger; time
  Falls down before them, all men's knees
Bow, all men's prayers and sorrows climb
  Like incense towards them; yea, for these
  Are gods, Félise.

Immortal are they, clothed with powers,
  Not to be comforted at all;
Lords over all the fruitless hours;
  Too great to appease, too high to appal,
  Too far to call.

For none shall move the most high gods,
  Who are most sad, being cruel; none
Shall break or take away the rods
  Wherewith they scourge us, not as one
  That smites a son.

By many a name of many a creed
  We have called upon them, since the sands
Fell through time's hour-glass first, a seed
  Of life; and out of many lands
  Have we stretched hands.

When have they heard us? who hath known
  Their faces, climbed unto their feet,
Felt them and found them? Laugh or groan,
  Doth heaven remurmur and repeat
  Sad sounds or sweet?

Do the stars answer? in the night
  Have ye found comfort? or by day
Have ye seen gods? What hope, what light,
  Falls from the farthest starriest way
  On you that pray?

Are the skies wet because we weep,
  Or fair because of any mirth?
Cry out; they are gods; perchance they sleep;
  Cry; thou shalt know what prayers are worth,
  Thou dust and earth.

O earth, thou art fair; O dust, thou art great;
  O laughing lips and lips that mourn,
Pray, till ye feel the exceeding weight
  Of God's intolerable scorn,
  Not to be borne.

Behold, there is no grief like this;
  The barren blossom of thy prayer,
Thou shalt find out how sweet it is.
  O fools and blind, what seek ye there,
  High up in the air?

Ye must have gods, the friends of men,
  Merciful gods, compassionate,
And these shall answer you again.
  Will ye beat always at the gate,
  Ye fools of fate?

Ye fools and blind; for this is sure,
  That all ye shall not live, but die.

Lo, what thing have ye found endure?
  Or what thing have ye found on high
  Past the blind sky?

The ghosts of words and dusty dreams,
  Old memories, faiths infirm and dead.
Ye fools; for which among you deems
  His prayer can alter green to red
  Or stones to bread?

Why should ye bear with hopes and fears
  Till all these things be drawn in one,
The sound of iron-footed years,
  And all the oppression that is done
  Under the sun?

Ye might end surely, surely pass
  Out of the multitude of things,
Under the dust, beneath the grass,
  Deep in dim death, where no thought stings,
  No record clings.

No memory more of love or hate,
  No trouble, nothing that aspires,
No sleepless labour thwarting fate,
  And thwarted; where no travail tires,
  Where no faith fires.

All passes, nought that has been is,
  Things good and evil have one end.
Can anything be otherwise
  Though all men swear all things would mend
  With God to friend?

Can ye beat off one wave with prayer,
  Can ye move mountains? bid the flower
Take flight and turn to a bird in the air?
  Can ye hold fast for shine or shower
  One wingless hour?

Ah sweet, and we too, can we bring
  One sigh back, bid one smile revive?
Can God restore one ruined thing,
  Or he who slays our souls alive
  Make dead things thrive?

Two gifts perforce he has given us yet,
  Though sad things stay and glad things fly;
Two gifts he has given us, to forget
  All glad and sad things that go by,
  And then to die.

We know not whether death be good,
  But life at least it will not be:
Men will stand saddening as we stood,
  Watch the same fields and skies as we
  And the same sea.

Let this be said between us here,
  One love grows green when one turns grey;
This year knows nothing of last year;
  To-morrow has no more to say
  To yesterday.

Live and let live, as I will do,
  Love and let love, and so will I.
But, sweet, for me no more with you:
  Not while I live, not though I die.
  Goodnight, goodbye.

Hendecasyllabics

In the month of the long decline of roses
I, beholding the summer dead before me,
Set my face to the sea and journeyed silent,
Gazing eagerly where above the sea-mark
Flame as fierce as the fervid eyes of lions
Half divided the eyelids of the sunset;
Till I heard as it were a noise of waters
Moving tremulous under feet of angels
Multitudinous, out of all the heavens;
Knew the fluttering wind, the fluttered foliage,
Shaken fitfully, full of sound and shadow;
And saw, trodden upon by noiseless angels,
Long mysterious reaches fed with moonlight,
Sweet sad straits in a soft subsiding channel,
Blown about by the lips of winds I knew not,
Winds not born in the north nor any quarter,
Winds not warm with the south nor any sunshine;
Heard between them a voice of exultation,
"Lo, the summer is dead, the sun is faded,
Even like as a leaf the year is withered,
All the fruits of the day from all her branches
Gathered, neither is any left to gather.
All the flowers are dead, the tender blossoms,
All are taken away; the season wasted,
Like an ember among the fallen ashes.
Now with light of the winter days, with moonlight,
Light of snow, and the bitter light of hoarfrost,
We bring flowers that fade not after autumn,
Pale white chaplets and crowns of latter seasons,
Fair false leaves (but the summer leaves were falser),
Woven under the eyes of stars and planets
When low light was upon the windy reaches
Where the flower of foam was blown, a lily
Dropt among the sonorous fruitless furrows
And green fields of the sea that make no pasture:

Since the winter begins, the weeping winter,
All whose flowers are tears, and round his temples
Iron blossom of frost is bound for ever."

Sapphics

All the night sleep came not upon my eyelids,
Shed not dew, nor shook nor unclosed a feather,
Yet with lips shut close and with eyes of iron
    Stood and beheld me.

Then to me so lying awake a vision
Came without sleep over the seas and touched me,
Softly touched mine eyelids and lips; and I too,
    Full of the vision,

Saw the white implacable Aphrodite,
Saw the hair unbound and the feet unsandalled
Shine as fire of sunset on western waters;
    Saw the reluctant

Feet, the straining plumes of the doves that drew her,
Looking always, looking with necks reverted,
Back to Lesbos, back to the hills whereunder
    Shone Mitylene;

Heard the flying feet of the Loves behind her
Make a sudden thunder upon the waters,
As the thunder flung from the strong unclosing
    Wings of a great wind.

So the goddess fled from her place, with awful
Sound of feet and thunder of wings around her;
While behind a clamour of singing women
    Severed the twilight.

Ah the singing, ah the delight, the passion!
All the Loves wept, listening; sick with anguish,
Stood the crowned nine Muses about Apollo;
    Fear was upon them,

While the tenth sang wonderful things they knew not.
Ah the tenth, the Lesbian! the nine were silent,
None endured the sound of her song for weeping;
    Laurel by laurel,

Faded all their crowns; but about her forehead,
Round her woven tresses and ashen temples
White as dead snow, paler than grass in summer,
    Ravaged with kisses,

Shone a light of fire as a crown for ever.
Yea, almost the implacable Aphrodite
Paused, and almost wept; such a song was that song.
    Yea, by her name too

Called her, saying, "Turn to me, O my Sappho;"
Yet she turned her face from the Loves, she saw not
Tears for laughter darken immortal eyelids,
    Heard not about her

Fearful fitful wings of the doves departing,
Saw not how the bosom of Aphrodite
Shook with weeping, saw not her shaken raiment,
    Saw not her hands wrung;

Saw the Lesbians kissing across their smitten
Lutes with lips more sweet than the sound of lute-strings,
Mouth to mouth and hand upon hand, her chosen,
    Fairer than all men;

Only saw the beautiful lips and fingers,
Full of songs and kisses and little whispers,
Full of music; only beheld among them
    Soar, as a bird soars

Newly fledged, her visible song, a marvel,
Made of perfect sound and exceeding passion,
Sweetly shapen, terrible, full of thunders,
    Clothed with the wind's wings.

Then rejoiced she, laughing with love, and scattered
Roses, awful roses of holy blossom;
Then the Loves thronged sadly with hidden faces
    Round Aphrodite,

Then the Muses, stricken at heart, were silent;
Yea, the gods waxed pale; such a song was that song.
All reluctant, all with a fresh repulsion,
    Fled from before her.

All withdrew long since, and the land was barren,
Full of fruitless women and music only.
Now perchance, when winds are assuaged at sunset,
    Lulled at the dewfall,

By the grey sea-side, unassuaged, unheard of,
Unbeloved, unseen in the ebb of twilight,
Ghosts of outcast women return lamenting,
    Purged not in Lethe,

Clothed about with flame and with tears, and singing
Songs that move the heart of the shaken heaven,
Songs that break the heart of the earth with pity,
    Hearing, to hear them.

At Eleusis

Men of Eleusis, ye that with long staves
Sit in the market-houses, and speak words
Made sweet with wisdom as the rare wine is
Thickened with honey; and ye sons of these
Who in the glad thick streets go up and down
For pastime or grave traffic or mere chance;
And all fair women having rings of gold
On hands or hair; and chiefest over these
I name you, daughters of this man the king,
Who dipping deep smooth pitchers of pure brass
Under the bubbled wells, till each round lip
Stooped with loose gurgle of waters incoming,
Found me an old sick woman, lamed and lean,
Beside a growth of builded olive-boughs
Whence multiplied thick song of thick-plumed throats—
Also wet tears filled up my hollow hands
By reason of my crying into them—
And pitied me; for as cold water ran
And washed the pitchers full from lip to lip,
So washed both eyes full the strong salt of tears.
And ye put water to my mouth, made sweet
With brown hill-berries; so in time I spoke
And gathered my loose knees from under me.
Moreover in the broad fair halls this month
Have I found space and bountiful abode
To please me. I Demeter speak of this,
Who am the mother and the mate of things:
For as ill men by drugs or singing words
Shut the doors inward of the narrowed womb
Like a lock bolted with round iron through,
Thus I shut up the body and sweet mouth
Of all soft pasture and the tender land,
So that no seed can enter in by it
Though one sow thickly, nor some grain get out
Past the hard clods men cleave and bite with steel

To widen the sealed lips of them for use.
None of you is there in the peopled street
But knows how all the dry-drawn furrows ache
With no green spot made count of in the black:
How the wind finds no comfortable grass
Nor is assuaged with bud nor breath of herbs;
And in hot autumn when ye house the stacks,
All fields are helpless in the sun, all trees
Stand as a man stripped out of all but skin.
Nevertheless ye sick have help to get
By means and stablished ordinance of God;
For God is wiser than a good man is.
But never shall new grass be sweet in earth
Till I get righted of my wound and wrong
By changing counsel of ill-minded Zeus.
For of all other gods is none save me
Clothed with like power to build and break the year.
I make the lesser green begin, when spring
Touches not earth but with one fearful foot;
And as a careful gilder with grave art
Soberly colours and completes the face,
Mouth, chin and all, of some sweet work in stone,
I carve the shapes of grass and tender corn
And colour the ripe edges and long spikes
With the red increase and the grace of gold.
No tradesman in soft wools is cunninger
To kill the secret of the fat white fleece
With stains of blue and purple wrought in it.
Three moons were made and three moons burnt away
While I held journey hither out of Crete
Comfortless, tended by grave Hecate
Whom my wound stung with double iron point;
For all my face was like a cloth wrung out
With close and weeping wrinkles, and both lids
Sodden with salt continuance of tears.
For Hades and the sidelong will of Zeus
And that lame wisdom that has writhen feet,
Cunning, begotten in the bed of Shame,

These three took evil will at me, and made
Such counsel that when time got wing to fly
This Hades out of summer and low fields
Forced the bright body of Persephone:
Out of pure grass, where she lying down, red flowers
Made their sharp little shadows on her sides,
Pale heat, pale colour on pale maiden flesh—
And chill water slid over her reddening feet,
Killing the throbs in their soft blood; and birds,
Perched next her elbow and pecking at her hair,
Stretched their necks more to see her than even to sing.
A sharp thing is it I have need to say;
For Hades holding both white wrists of hers
Unloosed the girdle and with knot by knot
Bound her between his wheels upon the seat,
Bound her pure body, holiest yet and dear
To me and God as always, clothed about
With blossoms loosened as her knees went down,
Let fall as she let go of this and this
By tens and twenties, tumbled to her feet,
White waifs or purple of the pasturage.
Therefore with only going up and down
My feet were wasted, and the gracious air,
To me discomfortable and dun, became
As weak smoke blowing in the under world.
And finding in the process of ill days
What part had Zeus herein, and how as mate
He coped with Hades, yokefellow in sin,
I set my lips against the meat of gods
And drank not neither ate or slept in heaven.
Nor in the golden greeting of their mouths
Did ear take note of me, nor eye at all
Track my feet going in the ways of them.
Like a great fire on some strait slip of land
Between two washing inlets of wet sea
That burns the grass up to each lip of beach
And strengthens, waxing in the growth of wind,
So burnt my soul in me at heaven and earth,

Each way a ruin and a hungry plague,
Visible evil; nor could any night
Put cool between mine eyelids, nor the sun
With competence of gold fill out my want.
Yea so my flame burnt up the grass and stones,
Shone to the salt-white edges of thin sea,
Distempered all the gracious work, and made
Sick change, unseasonable increase of days
And scant avail of seasons; for by this
The fair gods faint in hollow heaven: there comes
No taste of burnings of the twofold fat
To leave their palates smooth, nor in their lips
Soft rings of smoke and weak scent wandering;
All cattle waste and rot, and their ill smell
Grows alway from the lank unsavoury flesh
That no man slays for offering; the sea
And waters moved beneath the heath and corn
Preserve the people of fin-twinkling fish,
And river-flies feed thick upon the smooth;
But all earth over is no man or bird
(Except the sweet race of the kingfisher)
That lacks not and is wearied with much loss.
Meantime the purple inward of the house
Was softened with all grace of scent and sound
In ear and nostril perfecting my praise;
Faint grape-flowers and cloven honey-cake
And the just grain with dues of the shed salt
Made me content: yet my hand loosened not
Its gripe upon your harvest all year long.
While I, thus woman-muffled in wan flesh
And waste externals of a perished face,
Preserved the levels of my wrath and love
Patiently ruled; and with soft offices
Cooled the sharp noons and busied the warm nights
In care of this my choice, this child my choice,
Triptolemus, the king's selected son:
That this fair yearlong body, which hath grown
Strong with strange milk upon the mortal lip

And nerved with half a god, might so increase
Outside the bulk and the bare scope of man:
And waxen over large to hold within
Base breath of yours and this impoverished air,
I might exalt him past the flame of stars,
The limit and walled reach of the great world.
Therefore my breast made common to his mouth
Immortal savours, and the taste whereat
Twice their hard life strains out the coloured veins
And twice its brain confirms the narrow shell.
Also at night, unwinding cloth from cloth
As who unhusks an almond to the white
And pastures curiously the purer taste,
I bared the gracious limbs and the soft feet,
Unswaddled the weak hands, and in mid ash
Laid the sweet flesh of either feeble side,
More tender for impressure of some touch
Than wax to any pen; and lit around
Fire, and made crawl the white worm-shapen flame,
And leap in little angers spark by spark
At head at once and feet; and the faint hair
Hissed with rare sprinkles in the closer curl,
And like scaled oarage of a keen thin fish
In sea-water, so in pure fire his feet
Struck out, and the flame bit not in his flesh,
But like a kiss it curled his lip, and heat
Fluttered his eyelids; so each night I blew
The hot ash red to purge him to full god.
Ill is it when fear hungers in the soul
For painful food, and chokes thereon, being fed;
And ill slant eyes interpret the straight sun,
But in their scope its white is wried to black:
By the queen Metaneira mean I this;
For with sick wrath upon her lips, and heart
Narrowing with fear the spleenful passages,
She thought to thread this web's fine ravel out,
Nor leave her shuttle split in combing it;
Therefore she stole on us, and with hard sight

Peered, and stooped close; then with pale open mouth
As the fire smote her in the eyes between
Cried, and the child's laugh, sharply shortening
As fire doth under rain, fell off; the flame
Writhed once all through and died, and in thick dark
Tears fell from mine on the child's weeping eyes,
Eyes dispossessed of strong inheritance
And mortal fallen anew. Who not the less
From bud of beard to pale-grey flower of hair
Shall wax vinewise to a lordly vine, whose grapes
Bleed the red heavy blood of swoln soft wine,
Subtle with sharp leaves' intricacy, until
Full of white years and blossom of hoary days
I take him perfected; for whose one sake
I am thus gracious to the least who stands
Filleted with white wool and girt upon
As he whose prayer endures upon the lip
And falls not waste: wherefore let sacrifice
Burn and run red in all the wider ways;
Seeing I have sworn by the pale temples' band
And poppied hair of gold Persephone
Sad-tressed and pleached low down about her brows,
And by the sorrow in her lips, and death
Her dumb and mournful-mouthèd minister,
My word for you is eased of its harsh weight
And doubled with soft promise; and your king
Triptolemus, this Celeus dead and swathed
Purple and pale for golden burial,
Shall be your helper in my services,
Dividing earth and reaping fruits thereof
In fields where wait, well-girt, well-wreathen, all
The heavy-handed seasons all year through;
Saving the choice of warm spear-headed grain,
And stooping sharp to the slant-sided share
All beasts that furrow the remeasured land
With their bowed necks of burden equable.

August

There were four apples on the bough,
Half gold half red, that one might know
The blood was ripe inside the core;
The colour of the leaves was more
Like stems of yellow corn that grow
Through all the gold June meadow's floor.

The warm smell of the fruit was good
To feed on, and the split green wood,
With all its bearded lips and stains
Of mosses in the cloven veins,
Most pleasant, if one lay or stood
In sunshine or in happy rains.

There were four apples on the tree,
Red stained through gold, that all might see
The sun went warm from core to rind;
The green leaves made the summer blind
In that soft place they kept for me
With golden apples shut behind.

The leaves caught gold across the sun,
And where the bluest air begun
Thirsted for song to help the heat;
As I to feel my lady's feet
Draw close before the day were done;
Both lips grew dry with dreams of it.

In the mute August afternoon
They trembled to some undertune
Of music in the silver air;
Great pleasure was it to be there
Till green turned duskier and the moon
Coloured the corn-sheaves like gold hair.

That August time it was delight
To watch the red moons wane to white
'Twixt grey seamed stems of apple-trees;
A sense of heavy harmonies
Grew on the growth of patient night,
More sweet than shapen music is.

But some three hours before the moon
The air, still eager from the noon,
Flagged after heat, not wholly dead;
Against the stem I leant my head;
The colour soothed me like a tune,
Green leaves all round the gold and red.

I lay there till the warm smell grew
More sharp, when flecks of yellow dew
Between the round ripe leaves had blurred
The rind with stain and wet; I heard
A wind that blew and breathed and blew,
Too weak to alter its one word.

The wet leaves next the gentle fruit
Felt smoother, and the brown tree-root
Felt the mould warmer: I too felt
(As water feels the slow gold melt
Right through it when the day burns mute)
The peace of time wherein love dwelt.

There were four apples on the tree,
Gold stained on red that all might see
The sweet blood filled them to the core:
The colour of her hair is more
Like stems of fair faint gold, that be
Mown from the harvest's middle floor.

St. Dorothy

It hath been seen and yet it shall be seen
That out of tender mouths God's praise hath been
Made perfect, and with wood and simple string
He hath played music sweet as shawm-playing
To please himself with softness of all sound;
And no small thing but hath been sometime found
Full sweet of use, and no such humbleness
But God hath bruised withal the sentences
And evidence of wise men witnessing;
No leaf that is so soft a hidden thing
It never shall get sight of the great sun;
The strength of ten has been the strength of one,
And lowliness has waxed imperious.
    There was in Rome a man Theophilus
Of right great blood and gracious ways, that had
All noble fashions to make people glad
And a soft life of pleasurable days;
He was a goodly man for one to praise,
Flawless and whole upward from foot to head;
His arms were a red hawk that alway fed
On a small bird with feathers gnawed upon,
Beaten and plucked about the bosom-bone
Whereby a small round fleck like fire there was:
They called it in their tongue lampadias;
This was the banner of the lordly man.
In many straits of sea and reaches wan
Full of quick wind, and many a shaken firth,
It had seen fighting days of either earth,
Westward or east of waters Gaditane
(This was the place of sea-rocks under Spain
Called after the great praise of Hercules)
And north beyond the washing Pontic seas,
Far windy Russian places fabulous,
And salt fierce tides of storm-swoln Bosphorus.
    Now as this lord came straying in Rome town

He saw a little lattice open down
And after it a press of maidens' heads
That sat upon their cold small quiet beds
Talking, and played upon short-stringèd lutes;
And other some ground perfume out of roots
Gathered by marvellous moons in Asia;
Saffron and aloes and wild cassia,
Coloured all through and smelling of the sun;
And over all these was a certain one
Clothed softly, with sweet herbs about her hair
And bosom flowerful; her face more fair
Than sudden-singing April in soft lands:
Eyed like a gracious bird, and in both hands
She held a psalter painted green and red.
    This Theophile laughed at the heart, and said,
Now God so help me hither and St. Paul,
As by the new time of their festival
I have good will to take this maid to wife.
And herewith fell to fancies of her life
And soft half-thoughts that ended suddenly.
This is man's guise to please himself, when he
Shall not see one thing of his pleasant things,
Nor with outwatch of many travailings
Come to be eased of the least pain he hath
For all his love and all his foolish wrath
And all the heavy manner of his mind.
Thus is he like a fisher fallen blind
That casts his nets across the boat awry
To strike the sea, but lo, he striketh dry
And plucks them back all broken for his pain
And bites his beard and casts across again
And reaching wrong slips over in the sea.
So hath this man a strangled neck for fee,
For all his cost he chuckles in his throat.
    This Theophile that little hereof wote
Laid wait to hear of her what she might be:
Men told him she had name of Dorothy,
And was a lady of a worthy house.

Thereat this knight grew inly glorious
That he should have a love so fair of place.
She was a maiden of most quiet face,
Tender of speech, and had no hardihood
But was nigh feeble of her fearful blood;
Her mercy in her was so marvellous
From her least years, that seeing her school-fellows
That read beside her stricken with a rod,
She would cry sore and say some word to God
That he would ease her fellow of his pain.
There is no touch of sun or fallen rain
That ever fell on a more gracious thing.
    In middle Rome there was in stone-working
The church of Venus painted royally.
The chapels of it were some two or three,
In each of them her tabernacle was
And a wide window of six feet in glass
Coloured with all her works in red and gold.
The altars had bright cloths and cups to hold
The wine of Venus for the services,
Made out of honey and crushed wood-berries
That shed sweet yellow through the thick wet red,
That on high days was borne upon the head
Of Venus' priest for any man to drink;
So that in drinking he should fall to think
On some fair face, and in the thought thereof
Worship, and such should triumph in his love.
For this soft wine that did such grace and good
Was new trans-shaped and mixed with Love's own blood,
That in the fighting Trojan time was bled;
For which came such a woe to Diomed
That he was stifled after in hard sea.
And some said that this wine-shedding should be
Made of the falling of Adonis' blood,
That curled upon the thorns and broken wood
And round the gold silk shoes on Venus' feet;
The taste thereof was as hot honey sweet
And in the mouth ran soft and riotous.

This was the holiness of Venus' house.
    It was their worship, that in August days
Twelve maidens should go through those Roman ways
Naked, and having gold across their brows
And their hair twisted in short golden rows,
To minister to Venus in this wise:
And twelve men chosen in their companies
To match these maidens by the altar-stair,
All in one habit, crowned upon the hair.
Among these men was chosen Theophile.
    This knight went out and prayed a little while,
Holding queen Venus by her hands and knees;
I will give thee twelve royal images
Cut in glad gold, with marvels of wrought stone
For thy sweet priests to lean and pray upon,
Jasper and hyacinth and chrysopras,
And the strange Asian thalamite that was
Hidden twelve ages under heavy sea
Among the little sleepy pearls, to be
A shrine lit over with soft candle-flame
Burning all night red as hot brows of shame,
So thou wilt be my lady without sin.
Goddess that art all gold outside and in,
Help me to serve thee in thy holy way.
Thou knowest, Love, that in my bearing day
There shone a laughter in the singing stars
Round the gold-ceilèd bride-bed wherein Mars
Touched thee and had thee in your kissing wise.
Now therefore, sweet, kiss thou my maiden's eyes
That they may open graciously towards me;
And this new fashion of thy shrine shall be
As soft with gold as thine own happy head.
    The goddess, that was painted with face red
Between two long green tumbled sides of sea,
Stooped her neck sideways, and spake pleasantly:
Thou shalt have grace as thou art thrall of mine.
And with this came a savour of shed wine
And plucked-out petals from a rose's head:

And softly with slow laughs of lip she said,
Thou shalt have favour all thy days of me.
    Then came Theophilus to Dorothy,
Saying: O sweet, if one should strive or speak
Against God's ways, he gets a beaten cheek
For all his wage and shame above all men.
Therefore I have no will to turn again
When God saith "go," lest a worse thing fall out.
Then she, misdoubting lest he went about
To catch her wits, made answer somewhat thus:
I have no will, my lord Theophilus,
To speak against this worthy word of yours;
Knowing how God's will in all speech endures,
That save by grace there may no thing be said.
Then Theophile waxed light from foot to head,
And softly fell upon this answering.
It is well seen you are a chosen thing
To do God service in his gracious way.
I will that you make haste and holiday
To go next year upon the Venus stair,
Covered none else, but crowned upon your hair,
And do the service that a maiden doth.
She said: but I that am Christ's maid were loth
To do this thing that hath such bitter name.
Thereat his brows were beaten with sore shame
And he came off and said no other word.
Then his eyes chanced upon his banner-bird,
And he fell fingering at the staff of it
And laughed for wrath and stared between his feet,
And out of a chafed heart he spake as thus:
Lo how she japes at me Theophilus,
Feigning herself a fool and hard to love;
Yet in good time for all she boasteth of
She shall be like a little beaten bird.
And while his mouth was open in that word
He came upon the house Janiculum,
Where some went busily, and other some
Talked in the gate called the gate glorious.

The emperor, which was one Gabalus,
Sat over all and drank chill wine alone.
To whom is come Theophilus anon,
And said as thus: *Beau sire, Dieu vous aide.*
And afterward sat under him, and said
All this thing through as ye have wholly heard.
　This Gabalus laughed thickly in his beard.
Yea, this is righteousness and maiden rule.
Truly, he said, a maid is but a fool.
And japed at them as one full villainous,
In a lewd wise, this heathen Gabalus,
And sent his men to bind her as he bade.
Thus have they taken Dorothy the maid,
And haled her forth as men hale pick-purses:
A little need God knows they had of this,
To hale her by her maiden gentle hair.
Thus went she lowly, making a soft prayer,
As one who stays the sweet wine in his mouth,
Murmuring with eased lips, and is most loth
To have done wholly with the sweet of it.
　Christ king, fair Christ, that knowest all men's wit
And all the feeble fashion of my ways,
O perfect God, that from all yesterdays
Abidest whole with morrows perfected,
I pray thee by thy mother's holy head
Thou help me to do right, that I not slip:
I have no speech nor strength upon my lip,
Except thou help me who art wise and sweet.
Do this too for those nails that clove thy feet,
Let me die maiden after many pains.
Though I be least among thy handmaidens,
Doubtless I shall take death more sweetly thus.
　Now have they brought her to King Gabalus,
Who laughed in all his throat some breathing-whiles:
By God, he said, if one should leap two miles,
He were not pained about the sides so much.
This were a soft thing for a man to touch.
Shall one so chafe that hath such little bones?

And shook his throat with thick and chuckled moans
For laughter that she had such holiness.
What aileth thee, wilt thou do services?
It were good fare to fare as Venus doth.
    Then said this lady with her maiden mouth,
Shamefaced, and something paler in the cheek:
Now, sir, albeit my wit and will to speak
Give me no grace in sight of worthy men,
For all my shame yet know I this again,
I may not speak, nor after downlying
Rise up to take delight in lute-playing,
Nor sing nor sleep, nor sit and fold my hands,
But my soul in some measure understands
God's grace laid like a garment over me.
For this fair God that out of strong sharp sea
Lifted the shapely and green-coloured land,
And hath the weight of heaven in his hand
As one might hold a bird, and under him
The heavy golden planets beam by beam
Building the feasting-chambers of his house,
And the large world he holdeth with his brows,
And with the light of them astonisheth
All place and time and face of life and death
And motion of the north wind and the south,
And is the sound within his angel's mouth
Of singing words and words of thanksgiving,
And is the colour of the latter spring
And heat upon the summer and the sun,
And is beginning of all things begun
And gathers in him all things to their end,
And with the fingers of his hand doth bend
The stretched-out sides of heaven like a sail,
And with his breath he maketh the red pale
And fills with blood faint faces of men dead,
And with the sound between his lips are fed
Iron and fire and the white body of snow,
And blossom of all trees in places low,
And small bright herbs about the little hills,

And fruit pricked softly with birds' tender bills,
And flight of foam about green fields of sea,
And fourfold strength of the great winds that be
Moved always outward from beneath his feet,
And growth of grass and growth of sheavèd wheat
And all green flower of goodly-growing lands;
And all these things he gathers with his hands
And covers all their beauty with his wings;
The same, even God that governs all these things,
Hath set my feet to be upon his ways.
Now therefore for no painfulness of days
I shall put off this service bound on me.
Also, fair sir, ye know this certainly,
How God was in his flesh full chaste and meek
And gave his face to shame, and either cheek
Gave up to smiting of men tyrannous.
    And here with a great voice this Gabalus
Cried out and said: By God's blood and his bones,
This were good game betwixen night and nones
For one to sit and hearken to such saws:
I were as lief fall in some big beast's jaws
As hear these women's jaw-teeth clattering;
By God a woman is the harder thing,
One may not put a hook into her mouth.
Now by St. Luke I am so sore adrouth
For all these saws I must needs drink again.
But I pray God deliver all us men
From all such noise of women and their heat.
That is a noble scripture, well I weet,
That likens women to an empty can;
When God said that he was a full wise man,
I trow no man may blame him as for that.
    And herewithal he drank a draught, and spat,
And said: Now shall I make an end hereof.
Come near all men and hearken for God's love,
And ye shall hear a jest or twain, God wot.
And spake as thus with mouth full thick and hot;
But thou do this thou shalt be shortly slain.

Lo, sir, she said, this death and all this pain
I take in penance of my bitter sins.
Yea now, quoth Gabalus, this game begins.
Lo, without sin one shall not live a span.
Lo, this is she that would not look on man
Between her fingers folded in thwart wise.
See how her shame hath smitten in her eyes
That was so clean she had not heard of shame.
Certes, he said, by Gabalus my name,
This two years back I was not so well pleased.
This were good mirth for sick men to be eased
And rise up whole and laugh at hearing of.
I pray thee show us something of thy love,
Since thou wast maid thy gown is waxen wide.
Yea, maid I am, she said, and somewhat sighed,
As one who thought upon the low fair house
Where she sat working, with soft bended brows
Watching her threads, among the school-maidens.
And she thought well now God had brought her thence
She should not come to sew her gold again.
    Then cried King Gabalus upon his men
To have her forth and draw her with steel gins.
And as a man hag-ridden beats and grins
And bends his body sidelong in his bed,
So wagged he with his body and knave's head,
Gaping at her, and blowing with his breath.
And in good time he gat an evil death
Out of his lewdness with his cursèd wives:
His bones were hewn asunder as with knives
For his misliving, certes it is said.
But all the evil wrought upon this maid,
It were full hard for one to handle it.
For her soft blood was shed upon her feet,
And all her body's colour bruised and faint.
But she, as one abiding God's great saint,
Spake not nor wept for all this travail hard.
Wherefore the king commanded afterward
To slay her presently in all men's sight.

And it was now an hour upon the night
And winter-time, and a few stars began.
The weather was yet feeble and all wan
For beating of a weighty wind and snow.
And she came walking in soft wise and slow,
And many men with faces piteous.
Then came this heavy cursing Gabalus,
That swore full hard into his drunken beard;
And faintly after without any word
Came Theophile some paces off the king.
And in the middle of this wayfaring
Full tenderly beholding her he said:
    There is no word of comfort with men dead
Nor any face and colour of things sweet;
But always with lean cheeks and lifted feet
These dead men lie all aching to the blood
With bitter cold, their brows withouten hood
Beating for chill, their bodies swathed full thin:
Alas, what hire shall any have herein
To give his life and get such bitterness?
Also the soul going forth bodiless
Is hurt with naked cold, and no man saith
If there be house or covering for death
To hide the soul that is discomforted.
    Then she beholding him a little said:
Alas, fair lord, ye have no wit of this;
For on one side death is full poor of bliss
And as ye say full sharp of bone and lean:
But on the other side is good and green
And hath soft flower of tender-coloured hair
Grown on his head, and a red mouth as fair
As may be kissed with lips; thereto his face
Is as God's face, and in a perfect place
Full of all sun and colour of straight boughs
And waterheads about a painted house
That hath a mile of flowers either way
Outward from it, and blossom-grass of May
Thickening on many a side for length of heat,

Hath God set death upon a noble seat
Covered with green and flowered in the fold,
In likeness of a great king grown full old
And gentle with new temperance of blood;
And on his brows a purfled purple hood,
They may not carry any golden thing;
And plays some tune with subtle fingering
On a small cithern, full of tears and sleep
And heavy pleasure that is quick to weep
And sorrow with the honey in her mouth;
And for this might of music that he doth
Are all souls drawn toward him with great love
And weep for sweetness of the noise thereof
And bow to him with worship of their knees;
And all the field is thick with companies
Of fair-clothed men that play on shawms and lutes
And gather honey of the yellow fruits
Between the branches waxen soft and wide:
And all this peace endures in either side
Of the green land, and God beholdeth all.
And this is girdled with a round fair wall
Made of red stone and cool with heavy leaves
Grown out against it, and green blossom cleaves
To the green chinks, and lesser wall-weed sweet,
Kissing the crannies that are split with heat,
And branches where the summer draws to head.
    And Theophile burnt in the cheek, and said:
Yea, could one see it, this were marvellous.
I pray you, at your coming to this house,
Give me some leaf of all those tree-branches;
Seeing how so sharp and white our weather is,
There is no green nor gracious red to see.
    Yea, sir, she said, that shall I certainly.
And from her long sweet throat without a fleck
Undid the gold, and through her stretched-out neck
The cold axe clove, and smote away her head:
Out of her throat the tender blood full red
Fell suddenly through all her long soft hair.

And with good speed for hardness of the air
Each man departed to his house again.
  Lo, as fair colour in the face of men
At seed-time of their blood, or in such wise
As a thing seen increaseth in men's eyes,
Caught first far off by sickly fits of sight,
So a word said, if one shall hear aright,
Abides against the season of its growth.
This Theophile went slowly, as one doth
That is not sure for sickness of his feet;
And counting the white stonework of the street,
Tears fell out of his eyes for wrath and love,
Making him weep more for the shame thereof
Than for true pain: so went he half a mile.
And women mocked him, saying: Theophile,
Lo, she is dead; what shall a woman have
That loveth such an one? so Christ me save,
I were as lief to love a man new-hung.
Surely this man has bitten on his tongue,
This makes him sad and writhled in his face.
  And when they came upon the paven place
That was called sometime the place amorous
There came a child before Theophilus
Bearing a basket, and said suddenly:
Fair sir, this is my mistress Dorothy
That sends you gifts; and with this he was gone.
In all this earth there is not such an one
For colour and straight stature made so fair.
The tender growing gold of his pure hair
Was as wheat growing, and his mouth as flame.
God called him Holy after his own name;
With gold cloth like fire burning he was clad.
But for the fair green basket that he had,
It was filled up with heavy white and red;
Great roses stained still where the first rose bled,
Burning at heart for shame their heart withholds:
And the sad colour of strong marigolds
That have the sun to kiss their lips for love;

The flower that Venus' hair is woven of,
The colour of fair apples in the sun,
Late peaches gathered when the heat was done
And the slain air got breath; and after these
The fair faint-headed poppies drunk with ease,
And heaviness of hollow lilies red.
    Then cried they all that saw these things, and said
It was God's doing, and was marvellous.
And in brief while this knight Theophilus
Is waxen full of faith, and witnesseth
Before the king of God and love and death,
For which the king bade hang him presently.
A gallows of a goodly piece of tree
This Gabalus hath made to hang him on.
Forth of this world lo Theophile is gone
With a wried neck, God give us better fare
Than his that hath a twisted throat to wear;
But truly for his love God hath him brought
There where his heavy body grieves him nought
Nor all the people plucking at his feet;
But in his face his lady's face is sweet,
And through his lips her kissing lips are gone:
God send him peace, and joy of such an one.
    This is the story of St. Dorothy.
I will you of your mercy pray for me
Because I wrote these sayings for your grace,
That I may one day see her in the face.

The Two Dreams

(FROM BOCCACCIO)

I will that if I say a heavy thing
Your tongues forgive me; seeing ye know that spring
Has flecks and fits of pain to keep her sweet,
And walks somewhile with winter-bitten feet.
Moreover it sounds often well to let
One string, when ye play music, keep at fret
The whole song through; one petal that is dead
Confirms the roses, be they white or red;
Dead sorrow is not sorrowful to hear
As the thick noise that breaks mid weeping were;
The sick sound aching in a lifted throat
Turns to sharp silver of a perfect note;
And though the rain falls often, and with rain
Late autumn falls on the old red leaves like pain,
I deem that God is not disquieted.
Also while men are fed with wine and bread,
They shall be fed with sorrow at his hand.
    There grew a rose-garden in Florence land
More fair than many; all red summers through
The leaves smelt sweet and sharp of rain, and blew
Sideways with tender wind; and therein fell
Sweet sound wherewith the green waxed audible,
As a bird's will to sing disturbed his throat
And set the sharp wings forward like a boat
Pushed through soft water, moving his brown side
Smooth-shapen as a maid's, and shook with pride
His deep warm bosom, till the heavy sun's
Set face of heat stopped all the songs at once.
The ways were clean to walk and delicate;
And when the windy white of March grew late,
Before the trees took heart to face the sun
With ravelled raiment of lean winter on,
The roots were thick and hot with hollow grass.
    Some roods away a lordly house there was,

Cool with broad courts and latticed passage wet
From rush-flowers and lilies ripe to set,
Sown close among the strewings of the floor;
And either wall of the slow corridor
Was dim with deep device of gracious things;
Some angel's steady mouth and weight of wings
Shut to the side; or Peter with straight stole
And beard cut black against the aureole
That spanned his head from nape to crown; thereby
Mary's gold hair, thick to the girdle-tie
Wherein was bound a child with tender feet;
Or the broad cross with blood nigh brown on it.
    Within this house a righteous lord abode,
Ser Averardo; patient of his mood,
And just of judgment; and to child he had
A maid so sweet that her mere sight made glad
Men sorrowing, and unbound the brows of hate;
And where she came, the lips that pain made strait
Waxed warm and wide, and from untender grew
Tender as those that sleep brings patience to.
Such long locks had she, that with knee to chin
She might have wrapped and warmed her feet therein.
Right seldom fell her face on weeping wise;
Gold hair she had, and golden-coloured eyes,
Filled with clear light and fire and large repose
Like a fair hound's; no man there is but knows
Her face was white, and thereto she was tall;
In no wise lacked there any praise at all
To her most perfect and pure maidenhood;
No sin I think there was in all her blood.
    She, where a gold grate shut the roses in,
Dwelt daily through deep summer weeks, through green
Flushed hours of rain upon the leaves; and there
Love made him room and space to worship her
With tender worship of bowed knees, and wrought
Such pleasure as the pained sense palates not
For weariness, but at one taste undoes
The heart of its strong sweet, is ravenous

Of all the hidden honey; words and sense
Fail through the tune's imperious prevalence.
    In a poor house this lover kept apart,
Long communing with patience next his heart
If love of his might move that face at all,
Tuned evenwise with colours musical;
Then after length of days he said thus: "Love,
For love's own sake and for the love thereof
Let no harsh words untune your gracious mood;
For good it were, if anything be good,
To comfort me in this pain's plague of mine;
Seeing thus, how neither sleep nor bread nor wine
Seems pleasant to me, yea no thing that is
Seems pleasant to me; only I know this,
Love's ways are sharp for palms of piteous feet
To travel, but the end of such is sweet:
Now do with me as seemeth you the best."
She mused a little, as one holds his guest
By the hand musing, with her face borne down:
Then said: "Yea, though such bitter seed be sown,
Have no more care of all that you have said;
Since if there is no sleep will bind your head,
Lo, I am fain to help you certainly;
Christ knoweth, sir, if I would have you die;
There is no pleasure when a man is dead."
Thereat he kissed her hands and yellow head
And clipped her fair long body many times;
I have no wit to shape in written rhymes
A scanted tithe of this great joy they had.
    They were too near love's secret to be glad;
As whoso deems the core will surely melt
From the warm fruit his lips caress, hath felt
Some bitter kernel where the teeth shut hard:
Or as sweet music sharpens afterward,
Being half disrelished both for sharp and sweet;
As sea-water, having killed over-heat
In a man's body, chills it with faint ache;
So their sense, burdened only for love's sake,

Failed for pure love; yet so time served their wit,
They saved each day some gold reserves of it,
Being wiser in love's riddle than such be
Whom fragments feed with his chance charity.
All things felt sweet were felt sweet overmuch;
The rose-thorn's prickle dangerous to touch,
And flecks of fire in the thin leaf-shadows;
Too keen the breathed honey of the rose,
Its red too harsh a weight on feasted eyes;
They were so far gone in love's histories,
Beyond all shape and colour and mere breath,
Where pleasure has for kinsfolk sleep and death,
And strength of soul and body waxen blind
For weariness, and flesh entoiled with mind,
When the keen edge of sense foretasteth sin.
    Even this green place the summer caught them in
Seemed half deflowered and sick with beaten leaves
In their strayed eyes; these gold flower-fumèd eves
Burnt out to make the sun's love-offering,
The midnoon's prayer, the rose's thanksgiving,
The trees' weight burdening the strengthless air,
The shape of her stilled eyes, her coloured hair,
Her body's balance from the moving feet—
All this, found fair, lacked yet one grain of sweet
It had some warm weeks back: so perisheth
On May's new lip the tender April breath:
So those same walks the wind sowed lilies in
All April through, and all their latter kin
Of languid leaves whereon the Autumn blows—
The dead red raiment of the last year's rose—
The last year's laurel, and the last year's love,
Fade, and grow things that death grows weary of.
    What man will gather in red summer-time
The fruit of some obscure and hoary rhyme
Heard last midwinter, taste the heart in it,
Mould the smooth semitones afresh, refit
The fair limbs ruined, flush the dead blood through
With colour, make all broken beauties new

For love's new lesson—shall not such find pain
When the marred music labouring in his brain
Frets him with sweet sharp fragments, and lets slip
One word that might leave satisfied his lip—
One touch that might put fire in all the chords?
This was her pain: to miss from all sweet words
Some taste of sound, diverse and delicate—
Some speech the old love found out to compensate
For seasons of shut lips and drowsiness—
Some grace, some word the old love found out to bless
Passionless months and undelighted weeks.
The flowers had lost their summer-scented cheeks,
Their lips were no more sweet than daily breath:
The year was plagued with instances of death.
    So fell it, these were sitting in cool grass
With leaves about, and many a bird there was
Where the green shadow thickliest impleached
Soft fruit and writhen spray and blossom bleached
Dry in the sun or washed with rains to white:
Her girdle was pure silk, the bosom bright
With purple as purple water and gold wrought in.
One branch had touched with dusk her lips and chin,
Made violet of the throat, abashed with shade
The breast's bright plaited work: but nothing frayed
The sun's large kiss on the luxurious hair.
Her beauty was new colour to the air
And music to the silent many birds.
Love was an-hungred for some perfect words
To praise her with; but only her low name
"Andrevuola" came thrice, and thrice put shame
In her clear cheek, so fruitful with new red
That for pure love straightway shame's self was dead.
    Then with lids gathered as who late had wept
She began saying: "I have so little slept
My lids drowse now against the very sun;
Yea, the brain aching with a dream begun
Beats like a fitful blood; kiss but both brows,
And you shall pluck my thoughts grown dangerous

Almost away." He said thus, kissing them:
"O sole sweet thing that God is glad to name,
My one gold gift, if dreams be sharp and sore
Shall not the waking time increase much more
With taste and sound, sweet eyesight or sweet scent?
Has any heat too hard and insolent
Burnt bare the tender married leaves, undone
The maiden grass shut under from the sun?
Where in this world is room enough for pain?"
    The feverish finger of love had touched again
Her lips with happier blood; the pain lay meek
In her fair face, nor altered lip nor cheek
With pallor or with pulse; but in her mouth
Love thirsted as a man wayfaring doth,
Making it humble as weak hunger is.
She lay close to him, bade do this and this,
Say that, sing thus: then almost weeping-ripe
Crouched, then laughed low. As one that fain would wipe
The old record out of old things done and dead,
She rose, she heaved her hands up, and waxed red
For wilful heart and blameless fear of blame;
Saying "Though my wits be weak, this is no shame
For a poor maid whom love so punisheth
With heats of hesitation and stopped breath
That with my dreams I live yet heavily
For pure sad heart and faith's humility.
Now be not wroth and I will show you this.
    "Methought our lips upon their second kiss
Met in this place, and a fair day we had
And fair soft leaves that waxed and were not sad
With shaken rain or bitten through with drouth;
When I, beholding ever how your mouth
Waited for mine, the throat being fallen back,
Saw crawl thereout a live thing flaked with black
Specks of brute slime and leper-coloured scale,
A devil's hide with foul flame-writhen grail
Fashioned where hell's heat festers loathsomest;
And that brief speech may ease me of the rest,

Thus were you slain and eaten of the thing.
My waked eyes felt the new day shuddering
On their low lids, felt the whole east so beat,
Pant with close pulse of such a plague-struck heat,
As if the palpitating dawn drew breath
For horror, breathing between life and death,
Till the sun sprang blood-bright and violent."
  So finishing, her soft strength wholly spent,
She gazed each way, lest some brute-hoovèd thing,
The timeless travail of hell's childbearing,
Should threat upon the sudden: whereat he,
For relish of her tasted misery
And tender little thornprick of her pain,
Laughed with mere love. What lover among men
But hath his sense fed sovereignly 'twixt whiles
With tears and covered eyelids and sick smiles
And soft disaster of a painèd face?
What pain, established in so sweet a place,
But the plucked leaf of it smells fragrantly?
What colour burning man's wide-open eye
But may be pleasurably seen? what sense
Keeps in its hot sharp extreme violence
No savour of sweet things? The bereaved blood
And emptied flesh in their most broken mood
Fail not so wholly, famish not when thus
Past honey keeps the starved lip covetous.
  Therefore this speech from a glad mouth began,
Breathed in her tender hair and temples wan
Like one prolonged kiss while the lips had breath.
"Sleep, that abides in vassalage of death
And in death's service wears out half his age,
Hath his dreams full of deadly vassalage,
Shadow and sound of things ungracious;
Fair shallow faces, hooded bloodless brows,
And mouths past kissing; yea, myself have had
As harsh a dream as holds your eyelids sad.
  "This dream I tell you came three nights ago;
In full mid sleep I took a whim to know

How sweet things might be; so I turned and thought;
But save my dream all sweet availed me not.
First came a smell of pounded spice and scent
Such as God ripens in some continent
Of utmost amber in the Syrian sea;
And breaths as though some costly rose could be
Spoiled slowly, wasted by some bitter fire
To burn the sweet out leaf by leaf, and tire
The flower's poor heart with heat and waste, to make
Strong magic for some perfumed woman's sake.
Then a cool naked sense beneath my feet
Of bud and blossom; and sound of veins that beat
As if a lute should play of its own heart
And fearfully, not smitten of either part;
And all my blood it filled with sharp and sweet
As gold swoln grain fills out the huskèd wheat;
So I rose naked from the bed, and stood
Counting the mobile measure in my blood
Some pleasant while, and through each limb there came
Swift little pleasures pungent as a flame,
Felt in the thrilling flesh and veins as much
As the outer curls that feel the comb's first touch
Thrill to the roots and shiver as from fire;
And blind between my dream and my desire
I seemed to stand and held my spirit still
Lest this should cease. A child whose fingers spill
Honey from cells forgotten of the bee
Is less afraid to stir the hive and see
Some wasp's bright back inside, than I to feel
Some finger-touch disturb the flesh like steel.
I prayed thus; Let me catch a secret here
So sweet, it sharpens the sweet taste of fear
And takes the mouth with edge of wine; I would
Have here some colour and smooth shape as good
As those in heaven whom the chief garden hides
With low grape-blossom veiling their white sides
And lesser tendrils that so bind and blind
Their eyes and feet, that if one come behind

To touch their hair they see not, neither fly;
This would I see in heaven and not die.
So praying, I had nigh cried out and knelt,
So wholly my prayer filled me: till I felt
In the dumb night's warm weight of glowing gloom
Somewhat that altered all my sleeping-room,
And made it like a green low place wherein
Maids mix to bathe: one sets her small warm chin
Against a ripple, that the angry pearl
May flow like flame about her: the next curl
Dips in some eddy coloured of the sun
To wash the dust well out; another one
Holds a straight ankle in her hand and swings
With lavish body sidelong, so that rings
Of sweet fierce water, swollen and splendid, fail
All round her fine and floated body pale,
Swayed flower-fashion, and her balanced side
Swerved edgeways lets the weight of water slide,
As taken in some underflow of sea
Swerves the banked gold of sea-flowers; but she
Pulls down some branch to keep her perfect head
Clear of the river: even from wall to bed,
I tell you, was my room transfigured so.
Sweet, green and warm it was, nor could one know
If there were walls or leaves, or if there was
No bed's green curtain, but mere gentle grass.
There were set also hard against the feet
Gold plates with honey and green grapes to eat,
With the cool water's noise to hear in rhymes:
And a wind warmed me full of furze and limes
And all hot sweets the heavy summer fills
To the round brim of smooth cup-shapen hills.
Next the grave walking of a woman's feet
Made my veins hesitate, and gracious heat
Made thick the lids and leaden on mine eyes:
And I thought ever, surely it were wise
Not yet to see her: this may last (who knows?)
Five minutes; the poor rose is twice a rose

Because it turns a face to her, the wind
Sings that way; hath this woman ever sinned,
I wonder? as a boy with apple-rind,
I played with pleasures, made them to my mind,
Changed each ere tasting. When she came indeed,
First her hair touched me, then I grew to feed
On the sense of her hand; her mouth at last
Touched me between the cheek and lip and past
Over my face with kisses here and there
Sown in and out across the eyes and hair.
Still I said nothing; till she set her face
More close and harder on the kissing-place,
And her mouth caught like a snake's mouth, and stung
So faint and tenderly, the fang scarce clung
More than a bird's foot: yet a wound it grew,
A great one, let this red mark witness you
Under the left breast; and the stroke thereof
So clove my sense that I woke out of love
And knew not what this dream was nor had wit;
But now God knows if I have skill of it."
    Hereat she laid one palm against her lips
To stop their trembling; as when water slips
Out of a beak-mouthed vessel with faint noise
And chuckles in the narrowed throat and cloys
The carven rims with murmuring, so came
Words in her lips with no word right of them,
A beaten speech thick and disconsolate,
Till his smile ceasing waxed compassionate
Of her sore fear that grew from anything—
The sound of the strong summer thickening
In heated leaves of the smooth apple-trees:
The day's breath felt about the ash-branches,
And noises of the noon whose weight still grew
On the hot heavy-headed flowers, and drew
Their red mouths open till the rose-heart ached;
For eastward all the crowding rose was slaked
And soothed with shade: but westward all its growth
Seemed to breathe hard with heat as a man doth

Who feels his temples newly feverous.
And even with such motion in her brows
As that man hath in whom sick days begin,
She turned her throat and spake, her voice being thin
As a sick man's, sudden and tremulous;
"Sweet, if this end be come indeed on us,
Let us love more;" and held his mouth with hers.
As the first sound of flooded hill-waters
Is heard by people of the meadow-grass,
Or ever a wandering waif of ruin pass
With whirling stones and foam of the brown stream
Flaked with fierce yellow: so beholding him
She felt before tears came her eyelids wet,
Saw the face deadly thin where life was yet,
Heard his throat's harsh last moan before it clomb:
And he, with close mouth passionate and dumb,
Burned at her lips: so lay they without speech,
Each grasping other, and the eyes of each
Fed in the other's face: till suddenly
He cried out with a little broken cry
This word, "O help me, sweet, I am but dead."
And even so saying, the colour of fair red
Was gone out of his face, and his blood's beat
Fell, and stark death made sharp his upward feet
And pointed hands; and without moan he died.
Pain smote her sudden in the brows and side,
Strained her lips open and made burn her eyes:
For the pure sharpness of her miseries
She had no heart's pain, but mere body's wrack;
But at the last her beaten blood drew back
Slowly upon her face, and her stunned brows
Suddenly grown aware and piteous
Gathered themselves, her eyes shone, her hard breath
Came as though one nigh dead came back from death;
Her lips throbbed, and life trembled through her hair.
    And in brief while she thought to bury there
The dead man that her love might lie with him
In a sweet bed under the rose-roots dim

And soft earth round the branchèd apple-trees,
Full of hushed heat and heavy with great ease,
And no man entering divide him thence.
Wherefore she bade one of her handmaidens
To be her help to do upon this wise.
And saying so the tears out of her eyes
Fell without noise and comforted her heart:
Yea, her great pain eased of the sorest part
Began to soften in her sense of it.
There under all the little branches sweet
The place was shapen of his burial;
They shed thereon no thing funereal,
But coloured leaves of latter rose-blossom,
Stems of soft grass, some withered red and some
Fair and fresh-blooded; and spoil splendider
Of marigold and great spent sunflower.
    And afterward she came back without word
To her own house; two days went, and the third
Went, and she showed her father of this thing.
And for great grief of her soul's travailing
He gave consent she should endure in peace
Till her life's end; yea, till her time should cease,
She should abide in fellowship of pain.
And having lived a holy year or twain
She died of pure waste heart and weariness.
And for love's honour in her love's distress
This word was written over her tomb's head;
"Here dead she lieth, for whose sake Love is dead."

The King's Daughter

We were ten maidens in the green corn,
   Small red leaves in the mill-water:
Fairer maidens never were born,

Apples of gold for the king's daughter.

We were ten maidens by a well-head,
Small white birds in the mill-water:
Sweeter maidens never were wed,
Rings of red for the king's daughter.

The first to spin, the second to sing,
Seeds of wheat in the mill-water;
The third may was a goodly thing,
White bread and brown for the king's daughter.

The fourth to sew and the fifth to play,
Fair green weed in the mill-water;
The sixth may was a goodly may,
White wine and red for the king's daughter.

The seventh to woo, the eighth to wed,
Fair thin reeds in the mill-water;
The ninth had gold work on her head,
Honey in the comb for the king's daughter.

The ninth had gold work round her hair,
Fallen flowers in the mill-water;
The tenth may was goodly and fair,
Golden gloves for the king's daughter.

We were ten maidens in a field green,
Fallen fruit in the mill-water;
Fairer maidens never have been,
Golden sleeves for the king's daughter.

By there comes the king's young son,
A little wind in the mill-water;
"Out of ten maidens ye'll grant me one,"
A crown of red for the king's daughter.

"Out of ten mays ye'll give me the best,"

A little rain in the mill-water;
A bed of yellow straw for all the rest,
A bed of gold for the king's daughter.

He's ta'en out the goodliest,
Rain that rains in the mill-water;
A comb of yellow shell for all the rest,
A comb of gold for the king's daughter.

He's made her bed to the goodliest,
Wind and hail in the mill-water;
A grass girdle for all the rest,
A girdle of arms for the king's daughter.

He's set his heart to the goodliest,
Snow that snows in the mill-water;
Nine little kisses for all the rest,
An hundredfold for the king's daughter.

He's ta'en his leave at the goodliest,
Broken boats in the mill-water;
Golden gifts for all the rest,
Sorrow of heart for the king's daughter.

"Ye'll make a grave for my fair body,"
Running rain in the mill-water;
"And ye'll streek my brother at the side of me,"
The pains of hell for the king's daughter.

After Death

The four boards of the coffin lid
Heard all the dead man did.

The first curse was in his mouth,
Made of grave's mould and deadly drouth.

The next curse was in his head,
Made of God's work discomfited.

The next curse was in his hands,
Made out of two grave-bands.

The next curse was in his feet,
Made out of a grave-sheet.

"I had fair coins red and white,
And my name was as great light;

I had fair clothes green and red,
And strong gold bound round my head.

But no meat comes in my mouth,
Now I fare as the worm doth;

And no gold binds in my hair,
Now I fare as the blind fare.

My live thews were of great strength,
Now am I waxen a span's length;

My live sides were full of lust,
Now are they dried with dust."

The first board spake and said:
"Is it best eating flesh or bread?"

The second answered it:
"Is wine or honey the more sweet?"

The third board spake and said:
"Is red gold worth a girl's gold head?"

The fourth made answer thus:
"All these things are as one with us."

The dead man asked of them:
"Is the green land stained brown with flame?

Have they hewn my son for beasts to eat,
And my wife's body for beasts' meat?

Have they boiled my maid in a brass pan,
And built a gallows to hang my man?"

The boards said to him:
"This is a lewd thing that ye deem.

Your wife has gotten a golden bed,
All the sheets are sewn with red.

Your son has gotten a coat of silk,
The sleeves are soft as curded milk.

Your maid has gotten a kirtle new,
All the skirt has braids of blue.

Your man has gotten both ring and glove,
Wrought well for eyes to love."

The dead man answered thus:
"What good gift shall God give us?"

The boards answered him anon:
"Flesh to feed hell's worm upon."

The Year of Love

There were four loves that one by one,
Following the seasons and the sun,
Passed over without tears, and fell
Away without farewell.

The first was made of gold and tears,
The next of aspen-leaves and fears,
The third of rose-boughs and rose-roots,
The last love of strange fruits.

These were the four loves faded. Hold
Some minutes fast the time of gold
When our lips each way clung and clove
To a face full of love.

The tears inside our eyelids met,
Wrung forth with kissing, and wept wet
The faces cleaving each to each
Where the blood served for speech.

The second, with low patient brows
Bound under aspen-coloured boughs
And eyes made strong and grave with sleep
And yet too weak to weep—

The third, with eager mouth at ease
Fed from late autumn honey, lees
Of scarce gold left in latter cells
With scattered flower-smells—

Hair sprinkled over with spoilt sweet
Of ruined roses, wrists and feet
Slight-swathed, as grassy-girdled sheaves
Hold in stray poppy-leaves—

The fourth, with lips whereon has bled
Some great pale fruit's slow colour, shed
From the rank bitter husk whence drips
Faint blood between her lips—

Made of the heat of whole great Junes
Burning the blue dark round their moons
(Each like a mown red marigold)
So hard the flame keeps hold—

These are burnt thoroughly away.
Only the first holds out a day
Beyond these latter loves that were
Made of mere heat and air.

And now the time is winterly
The first love fades too: none will see,
When April warms the world anew,
The place wherein love grew.

From SONGS BEFORE SUNRISE (1871)

Prelude

Between the green bud and the red
Youth sat and sang by Time, and shed
    From eyes and tresses flowers and tears,
    From heart and spirit hopes and fears,
Upon the hollow stream whose bed
    Is channelled by the foamless years;
And with the white the gold-haired head
    Mixed running locks, and in Time's ears
Youth's dreams hung singing, and Time's truth
Was half not harsh in the ears of Youth.

Between the bud and the blown flower
Youth talked with joy and grief an hour,
    With footless joy and wingless grief
    And twin-born faith and disbelief
Who share the seasons to devour;
    And long ere these made up their sheaf
Felt the winds round him shake and shower
    The rose-red and the blood-red leaf,
Delight whose germ grew never grain,
And passion dyed in its own pain.

Then he stood up, and trod to dust
Fear and desire, mistrust and trust,
    And dreams of bitter sleep and sweet,

And bound for sandals on his feet
Knowledge and patience of what must
And what things may be, in the heat
And cold of years that rot and rust
And alter; and his spirit's meat
Was freedom, and his staff was wrought
Of strength, and his cloak woven of thought.

For what has he whose will sees clear
To do with doubt and faith and fear,
Swift hopes and slow despondencies?
His heart is equal with the sea's
And with the sea-wind's, and his ear
Is level to the speech of these,
And his soul communes and takes cheer
With the actual earth's equalities,
Air, light, and night, hills, winds, and streams,
And seeks not strength from strengthless dreams.

His soul is even with the sun
Whose spirit and whose eye are one,
Who seeks not stars by day, nor light
And heavy heat of day by night.
Him can no God cast down, whom none
Can lift in hope beyond the height
Of fate and nature and things done
By the calm rule of might and right
That bids men be and bear and do,
And die beneath blind skies or blue.

To him the lights of even and morn
Speak no vain things of love or scorn,
Fancies and passions miscreate
By man in things dispassionate.
Nor holds he fellowship forlorn
With souls that pray and hope and hate,
And doubt they had better not been born,
And fain would lure or scare off fate

And charm their doomsman from their doom
And make fear dig its own false tomb.

He builds not half of doubts and half
Of dreams his own soul's cenotaph,
    Whence hopes and fears with helpless eyes,
    Wrapt loose in cast-off cerecloths, rise
And dance and wring their hands and laugh,
    And weep thin tears and sigh light sighs,
And without living lips would quaff
    The living spring in man that lies,
And drain his soul of faith and strength
It might have lived on a life's length.

He hath given himself and hath not sold
To God for heaven or man for gold,
    Or grief for comfort that it gives,
    Or joy for grief's restoratives.
He hath given himself to time, whose fold
    Shuts in the mortal flock that lives
On its plain pasture's heat and cold
    And the equal year's alternatives.
Earth, heaven, and time, death, life, and he,
Endure while they shall be to be.

"Yet between death and life are hours
To flush with love and hide in flowers;
    What profit save in these?" men cry:
    "Ah, see, between soft earth and sky,
What only good things here are ours!"
    They say, "what better wouldst thou try,
What sweeter sing of? or what powers
    Serve, that will give thee ere thou die
More joy to sing and be less sad,
More heart to play and grow more glad?"

Play then and sing; we too have played,
We likewise, in that subtle shade.

We too have twisted through our hair
Such tendrils as the wild Loves wear,
And heard what mirth the Maenads made,
Till the wind blew our garlands bare
And left their roses disarrayed,
And smote the summer with strange air,
And disengirdled and discrowned
The limbs and locks that vine-wreaths bound.

We too have tracked by star-proof trees
The tempest of the Thyiades
Scare the loud night on hills that hid
The blood-feasts of the Bassarid,
Heard their song's iron cadences
Fright the wolf hungering from the kid,
Outroar the lion-throated seas,
Outchide the north-wind if it chid,
And hush the torrent-tongued ravines
With thunders of their tambourines.

But the fierce flute whose notes acclaim
Dim goddesses of fiery fame,
Cymbal and clamorous kettledrum,
Timbrels and tabrets, all are dumb
That turned the high chill air to flame;
The singing tongues of fire are numb
That called on Cotys by her name
Edonian, till they felt her come
And maddened, and her mystic face
Lightened along the streams of Thrace.

For Pleasure slumberless and pale,
And Passion with rejected veil,
Pass, and the tempest-footed throng
Of hours that follow them with song
Till their feet flag and voices fail,
And lips that were so loud so long
Learn silence, or a wearier wail;

So keen is change, and time so strong,
To weave the robes of life and rend
And weave again till life have end.

But weak is change, but strengthless time,
To take the light from heaven, or climb
The hills of heaven with wasting feet.
Songs they can stop that earth found meet,
But the stars keep their ageless rhyme;
Flowers they can slay that spring thought sweet,
But the stars keep their spring sublime;
Passions and pleasures can defeat,
Actions and agonies control,
And life and death, but not the soul.

Because man's soul is man's God still,
What wind soever waft his will
Across the waves of day and night
To port or shipwreck, left or right,
By shores and shoals of good and ill;
And still its flame at mainmast height
Through the rent air that foam-flakes fill
Sustains the indomitable light
Whence only man hath strength to steer
Or helm to handle without fear.

Save his own soul's light overhead,
None leads him, and none ever led,
Across birth's hidden harbour-bar,
Past youth where shoreward shallows are,
Through age that drives on toward the red
Vast void of sunset hailed from far,
To the equal waters of the dead;
Save his own soul he hath no star,
And sinks, except his own soul guide,
Helmless in middle turn of tide.

No blast of air or fire of sun
Puts out the light whereby we run
    With girded loins our lamplit race,
    And each from each takes heart of grace
And spirit till his turn be done,
    And light of face from each man's face
In whom the light of trust is one;
    Since only souls that keep their place
By their own light, and watch things roll,
And stand, have light for any soul.

A little time we gain from time
To set our seasons in some chime,
    For harsh or sweet or loud or low,
    With seasons played out long ago
And souls that in their time and prime
    Took part with summer or with snow,
Lived abject lives out or sublime,
    And had their chance of seed to sow
For service or disservice done
To those days dead and this their son.

A little time that we may fill
Or with such good works or such ill
    As loose the bonds or make them strong
    Wherein all manhood suffers wrong.
By rose-hung river and light-foot rill
    There are who rest not; who think long
Till they discern as from a hill
    At the sun's hour of morning song,
Known of souls only, and those souls free,
The sacred spaces of the sea.

Hertha

I am that which began;
  Out of me the years roll;
Out of me God and man;
  I am equal and whole;
God changes, and man, and the form of them bodily; I am
 the soul.

Before ever land was,
  Before ever the sea,
Or soft hair of the grass,
  Or fair limbs of the tree,
Or the flesh-coloured fruit of my branches, I was, and thy
 soul was in me.

First life on my sources
  First drifted and swam;
Out of me are the forces
  That save it or damn;
Out of me man and woman, and wild-beast and bird; before
 God was, I am.

Beside or above me
  Nought is there to go;
Love or unlove me,
  Unknow me or know,
I am that which unloves me and loves; I am stricken, and I
 am the blow.

I the mark that is missed
  And the arrows that miss,
I the mouth that is kissed
  And the breath in the kiss,
The search, and the sought, and the seeker, the soul and the
 body that is.

From SONGS BEFORE SUNRISE (1871)

I am that thing which blesses
My spirit elate;
That which caresses
With hands uncreate
My limbs unbegotten that measure the length of the measure of fate.

But what thing dost thou now,
Looking Godward, to cry
"I am I, thou art thou,
I am low, thou art high"?
I am thou, whom thou seekest to find him; find thou but thyself, thou art I.

I the grain and the furrow,
The plough-cloven clod
And the ploughshare drawn thorough,
The germ and the sod,
The deed and the doer, the seed and the sower, the dust which is God.

Hast thou known how I fashioned thee,
Child, underground?
Fire that impassioned thee,
Iron that bound,
Dim changes of water, what thing of all these hast thou known of or found?

Canst thou say in thine heart
Thou hast seen with thine eyes
With what cunning of art
Thou wast wrought in what wise,
By what force of what stuff thou wast shapen, and shown on my breast to the skies?

Who hath given, who hath sold it thee,
Knowledge of me?
Hath the wilderness told it thee?

Hast thou learnt of the sea?
Hast thou communed in spirit with night? have the winds taken counsel with thee?

Have I set such a star
To show light on thy brow
That thou sawest from afar
What I show to thee now?
Have ye spoken as brethren together, the sun and the mountains and thou?

What is here, dost thou know it?
What was, hast thou known?
Prophet nor poet
Nor tripod nor throne
Nor spirit nor flesh can make answer, but only thy mother alone.

Mother, not maker,
Born, and not made;
Though her children forsake her,
Allured or afraid,
Praying prayers to the God of their fashion, she stirs not for all that have prayed.

A creed is a rod,
And a crown is of night;
But this thing is God,
To be man with thy might,
To grow straight in the strength of thy spirit, and live out thy life as the light.

I am in thee to save thee,
As my soul in thee saith;
Give thou as I gave thee,
Thy life-blood and breath,
Green leaves of thy labour, white flowers of thy thought, and red fruit of thy death.

Be the ways of thy giving
  As mine were to thee;
The free life of thy living,
  Be the gift of it free;
Not as servant to lord, nor as master to slave, shalt thou give
  thee to me.

O children of banishment,
  Souls overcast,
Were the lights ye see vanish meant
  Alway to last,
Ye would know not the sun overshining the shadows and
  stars overpast.

I that saw where ye trod
  The dim paths of the night
Set the shadow called God
  In your skies to give light;
But the morning of manhood is risen, and the shadowless
  soul is in sight.

The tree many-rooted
  That swells to the sky
With frondage red-fruited,
  The life-tree am I;
In the buds of your lives is the sap of my leaves: ye shall live
  and not die.

But the Gods of your fashion
  That take and that give,
In their pity and passion
  That scourge and forgive,
They are worms that are bred in the bark that falls off; they
  shall die and not live.

My own blood is what stanches
  The wounds in my bark;
Stars caught in my branches

Make day of the dark,
And are worshipped as suns till the sunrise shall tread out
their fires as a spark.

Where dead ages hide under
The live roots of the tree,
In my darkness the thunder
Makes utterance of me;
In the clash of my boughs with each other ye hear the waves
sound of the sea.

That noise is of Time,
As his feathers are spread
And his feet set to climb
Through the boughs overhead,
And my foliage rings round him and rustles, and branches
are bent with his tread.

The storm-winds of ages
Blow through me and cease,
The war-wind that rages,
The spring-wind of peace,
Ere the breath of them roughen my tresses, ere one of my
blossoms increase.

All sounds of all changes,
All shadows and lights
On the world's mountain-ranges
And stream-riven heights,
Whose tongue is the wind's tongue and language of
storm-clouds on earth-shaking nights;

All forms of all faces,
All works of all hands
In unsearchable places
Of time-stricken lands,
All death and all life, and all reigns and all ruins, drop
through me as sands.

Though sore be my burden
And more than ye know,
And my growth have no guerdon
But only to grow,
Yet I fail not of growing for lightnings above me or deathworms below.

These too have their part in me,
As I too in these;
Such fire is at heart in me,
Such sap is this tree's,
Which hath in it all sounds and all secrets of infinite lands and of seas.

In the spring-coloured hours
When my mind was as May's,
There brake forth of me flowers
By centuries of days,
Strong blossoms with perfume of manhood, shot out from my spirit as rays.

And the sound of them springing
And smell of their shoots
Were as warmth and sweet singing
And strength to my roots;
And the lives of my children made perfect with freedom of soul were my fruits.

I bid you but be;
I have need not of prayer;
I have need of you free
As your mouths of mine air;
That my heart may be greater within me, beholding the fruits of me fair.

More fair than strange fruit is
Of faiths ye espouse;
In me only the root is

That blooms in your boughs;
Behold now your God that ye made you, to feed him with faith of your vows.

In the darkening and whitening
Abysses adored,
With dayspring and lightning
For lamp and for sword,
God thunders in heaven, and his angels are red with the wrath of the Lord.

O my sons, O too dutiful
Toward Gods not of me,
Was not I enough beautiful?
Was it hard to be free?
For behold, I am with you, am in you and of you; look forth now and see.

Lo, winged with world's wonders,
With miracles shod,
With the fires of his thunders
For raiment and rod,
God trembles in heaven, and his angels are white with the terror of God.

For his twilight is come on him,
His anguish is here;
And his spirits gaze dumb on him,
Grown grey from his fear;
And his hour taketh hold on him stricken, the last of his infinite year.

Thought made him and breaks him,
Truth slays and forgives;
But to you, as time takes him,
This new thing it gives,
Even love, the beloved Republic, that feeds upon freedom and lives.

For truth only is living,
Truth only is whole,
And the love of his giving
Man's polestar and pole;
Man, pulse of my centre, and fruit of my body, and seed of my soul.

One birth of my bosom;
One beam of mine eye;
One topmost blossom
That scales the sky;
Man, equal and one with me, man that is made of me, man that is I.

Before a Crucifix

Here, down between the dusty trees,
At this lank edge of haggard wood,
Women with labour-loosened knees,
With gaunt backs bowed by servitude,
Stop, shift their loads, and pray, and fare
Forth with souls easier for the prayer.

The suns have branded black, the rains
Striped grey this piteous God of theirs;
The face is full of prayers and pains,
To which they bring their pains and prayers;
Lean limbs that shew the labouring bones,
And ghastly mouth that gapes and groans.

God of this grievous people, wrought
After the likeness of their race,
By faces like thine own besought,
Thine own blind helpless eyeless face,

I too, that have nor tongue nor knee
For prayer, I have a word to thee.

It was for this then, that thy speech
  Was blown about the world in flame
And men's souls shot up out of reach
  Of fear or lust or thwarting shame—
That thy faith over souls should pass
As sea-winds burning the grey grass?

It was for this, that prayers like these
  Should spend themselves about thy feet,
And with hard overlaboured knees
  Kneeling, these slaves of men should beat
Bosoms too lean to suckle sons
And fruitless as their orisons?

It was for this, that men should make
  Thy name a fetter on men's necks,
Poor men's made poorer for thy sake,
  And women's withered out of sex?
It was for this, that slaves should be,
Thy word was passed to set men free?

The nineteenth wave of the ages rolls
  Now deathward since thy death and birth.
Hast thou fed full men's starved-out souls?
  Hast thou brought freedom upon earth?
Or are there less oppressions done
In this wild world under the sun?

Nay, if indeed thou be not dead,
  Before thy terrene shrine be shaken,
Look down, turn usward, bow thine head;
  O thou that wast of God forsaken,
Look on thine household here, and see
These that have not forsaken thee.

Thy faith is fire upon their lips,
  Thy kingdom golden in their hands;
They scourge us with thy words for whips,
  They brand us with thy words for brands;
The thirst that made thy dry throat shrink
To their moist mouths commends the drink.

The toothed thorns that bit thy brows
  Lighten the weight of gold on theirs;
Thy nakedness enrobes thy spouse
  With the soft sanguine stuff she wears
Whose old limbs use for ointment yet
Thine agony and bloody sweat.

The blinding buffets on thine head
  On their crowned heads confirm the crown;
Thy scourging dyes their raiment red,
  And with thy bands they fasten down
For burial in the blood-bought field
The nations by thy stripes unhealed.

With iron for thy linen bands
  And unclean cloths for winding-sheet
They bind the people's nail-pierced hands,
  They hide the people's nail-pierced feet;
And what man or what angel known
Shall roll back the sepulchral stone?

But these have not the rich man's grave
  To sleep in when their pain is done.
These were not fit for God to save.
  As naked hell-fire is the sun
In their eyes living, and when dead
These have not where to lay their head.

They have no tomb to dig, and hide;
  Earth is not theirs, that they should sleep.
On all these tombless crucified

No lovers' eyes have time to weep.
So still, for all man's tears and creeds,
The sacred body hangs and bleeds.

Through the left hand a nail is driven,
Faith, and another through the right,
Forged in the fires of hell and heaven,
Fear that puts out the eye of light:
And the feet soiled and scarred and pale
Are pierced with falsehood for a nail.

And priests against the mouth divine
Push their sponge full of poison yet
And bitter blood for myrrh and wine,
And on the same reed is it set
Wherewith before they buffeted
The people's disanointed head.

O sacred head, O desecrate,
O labour-wounded feet and hands,
O blood poured forth in pledge to fate
Of nameless lives in divers lands,
O slain and spent and sacrificed
People, the grey-grown speechless Christ!

Is there a gospel in the red
Old witness of thy wide-mouthed wounds?
From thy blind stricken tongueless head
What desolate evangel sounds
A hopeless note of hope deferred?
What word, if there be any word?

O son of man, beneath man's feet
Cast down, O common face of man
Whereon all blows and buffets meet,
O royal, O republican
Face of the people bruised and dumb
And longing till thy kingdom come!

The soldiers and the high priests part
  Thy vesture: all thy days are priced,
And all the nights that eat thine heart.
  And that one seamless coat of Christ,
The freedom of the natural soul,
They cast their lots for to keep whole.

No fragment of it save the name
  They leave thee for a crown of scorns
Wherewith to mock thy naked shame
  And forehead bitten through with thorns
And, marked with sanguine sweat and tears,
The stripes of eighteen hundred years.

And we seek yet if God or man
  Can loosen thee as Lazarus,
Bid thee rise up republican
  And save thyself and all of us;
But no disciple's tongue can say
When thou shalt take our sins away.

And mouldering now and hoar with moss
  Between us and the sunlight swings
The phantom of a Christless cross
  Shadowing the sheltered heads of kings
And making with its moving shade
The souls of harmless men afraid.

It creaks and rocks to left and right
  Consumed of rottenness and rust,
Worm-eaten of the worms of night,
  Dead as their spirits who put trust,
Round its base muttering as they sit,
In the time-cankered name of it.

Thou, in the day that breaks thy prison,
  People, though these men take thy name,
And hail and hymn thee rearisen,

Who made songs erewhile of thy shame,
Give thou not ear; for these are they
Whose good day was thine evil day.

Set not thine hand unto their cross.
Give not thy soul up sacrificed.
Change not the gold of faith for dross
Of Christian creeds that spit on Christ.
Let not thy tree of freedom be
Regrafted from that rotting tree.

This dead God here against my face
Hath help for no man; who hath seen
The good works of it, or such grace
As thy grace in it, Nazarene,
As that from thy live lips which ran
For man's sake, O thou son of man?

The tree of faith ingraffed by priests
Puts its foul foliage out above thee,
And round it feed man-eating beasts
Because of whom we dare not love thee;
Though hearts reach back and memories ache,
We cannot praise thee for their sake.

O hidden face of man, whereover
The years have woven a viewless veil,
If thou wast verily man's lover,
What did thy love or blood avail?
Thy blood the priests make poison of,
And in gold shekels coin thy love.

So when our souls look back to thee
They sicken, seeing against thy side,
Too foul to speak of or to see,
The leprous likeness of a bride,
Whose kissing lips through his lips grown
Leave their God rotten to the bone.

When we would see thee man, and know
  What heart thou hadst toward men indeed,
Lo, thy blood-blackened altars; lo,
  The lips of priests that pray and feed
While their own hell's worm curls and licks
The poison of the crucifix.

Thou bad'st let children come to thee;
  What children now but curses come?
What manhood in that God can be
  Who sees their worship, and is dumb?
No soul that lived, loved, wrought, and died,
Is this their carrion crucified.

Nay, if their God and thou be one,
  If thou and this thing be the same,
Thou shouldst not look upon the sun;
  The sun grows haggard at thy name.
Come down, be done with, cease, give o'er;
Hide thyself, strive not, be no more.

Genesis

In the outer world that was before this earth,
  That was before all shape or space was born,
Before the blind first hour of time had birth,
  Before night knew the moonlight or the morn;

Yea, before any world had any light,
  Or anything called God or man drew breath,
Slowly the strong sides of the heaving night
  Moved, and brought forth the strength of life and death.

And the sad shapeless horror increate
  That was all things and one thing, without fruit,
Limit, or law; where love was none, nor hate,
  Where no leaf came to blossom from no root;

The very darkness that time knew not of,
  Nor God laid hand on, nor was man found there,
Ceased, and was cloven in several shapes; above
  Light, and night under, and fire, earth, water, and air.

Sunbeams and starbeams, and all coloured things,
  All forms and all similitudes began;
And death, the shadow cast by life's wide wings,
  And God, the shade cast by the soul of man.

Then between shadow and substance, night and light,
  Then between birth and death, and deeds and days,
The illimitable embrace and the amorous fight
  That of itself begets, bears, rears, and slays,

The immortal war of mortal things that is
  Labour and life and growth and good and ill,
The mild antiphonies that melt and kiss,
  The violent symphonies that meet and kill,

All nature of all things began to be.
  But chiefliest in the spirit (beast or man,
Planet of heaven or blossom of earth or sea)
  The divine contraries of life began.

For the great labour of growth, being many, is one;
  One thing the white death and the ruddy birth;
The invisible air and the all-beholden sun,
  And barren water and many-childed earth.

And these things are made manifest in men
  From the beginning forth unto this day:
Time writes and life records them, and again
  Death seals them lest the record pass away.

For if death were not, then should growth not be,
  Change, nor the life of good nor evil things;
Nor were there night at all nor light to see,
  Nor water of sweet nor water of bitter springs.

For in each man and each year that is born
  Are sown the twin seeds of the strong twin powers;
The white seed of the fruitful helpful morn,
  The black seed of the barren hurtful hours.

And he that of the black seed eateth fruit,
  To him the savour as honey shall be sweet;
And he in whom the white seed hath struck root,
  He shall have sorrow and trouble and tears for meat.

And him whose lips the sweet fruit hath made red
  In the end men loathe and make his name a rod;
And him whose mouth on the unsweet fruit hath fed
  In the end men follow and know for very God.

And of these twain, the black seed and the white,
  All things come forth, endured of men and done;
And still the day is great with child of night,
  And still the black night labours with the sun.

And each man and each year that lives on earth
  Turns hither or thither, and hence or thence is fed;
And as a man before was from his birth,
  So shall a man be after among the dead.

The Oblation

Ask nothing more of me, sweet;
  All I can give you I give.
    Heart of my heart, were it more,
More would be laid at your feet:
  Love that should help you to live,
    Song that should spur you to soar.

All things were nothing to give
  Once to have sense of you more,
    Touch you and taste of you sweet,
Think you and breathe you and live,
  Swept of your wings as they soar,
    Trodden by chance of your feet.

I that have love and no more
  Give you but love of you, sweet:
    He that hath more, let him give;
He that hath wings, let him soar;
  Mine is the heart at your feet
    Here, that must love you to live.

From BOTHWELL (1874)

From Act 1, scene 3

The Queen grants audience to John Knox.

QUEEN. With what sign-manual has God warranted
Your inquisition of us? What am I
That my most secret sanctuaries of life
And private passages of hours should be
Food for men's eyes or pavement for men's feet
To peer and pasture, track and tread upon,
Insult with instance? Am I only bound
To let the common mouth communicate
In my life's sweet or bitter sacrament,
The wine poured, the bread broken every day?
To walk before men bare that they may judge
If I were born with any spot or no,
And praise my naked nature? to subject
Mine unsubmitted soul subordinate
To popular sight and sentence? What am I
That I should be alone debarred, deposed,
From the poor right of poor men, who may live
Some hour or twain unchallenged of the day
And make to no man answer what they do
As I to mine must render? who is this
That takes in hand such hard things and such high?
Sir, what man are you that I need account
For this word said or that, or such things done,

Only to you or mainly, of myself?
Yea, what are you within this commonwealth?
JOHN KNOX. A man within it and a subject born,
Madam; and howsoever no great man,
Earl, lord, nor baron to bear rule therein,
Yet has God made me a profitable man,
How abject I seem ever in your eye,
No member of the same unmeritable.
Yea, madam, this pertains not less to me
Than any of all your noble-nurtured men,
To warn men of what things may hurt the same,
So as I see them dangerous: and herein
My conscience and mine office with one tongue
Crave plainness of me: wherefore to yourself
I say the thing I speak in public place,
That what great men soever at any time
Shall be consenting to your lord's unfaith
Or flattering furtherance of unfaith in you,
They do what in them lieth to cast out Christ,
Banish his truth, betray his liberty
And free right of this realm, and in the end
Shall haply do small comfort to yourself.
And for him too, your husband, it may be
That as he spares not to dishonour God
For your delight, by service of the mass,
God will not spare to smite him by your hand
That faithlessly he fawns on to his loss.
QUEEN. When was there queen so handled in the world?
I would I could not weep; for being thus used
I needs must never or now. Is this light day?
Am I asleep, or mad, or in a trance,
That have such words to beat about mine ears
And in mine eyes his present face who speaks?
ERSKINE OF DUN. Madam, I pray your grace contain your mood,
And keep your noble temperance of yourself,
For your high sake and honour, who are held
For excellence of spirit and natural soul
As sovereign born as for your face and place,

Kingdom and kingly beauty; to whose might
The worthiest of the world, all Europe's chief,
Her choice of crowns, might gladly bow themselves
To find your favour. I beseech you think
That here is no disloyalty designed
Nor thing dishonourable; for were men mad
Whose wits are whole, and false whose faiths are sound,
The very mouth of madness would speak sense,
The very tongue of treason would speak truth,
For love and service of your royalty;
Blind curses bless, and red rebellion bow,
That came to burn and threaten. Do not dream
That a man faithful Godward and well loved
Can be to youward evil-willed, who have
Power on your natural and your born unfriends
To bind their good-will to you.
QUEEN. Words, all words;
I am weary of words: I have heard words enough
To build and break, if breath could break or build,
Centuries of men. What would they with me, sir?
These my liege folk that love me to the death,
Their death or mine, no matter—my fast friends
Whose comfortable balms so bruise my head
It cannot hold the crown up—these good hands
That wring my wrist round to wrench out the staff
God set into mine own—these loving lips
That take my name upon them as to kiss
And leave it rank with foam of hateful speech?
Must I be dead deposed, or must I live
Stript shameless, naked to the very name,
A crestless creature and displumed, that feeds
On charities and chances? will they give
Me, their queen born, me, bread or dust to eat,
With a mouth water-moisted or a dry,
Beggared or buried? shall I hold my head
In shameful fief and tenantry of these
For their least wind of any wrath that blows
To storm it off my shoulders? What were I

That being so born should be born such a thing
As bondsmen might bemock the bondage of
And slaves contemn for slavery? Nay, no words:
A word may wound and no word heal again,
As none can me—whom all men's words may wound—
Who am liable to all buffets of men's tongues,
All stripes of all their scandals—and was born
To no such fear—and have nor tongue nor wit
To plead and gather favour—no such grace
As may get grace, no piteous skilfulness—
Only my truth and tears—and would to God
My tears and truth for you were wind and fire
To burn and blow corruption from the world,
And leave pure peace to breed where you plant war
And make the furrows fat with pestilence
And the grain swell with treason—but, too sure,
They too can hurt and heal not. I am soul-sick
With shame and bitter weakness; yet, God's will,
I may take strength about me to put off
Some part of shame. Sir, you that make me weep,
By these my tears and my sharp shame of them
I swear you will not laugh to see me laugh,
When my time comes: you shall not; I will have
Time to my friend yet—I shall see you, sir,
If you can weep or no, that with dry eyes
Have seen mine wet—I will try that—look to it.
JOHN KNOX. Madam, I speak in very eye of God,
I never took delight in any tears
Shed of God's creatures; yea, for my self-sake,
I can but very hardly abide the tears
Of mine own boys whom mine own hand and love
Chastens, and much less can take any joy
In this the weeping of your majesty.
But seeing I have given you no offensive cause
Nor just occasion, but have spoken truth
After mine office as mine own place craves
Lest I, God's man, be mansworn to God's truth,
I must sustain, howbeit unwillingly,

Rather these tears drawn of your majesty
Than blood of mine own conscience stabbed to death
Or through my silence of my commonwealth
By my dumb treason wounded.
QUEEN. A fair word—
I thought it was forgotten of men's mouths
And only lived in the inner heat of the heart
Too sure to want the spelling of their speech.
Sir, you shall find it in my very tears,
This blood you fear for of your commonwealth,
And in the hurts of mine authority
The wounds it lies abed with; what, God help,
Can the head bleed and not the body faint?
Or wherein should the kingdom feel such maim
As in the kingship stricken? there are you,
If you be true man, and each true man born
Subject and circled with the bond of rule,
Hurt to the heart. But heartless things are words;
Henceforth I will not mix my speech with yours
In the way of disputation ever more,
Nor set against your tongue the plea of mine
To reason as its equal. Wait you here,
Here in the chamber: you, sir, come with me
To counsel in my cabinet somewhile;
We will return his answer.

From Act 1, scene 5

After the interview with Knox.

QUEEN. … nay, I think
We shall get vantage of your lord's friend Knox
Ere many days be.
COUNTESS OF ARGYLE. Speed your majesty!

The cord were hallowed that should silence him.
QUEEN. Ay, though mine own hands twist it. To spin hemp
For such a throat, so loud and eloquent,
Should better please me and seem a queenlier thing
Than to weave silk and flower it with fine gold.
He hath a tongue to tame a tiger with,
Fright into fierce and violent reverence
The fearfullest earth's monsters. I do think
I like him better than his creed-fellows
Whose lips are softer toward me; 'tis some sport
To set my wit to his, and match with mine
The shrewd and fiery temper of his spirit
For trial of true mastery; yet to-day
He made me weep, weep mightily—by faith,
If there be faith in any lips of earth,
I think to live and laugh at his tears yet.

From Act 2, scene 1

Escape from Holyrood.

QUEEN. … by this light,
I feel a heat and hurry of the heart
That burns like joy; my blood is light and quick,
And my breath comes triumphantly as his
That has long laboured for a mountainous goal
And sets fast foot on the utmost cliff of all.
If ere the race be run my spirit be glad,
What when it puts the palm of peril on
And breathes clear air and conquers? Nay, I think
The doubt itself and danger are as food
To strengthen and bright wine to quicken me
And lift my heart up higher than my need,
Though that be high upon me.

Re-enter ERSKINE *with* TRAQUAIR *and* STANDEN.

                                        Now, my friends,
Ye come unlike to courtiers, come to serve
Me most unlike a queen: shall I think yet
I have some poor part in your memories safe,
And you some care of what I was, and thought
How I fare now? Shall I take up my hope,
That was cast down into the pit of death,
To keep the name God gave me, and the seal
That signs me royal, by your loves and faiths
Recrowned and reinstated? Say but no,
Or say but nought, this hope of mine and heart
Are things as dead as yesterday: my cause
Lies in your lips, to comfort or confound,
As ye see reason. Yet, as power is yours,
So let remembrance in you be for light
To see the face of the time by; so let faith,
Let noble pity and love be part of you,
To make you mindful what a cause it is
That ye must put in judgment, and what life
For fame or shame to you through all time born
Ensues upon your sentence; for ye choose
If ye will match my dangers with your faiths
And help me helpless with your hearts, who lie
By grief and fear made heartless; or lend hand
To make my weakness weaker, and break down
My broken wall of sovereignty; which now
Ye wot were no sore labour.

STANDEN.   Let him die
As heartless toward the grace of God, who hath
No heart in him to give its blood for yours!

TRAQUAIR. So say we all your servants.

QUEEN.   Did I know it?
Methinks I knew when I bade send for you,
Ye should so say. Ah friends, I had no fear
But I should find me friends in this fierce world,
Or I had died unfriended. Shall I thank you
For being the true men and the kind ye are,

Or take your service thankless, since I thought
Ye could not else, being young and of your kinds,
But needs must be my help? ye have not hearts
To strike but at men weaponed; ye would not
Lay hard hand on a woman weak with child,
A sick sad woman that was no man's queen
Of all that stood against her; yet her son,
The unborn thing that pleads again with you
As it could plead not with them, this dumb voice,
This sightless life and sinless, was their king's,
If ever they would let it come to life.
Lo, here their aim was; here the weapons went
That should have stabbed to death the race of kings
And cut their stem down to the root; here, here
The pistol's mouth that bruised my breast, the hand
That struck athwart my shoulder, found their mark,
Made here their point to shoot at; in my womb
By them the bud of empire should have died
That yet by you may live and yet give thanks
For flower and fruit to them that saved the seed.
STANDEN. They shall die first.
TRAQUAIR. Command us what next way
There is to serve you, though the way were fire
We would be through it.
QUEEN. To-night then at first watch
I purpose with the man's help—nay, what name
Shall his be now? king, husband, or, God help,
King's father?—with the man that you called king
As I called husband, to win forth of bonds
By the close covered passage underground
That by strange turns and strait blind working ways
Winds up into the sovereign cemetery
Whose dust is of my fathers; therewithout
Wait you with horse; and when you see us rise
Out of the hollow earth among the dead,
Be ready to receive and bear us thence.
Some two hours' haste will speed us to Dunbar,
Where friends lie close, and whence with sudden strength

I trust to turn on these good lords again.
Do this for such poor love's sake as your queen's,
And if there be thanks worthy in the world,
Them shall she give; not silver, sirs, nor gold,
Nor the coined guerdon that is cast on churls
To coin them into service; but a heart,
If not worth love, yet loving, and a faith
That will die last of all that dies in me
And last of all remembrances foregone
Let your names go. God speed you, and farewell.

From Act 2, scene 6

At the Castle of Alloa.

QUEEN. Is not that light red oversea?
BOTHWELL. Blood-red.
QUEEN. The wind has fallen; but there the clouds come up;
We shall not sail to-day.
BOTHWELL. No; here will be
No woman's weather.
QUEEN. Yet I had in mind
Either to sail or drive the deer to-day.
I fear not so much rainfall or sea-drift
That I should care to house and hide my head.
I never loved the windless weather, nor
The dead face of the water in the sun;
I had rather the live wave leapt under me,
And fits of foam struck light on the dark air,
And the sea's kiss were keen upon my lip
And bold as love's and bitter; then my soul
Is a wave too that springs against the light
And beats and bursts with one great strain of joy
As the sea breaking. You said well; this light

Is like shed blood spilt here by drops and there
That overflows the red brims of the cloud
And stains the moving water: yet the waves
Pass, and the spilt light of the broken sun
Rests not upon them but a minute's space;
No longer should a deed, methinks, once done
Endure upon the life of memory
To stain the days thereafter with remorse
And mar the better seasons.
BOTHWELL. So think I.
QUEEN. If I were man I would be man like you.
BOTHWELL. What then?
QUEEN. And being so loved as you of me,
I would make use of love, and in good time
Put the scythe to it and reap; it should not rot
As corn ungarnered, it should bring forth bread
And fruit of life to strengthen me: but, mark,
Who would eat bread must earn bread: would you be King?
BOTHWELL. Nay, but servant ever to my queen.
QUEEN. Let us go forth; the evening will be fair.

From Act 2, scene 9

The Queen's illness at Jedburgh.

Enter the QUEEN, *supported by attendants.*
QUEEN. What word was in your lips?
That I must die?
MARY SEYTON. Heaven hath not such hard heart.
QUEEN. I think I shall not, surely, by God's grace;
Yet no man knows of God when he will bring
His hour upon him. I am sick and weak,
And yet unsure if I be whole of mind.
I think I have been estranged from my right wits

These some days back; I know not. Prithee tell me,
Have I not slept? I know you who you are;
You were about me thus in our first days,
When days and nights were roseleaves that fell off
Without a wind or taint of chafing air
But passed with perfume from us, and their death
Had on it still the tender dew of birth.
We were so near the sweet warm wells of life
We lay and laughed in bosom of the dawn
And knew not if the noon had heat to burn
Or the evening rain to smite us; being grown tall,
Our heads were raised more near the fires of heaven
And bitter strength of storms; then we were glad,
Ay, glad and good. Is there yet one of you
Keeps in her mind what hovers now in mine,
That sweet strait span of islanded green ground
Where we played once, and set us flowers that died
Before even our delight in them was dead?
Now we are old, delights are first to die
Before the things that breed them.

MARY SEYTON *(aside)*. She roams yet

MARY BEATON. I do remember.

QUEEN. Yea, I knew it; one day
We wrangled for a rose' sake and fell out
With tears and words protesting each 'twas she,
She 'twas that set it; and for very wrath
I plucked up my French lilies and set foot
On their gold heads, because you had chafed me, saying
Those were her flowers who should be queen in France,
And leave you being no queen your Scottish rose
With simpler leaves ungilt and innocent
That smelt of homelier air; and I mind well
I rent the rose out of your hand and cast
Upon the river's running; and a thorn
Pierced through mine own hand, and I wept not then,
But laughed for anger at you and glad heart
To have made you weep, being worsted. What light things
Come back to the light brain that sickness shakes

And makes the heaviest thought that it can hold
No heavier than a leaf, or gossamer
That seems to link two leaves a minute, then
A breath unlinks them; so my thoughts are: nay,
And should not so; it may be I shall die,
And as a fool I would not pass away
With babbling lips unpurged and graceless heart
Unreconciled to mercy. Let me see
That holy lord I bade be not far off
While I lay sick—I have not here his name—
My head is tired, yet have I strength at heart
To say one word shall make me friends with God,
Commending to him in the hour of unripe death
The spirit so rent untimely from its house
And ere the natural night lay hold on it
Darkly divided from the light of life.
Pray him come to me.

MARY BEATON. It is my lord of Ross
The queen would see? my lord is at her hand.

Enter the BISHOP OF ROSS.

QUEEN. Most reverend father, my soul's friend, you see
How little queenlike I sit here at wait
Till God lay hand on me for life or death,
With pain for that gold garland of my head
Men call a crown, and for my body's robe
Am girt with mortal sickness: I would fain,
Before I set my face to look on death,
Mine eyes against his eyes, make straight the way
My soul must travel with this flesh put off
At the dark door; I pray you for God's grace
Give me that holy help that is in you
To lighten my last passage out of sight.
For this world's works, I have done with them this day,
With mine own lips while yet their breath was warm
Commending to my lords the natural charge
Of their born king, and by my brother's mouth
To the English queen the wardship of her heir,
And by the ambassador's of France again

To his good mistress and my brother king
The care of mine unmothered child, who has
No better friends bequeathable than these:
And for this land have I besought them all,
Who may beseech of no man aught again,
That here may no man for his faith be wronged
Whose faith is one with mine that all my life
I have kept, and fear not in it now to die.
BISHOP OF ROSS. Madam, what comfort God hath given his priests
To give again, what stay of spirit and strength
May through their mean stablish the souls of men
To live or die unvexed of life or death,
Unwounded of the fear and fang of hell,
Doubt not to have; seeing though no man be good
But one is good, even God, yet in his eye
The man that keeps faith sealed upon his soul
Shall through the bloodshedding of Christ be clean.
And in this time of cursing and flawed faith
Have you kept faith unflawed, and on your head
The immediate blessing of the spouse of God.
Have no fear therefore but your sins of life,
Or stains and shadows such as all men take,
In this world's passage, from the touch of time,
Shall fall from off you as a vesture changed
And leave your soul for whiteness as a child's.
QUEEN. I would have absolution ere I die,
But of what sins I have not strength to say
Nor hardly to remember. I do think
I have done God some service, holding fast
Faith, and his Church's fear; and have loved well
His name and burden set on me to serve,
To bear his part in the eye of this thwart world
And witness of his cross; yet know myself
To be but as a servant without grace
Save of his lord's love's gift; I have sinned in pride,
Perchance, to be his servant first and fight,
In face of all men's hate and might, alone,

Here sitting single-sceptred, and compel
For all its many-mouthed inveteracy
The world with bit and bridle like a beast
Brought back to serve him, and bowed down to me
Whose hand should take and hale it by the mane
And bend its head to worship as I bade,
I, first among his faithful; so I said,
And foolishly; for I was high of heart;
And now, behold, I am in God's sight and man's
Nothing; but though I have not so much grace
To bind again this people fast to God,
I have held mine own faith fast and with my lips
Have borne him witness if my heart were whole.
BISHOP OF ROSS. Therefore shall he forget not in your hour
Nor for his child reject you; and shall make
The weight and colour of your sins on earth
More white and light than wool may be or snow.
QUEEN. Yea, so my trust is of him; though as now
Scarce having in me breath or spirit of speech
I make not long confession, and my words
Through faintness of my flesh lack form; yet, pray you,
Think it but sickness and my body's fault
That comes between me and my will, who fain
Would have your eye look on my naked soul
And read what writing there should be washed out
With mine own heart's tears, and with God's dear blood,
Who sees me for his penitent; for surely
My sins of wrath and of light-mindedness,
And waste of wanton will and wandering eyes,
Call on me with dumb tongues for penitence;
Which I beseech you let not God reject
For lack of words that I lack strength to say.
For here as I repent and put from me
In perfect hope of pardon all ill thoughts,
So I remit all faults against me done,
Forgive all evil toward me of all men,
Deed or device to hurt me; yea, I would not
There were one heart unreconciled with mine

When mine is cold; I will not take death's hand
With any soil of hate or wrath or wrong
About me, but being friends with this past world
Pass from it in the general peace of love.
MARY BEATON. Here is some message from the world of friends
Brought to your brother: shall my lord come in?
QUEEN. What lord? ye have no lord of any man
While I am lady of all you. Who is this?
Message? what message? whence?
Enter MURRAY.
MURRAY. From Edinburgh
Your husband new alighted in sharp speed
Craves leave of access to your majesty.
QUEEN. By heaven, I had rather death had leave than he.
What comes he for? to vex me quick or dead
With his lewd eyes and sodden sidelong face
That I may die again with loathing of him?
By God, as God shall look upon my soul,
I will not see him. Bid him away, and keep
Far off as Edinburgh may hold him hence
Among his fellows of the herded swine
That not for need but love he wallows with
To expend his patrimony of breath and blood
In the dear service of dishonouring days.
MURRAY. Let him but bide the night here.
QUEEN. Not an hour;
Not while his horse may breathe. I will not see him.
MURRAY. Nay, for the world's sake, and lest worse be said;
Let him sleep here and come not in your sight.
QUEEN. Unless by some means I be freed of him
I have no pleasure upon earth to live.
I will put hand to it first myself. My lord,
See how this ill man's coming shakes my soul
And stains its thoughts with passionate earth again
That were as holy water, white and sweet,
For my rechristening; I could weep with wrath
To find between my very prayer and God
His face thrust like a shameful thought in sleep.

I cannot pray nor fix myself on heaven
But he must loose my hold, break up my trust,
Unbind my settled senses, and pluck down
My builded house of hope. Would he were dead
That puts my soul out of its peace with God.
Comfort me, father; let him not have way;
Keep my soul for me safe and full of heaven
As it was late.—See that you rid him hence,
I charge you, sir, with morning.

From Act 2, scene 15

Bothwell meditates the murder of Darnley (I).

BOTHWELL. This is the time and here the point of earth
That is to try what fate will make of me.
I hold here in my hand my hand's desire,
The fruit my life has climbed for; day on day
Have I strid over, stretching toward this prize
With all my thews and spirits. I must be glad,
If I could think; yet even my cause of joy
Doth somewhat shake me, that my sense and soul
Seem in their springs confused, even as two streams
Violently mingling: what is here to do
Is less now than the least I yet have done,
Being but the putting once of the mere hand
To the thing done already in device,
Wrought many times out in the working soul.
Yet my heart revels not, nor feel I now
The blood again leap in me for delight
That in the thought grew riotous and beat high
With foretaste of possession unpossessed.
Is it that in all alike fruition slacks
The shrunk imagination? in all deeds

The doing undoes the spirit to do, the joy
Sickens, the lust is swallowed as of sand?
Why, yet the stream should run of my desire
Unshrunken, and no deserts drink it up,
Being unfulfilled; no satiate sluggishness
Gape with dry lips at the edge of the dry cup
For the poor lees of longing. I am here
Not royal yet, nor redder in the hand
Than war has dyed me fighting; the thing done
Is but for me done, since I hold it so,
Not yet for him that in the doing must bleed;
I that stand up to do it, and in my mind
Behold across it mightier days for deeds,
Should not be way-sick yet nor travel-tired
Before I drink fulfilment as a wine;
And here must it restore me.

From Act 2, scene 18

Bothwell meditates the murder of Darnley (II).

BOTHWELL. I would the winds would muster, or the sun
Show half an eye-blink of his face that hangs
Now downward to the sea, curbed in with cloud,
And with a brief breath fire the rack that flies.
Why should not flame break over Arthur's Seat
This hour, and all the heaven with burning tongues
Cry from the world's height to the under line
That ends it for us gazing? If the sky
Had speech as it hath fire, or night or day
Voice to declare God's pleasure or his wrath
With their dumb lips of light, from moon or sun
Or the mute mouths of stars, would earth that heard
Take thought and counsel of the cause, to stir

Men's hearts up for our deed's sake here? I am wrought
Out of myself even by this pause and peace
In heaven and earth, that will not know of us
Nor what we compass; in this face of things,
Here in this eye of everduring life
That changes not in changing, fear and hope,
The life we live, the life we take, alike
Decline and dwindle from the shape they held,
Their import and significance; all seem
Less good and evil, worth less hate and love,
Than we would have them for our high heart's sake.
How shall this day when all these days are done
Seem to me standing where it sets my feet?
Nay, whence shall I behold it? or who knows
What crest or chasm, what pit or pinnacle,
Shall feel my foot or gulf my body down,
Bear up or break me falling? Fall or stand,
At least I live not as the beasts that serve,
But with a king's life or man's death at last
Make all my travails perfect; and a queen,
The fairest face I have loved and fieriest heart,
Shines with my star or sets.

From Act 3, scene 2

The Queen takes her leave of the murdered Darnley.

QUEEN. Let me look on him. It is marred not much;
This was a fair face of a boy's alive.
BOTHWELL. It had been better had he died ere man.
QUEEN. That hardly was he yesterday; a man!
What heart, what brain of manhood had God sown
In this poor fair fool's flesh to bear him fruit?
What seed of spirit or counsel? what good hope

That might have put forth flower in any sun?
We have plucked none up who cut him off at root,
But a tare only or a thorn. His cheek
Is not much changed, though since I wedded him
His eyes had shrunken and his lips grown wan
With sickness and ill living. Yesterday,
Man or no man, this was a living soul;
What is this now? This tongue that mourned to me,
These lips that mine were mixed with, these blind eyes
That fastened on me following, these void hands
That never plighted faith with man and kept.
Poor hands that paddled in the sloughs of shame,
Poor lips athirst for women's lips and wine,
Poor tongue that lied, poor eyes that looked askant
And had no heart to face men's wrath or love,
As who could answer either,—what work now
Doth that poor spirit which moved them? To what use
Of evil or good should hell put this or heaven,
Or with what fire of purgatory annealed
Shall it be clean and strong, yet keep in it
One grain for witness of what seed it was,
One thread, one shred enwoven with it alive,
To show what stuff time spun it of, and rent?
I have more pity such things should be born
Than of his death; yea, more than I had hate,
Living, of him. [...]
For him of whose dead face mine eyes take leave
As my free soul of shameful thought on him,
Let him have private burial some fit night
By David whom he slew. I mind me now
'Tis not a year since I fled forth with him
Even through the graves where he shall lie alone,
And passing through their dusty deadly ways
For some few minutes of the rustling night
I felt his hand quake; he will quake not now
To sleep there all night long. See you to that.

From Act 5, scene 2

The Queen incarcerated at Lochleven.

I tell thee yet, I thought indeed to die
When I came hither. 'Tis but five weeks gone—
Five, and two days; I keep the count of days
Here; I can mind the smell of the moist air
As we took land, and when we got to horse
I thought I never haply might ride more,
Nor hear a hoof's beat on the glad green ground,
Nor feel the free steed stretch him to the way
Nor his flank bound to bear me: then meseemed
Men could not make me live in prison long;
It were unlike my being, out of my doom;
Free should I live, or die. Then came these walls
And this blind water shuddering at the sun
That rose ere we had ten miles ridden; and here
The black boat rocked that took my feet off shore,
And set them in this prison; and as I came
The honey-heavy heather touched my sense
Wellnigh to weeping; I did think to die
And smell nought sweeter than the naked grave.
Yet sit we not among the worms and roots,
But can see this much—from the round tower here
The square walls of the main tower opposite
And the bare court between; a gracious sight.
Yet did they not so well to let me live,
If they love life too; I will find those friends
That found these walls and fears to fence me with
A narrower lodging than this seven feet's space
That yet I move in, where nor lip nor limb
Shall breathe or move for ever.

MARY BEATON. Do you think
You shall not long live bound?

QUEEN. Impossible.
I would have violent death, or life at large;

And either speedy. Were it in their mind
To slay me here and swiftly, as I thought,
Thou wouldst not here sit by their leave with me;
They get not so much grace who are now to die
And could not need it; yet I have heard it said
The headsman grants what sort of grace he may—
A grievous grace—to one about to bleed
That asks some boon before his neck lie down;
Thy face was haply such a boon to me,
Being cradle-fellows and fast-hearted friends,
To see before I died, and this the gift
Given of my headsmen's grace; what think'st thou?

MARY BEATON. Nay,
That I know nought of headsmen.

QUEEN. Thou hast seen—
It is a sharp strange thing to see men die.
I have prayed these men for life, thou knowest, have sent
Prayers in my son's and my dead father's name,
Their kings that were and shall be, and men say
One was well loved of the people, and their love
Is good to have, a goodly stay—and yet
I do not greatly think I fear to die.
I would not put off life yet; if I live,
For one thing most shall these men pay me dear,
That I was ever touched with fear of death.
Thou hast heard how seeing a child on the island once
Strayed over from the shore, I cried to him
Through the pierced wall between five feet of stone
To bid my friends pray God but for my soul,
My body was worth little; and they thought
I was cast down with bitter dread of heart;
Please God, for that will I get good revenge.

The Queen is presented with a bond to sign.

Enter LINDSAY *and* RUTHVEN.

QUEEN. 'Tis five weeks gone, my lord, *[To Lindsay*
Since last we looked on you; for you, fair sir, *[To Ruthven*

A year I think and four good months are sped
Since at that father's back whose name you bear
I saw your face dashed red with blood. My lords,
Ye come to treat with us ambassadors
Sent from our subjects; and we cannot choose,
Being held of them in bonds from whom ye come,
But give you leave to speak.
LINDSAY. Thus, briefly, madam.
If you will live to die no death by doom,
This threefold bond of contract that we bring
Requires your hand; wherein of your free will
First must you yield the crown of Scotland up
To your child's hand; then by this second deed
The place and name of regent through this realm
To the earl of Murray shall you here assign
Or, if he list not take this coil in hand,
Then to the council; last, this deed empowers
The lords of Mar and Morton with myself
To set the crown upon the young king's head.
These shall you sign.
QUEEN. These I shall sign, or die.
But hear you, sirs; when hither you brought these,
Burned not your hearts within you by the way
Thinking how she that should subscribe was born
King James's daughter? that this shameful hand,
Fit to sustain nor sword nor staff o' the realm,
Hath the blood in it of those years of kings
That tamed the neck and drove with spurs the sides
Of this beast people that now casts off me?
Ay, this that is to sign, no hand but this
Throbs with their sole inheritance of life
Who held with bit and bridle this bound land
And made it pace beneath them. What are ye
That I should tell you so, whose fathers fought
Beneath my fathers? Where my grandsire fell
And all this land about him, was there none
That bore on Flodden, sirs, such names as yours,
And shamed them not? Heard no men past of lords

That for the king's crown gave their crown of life
For death to harry? Did these grieve or grudge
To be built up into that bloody wall
That could not fence the king? Were no dead found
Of that huge cirque wherein my grandsire lay
But of poor men and commons? Yea, my lords,
I think the sires that bred you had not heart
As men have writ of them, but sent to fight
For them their vassals visored with their crests,
And these did well, and died, and left your sires
That hid their heads for ever and lived long
The name and false name of their deeds and death.
How should their sons else, how should ye, being born,
If born ye be, not bastards, of those lords
Who gat this lying glory to be called
Loyal, and in the reek of a false field
To fall so for my fathers—how, I say,
Dare sons of such come hither, how stand here,
From off the daughter's head of all those kings
To pluck the crown that on my fathers' heads
Ye say they died to save? I will not sign;
No, let some Flodden sword dip in my blood;
Here I sit fast, and die. [...]
                                        I had no skill
To shape false letters.
    RUTHVEN.   Madam, no man here
But knows by heart the height of your stout words
And strength of speech or sweetness; all this breath
Can blow not back the storm yourself raised up
Whose tempest shakes the kingdom from your hand,
And not men's hate. You have been loved of men;
All faith of heart, all honour possible,
While man might give, men gave you. Now, those deeds
Which none against your will enforced you do
Have set that spirit against you in men's minds
That till you die (as then your memory may)
Nor your fair beauty nor your fiery heart
Can lay with spells asleep.

From Act 5, scene 4

The Queen's conference with Murray, appointed Regent of Scotland.

QUEEN. Must I too
Bleed to make Scotland clean of baser blood
Than this she seeks of mine?
MURRAY. If you shall die,
Bethink you for what cause, and that sole thought
Shall seal your lips up from all pride of plea
That would put in between your deed and doom
The name of queen to cover you. No age
That lived on earth red-handed without law
Ever let pass in peace and unchastised
Such acts as this that yet in all men's ears
Rings as a cry unanswered. When your lord
Lay newly murdered, and all tongues of friends
Were loud in prayer to you to save your name
From stain of accusation, and yield up
That head to judgment which the whole world held
Blood-guilty, first with subtle stretch of time
Did you put back the trial, then devise
To make it fruitless save of mockery; next,
I cannot say for shame what shame foregone
Moved you to put upon this loathing land
That great dishonour to behold and bear
The man your lover for its lord, and you,
Queen of all Scots and thrall of one most base,
While yet the ring was from his finger warm
That sealed it first, and on his wedded hand
The young blood of your husband, ere the print
Had cooled of marriage or of murder, you
In the hot circle of his amorous arms
A new-espoused adulteress. Will you say
You were enforced or by false counsels bent
To take him to your bosom? In what eye
Was not the foregone commerce of your loves

As bare as shame? what ear had heard not blown
His name that was your sword and paramour,
Whose hand in yours was now as steel to slay,
Now as a jewel for love to wear, a pledge
Hot from your lips and from your husband's heart?
Who knew not what should make this man so proud
That none durst speak against him of your friends
But must abide for answer unaware
The peril of the swords that followed him?
Went he not with you where you went, and bade
Men come and go, do this or do not, stand
Or pass as pleased him, ere that day had risen
Which gave the mockery of a ravished bride
To the false violence of his fraudful rape
That hardly she could feign to fear, or hide
The sweetness of the hour when she might yield
That which was his before, and in men's eyes
Make proof of her subjection? Nay, forbear;
Plead not for shame that force was put on you
To bear that burden and embrace that shame
For which your heart was hungry; foe nor friend
Could choose but see it, and that the food desired
Must be but mortal to you. Think on this,
How you came hither crowned these six years gone
In this same summer month, and with what friends
Girt round about and guarded with what hopes,
And to a land how loving; and these years,
These few brief years, have blown from off your boughs
All blossom of that summer, though nor storm
Nor fire from heaven hath wrecked nor wind laid low
That stately tree that shadowed a glad land,
But now being inly gnawn of worms to death
And made a lurking-place for poisonous things
To breed and fester at its rotten root,
The axe is come against it. None save you
Could have done this, to turn all hearts and hands
That were for love's sake laid before your feet
To fire and iron whetted and made hot

To war against you. No man lives that knows
What is your cause, and loathes not; though for craft
Or hope of vantage some that know will seem
To know not, and some eyes be rather blind
Than see what eyeless ignorance in its sleep,
If but it would, must needs take note of; none
Whose mind is maimed not by his own mere will
And made perforce of its own deed perverse
Can read this truth awry. What have you done?
Men might weep for you, yea, beholding it
The eyes of angels melt; no tide of tears
Could wash from hand or soul the sinful sign
That now stands leprous there; albeit God knows
Myself for very pity could be glad
By mine own loss to ransom you, and set
Upon your soul again the seal of peace
And in your hand its empire; but your act
Has plucked out of men's hearts that fain would keep
The privilege of mercy; God alone
Can lose not that for ever, but retains
For all sins done that cry for judgment here
The property of pity, which in man
Were mere compliance and confederacy
With the sin pardoned; so shall you do best,
Being thus advised, to entertain the hope
Of nothing but God's mercy, and henceforth
Seek that as chiefest refuge; for in man
There shall no trust deliver you, nor free
Body nor soul from bonds. Weep not for that;
But let your tears be rather as were hers
That wept upon the feet of God, and bought
With that poor price her pardon.
QUEEN. So should I,
If grief more great may buy it than any of theirs
That had sinned more than I; nay, such have been
And have been pardoned. I have done ill, and given
My name for shame to feed on, put mine honour
Into mine enemies' keeping, made my fame

A prey and pasture for the teeth of scorn;
I dare not say I wist not by what mean
I should be freed of one that marred my life,
Who could by no mean else be quit of him
Save this blind way of blood; yet men there were
More wise than I, men much less wronged of him,
That led me to it and left me; but indeed
I cite not them to extenuate by strange aid
Mine own rash mind and unadvisedness
That brought forth fruit of death; yet must you know
What counsels led me by the hand, and whence
My wrath was fostered; and how all alone,
How utterly uncomforted, and girt
With how great peril, when the man was slain,
I stood and found not you to counsel me,
And no man else that loved; and in such need
If I did ill to seek to that strong hand
Which had for me done evil, if evil it were
To avenge me of mine enemy, what did they
That by their hands and voices on his side
Put force on me to wed him? yet I say not
I was indeed enforced; I will not mock
With one false plea my penitent heart, nor strive
With words to darken counsel, nor incense
By foolishness your wisdom, to provoke
A judgment heavier than I wait for; nay,
You have not said that bitter thing of me
That I may dare unsay; what most I would,
I must deny not; yet I pray you think,
Even as might God, being just, what cause I had,
What plea to lighten my sore load of sin,
Mismated and miscounselled, and had seen
Of my sad life not wholly nineteen years
When I came hither crowned; as yet would God
Your head, my brother, had endured for mine
That heaviness of honour, and this hand
The weight of Scotland, that being laid in mine
Has fallen and left it maimed, and on my brows

A mark as his whose temples for his crime
Were ringed with molten iron. Take them now,
Though but for pity of me that pray you take,
And bear them better than I did; for me,
Though no plea serve me in the sight of man
Nor grace excuse my fault, I am yet content,
If I may live but so much time in bonds
As may suffice for God to pardon me,
Who shall not long put off to pardon, then
Shut eyes and sleep to death.
MURRAY. I had thought to-night
To speak no more with you, but let that hope
Which only in God's name I gave you bear
What fruit it might with prayer and watching; yet
Take comfort, and assure yourself of life,
And, if it may be, honour; one of these
I may take on me to redeem, and one
So as I may will I preserve from death
Dealt of men's tongues that murder it; but you,
Keep these things in your heart; that if you raise
Within this realm a faction, or devise
To break these bonds, I shall not keep an hour
This power I have to save you; nor shall keep,
If France or England be by word of yours
Stirred up to strike at our frail peace; nor yet
If you shall cleave to him that should for shame
As from this land be cast out from your heart;
But if toward God your faults be faithfully
In good men's sight acknowledged, and that life
You led with your false lord and all sins past
Loathed and lamented, and in days to be
The living purpose in you manifest
Of a more modest habit and a life
More nobly fashioned—if the slaughter done
On your dead husband seem of you abhorred
And those ill days misliked wherein your fame
Drank mortal poison from his murderer's hand—
If this be seen, and that your mind lives clear

From counsel of revenge upon those lords
Who sought your reformation, nor with hope
Nor dangerous forethought of device to be
Renews itself to do them some day wrong;
Then may you now sit safe, and unreproved
Expect an end of bondage; for at large
You cannot think to live yet, who in time
May haply by repentance be restored
And for your prison somewhile here endured
Find yet your throne again, and sit renewed
More royal than men wist who saw the ship
Put in from France that bore you.

From Act 5, scene 11

The Queen flees from the Battle of Langside.

QUEEN. Come, help me then to horse;
If I must ride some hundred miles to breathe,
As we must fly no less, I think, or fall
Among our foes that follow, in my mind
The worst it were not nor the unkindliest death
To die in saddle. I will not give again,
So please it God, into mine enemies' hands
My body up for bondage; twice or thrice
I have ridden hard by stars of March or May
With false or true men to my left and right
The wild night through for death or kingly life,
And if I ride now with few friends at hand
I have none false of them; or if as once
One ride with me that had my hate alive
Who rode with me to his own grave, and now
Holds me in chase toward mine—O, thou that wast
My hate and husband, whom these men to-day

Take on them to revenge, and in thy name
Turn all men's hearts against me that were born
Mine and all swords that served me, if thou be
A shadow at hand, a ghost unreconciled,
That waits to take his triumph, hear and see
If in this hour that smites me, which is thine,
Thou find one thought in me that bows my heart,
One pang that turns it from the thing it was,
One pulse that moves me to repent or fear
For what was done or shall be; if thou have
But so much power upon me to be called
Less hateful or more fearful, and thy death
With aught of dread have clothed the thought of thee
That thy life had not; if thou seest me fly,
Then must thou see too that thou shalt not see
In death or life one part of spirit or sense
In me that calls thee master. To God's hand
I give the rest; but in mine own I hold
The perfect power for good or evil days
To keep the heart I had, and on myself
Lose not one jot of lordship; so may God
Love me no less and be no slower, I think,
To help my soul than theirs more vile than mine
And made for chance to mar, whereon their fate
Has power as on their bodies. If he will,
Now should he help, or never; for we have
A field more fatal to us and day more foul
Than ever cast out hope. I am loth to go
More than to die; yet come what will soe'er,
I shall no more.

From Act 5, scene 13

The Queen's departure for England. At the shore of Solway Firth.

QUEEN. Methinks the sand yet cleaving to my foot
Should not with no more words be shaken off,
Nor this my country from my parting eyes
Pass unsaluted; for who knows what year
May see us greet hereafter? Yet take heed,
Ye that have ears, and hear me; and take note,
Ye that have eyes, and see with what last looks
Mine own take leave of Scotland; seven years since
Did I take leave of my fair land of France,
My joyous mother, mother of my joy,
Weeping; and now with many a woe between
And space of seven years' darkness, I depart
From this distempered and unnatural earth
That casts me out unmothered, and go forth
On this grey sterile bitter gleaming sea
With neither tears nor laughter, but a heart
That from the softest temper of its blood
Is turned to fire and iron. If I live,
If God pluck not all hope out of my hand,
If aught of all mine prosper, I that go
Shall come back to men's ruin, as a flame
The wind bears down, that grows against the wind,
And grasps it with great hands, and wins its way,
And wins its will, and triumphs; so shall I
Let loose the fire of all my heart to feed
On these that would have quenched it. I will make
From sea to sea one furnace of the land
Whereon the wind of war shall beat its wings
Till they wax faint with hopeless hope of rest,
And with one rain of men's rebellious blood
Extinguish the red embers. I will leave
No living soul of their blaspheming faith
Who war with monarchs; God shall see me reign

As he shall reign beside me, and his foes
Lie at my foot with mine; kingdoms and kings
Shall from my heart take spirit, and at my soul
Their souls be kindled to devour for prey
The people that would make its prey of them
And leave God's altar stripped of sacrament
As all king's heads of sovereignty, and make
Bare as their thrones his temples; I will set
Those old things of his holiness on high
That are brought low, and break beneath my feet
These new things of men's fashion; I will sit
And see tears flow from eyes that saw me weep
And dust and ashes and the shadow of death
Cast from the block beneath the axe that falls
On heads that saw me humbled; I will do it,
Or bow mine own down to no royal end
And give my blood for theirs if God's will be,
But come back never as I now go forth
With but the hate of men to track my way
And not the face of any friend alive.

MARY BEATON. But I will never leave you till you die.

From POEMS AND BALLADS, SECOND SERIES (1878)

A Forsaken Garden

In a coign of the cliff between lowland and highland,
   At the sea-down's edge between windward and lee,
Walled round with rocks as an inland island,
   The ghost of a garden fronts the sea.
A girdle of brushwood and thorn encloses
   The steep square slope of the blossomless bed
Where the weeds that grew green from the graves of its roses
      Now lie dead.

The fields fall southward, abrupt and broken,
   To the low last edge of the long lone land.
If a step should sound or a word be spoken,
   Would a ghost not rise at the strange guest's hand?
So long have the grey bare walks lain guestless,
   Through branches and briars if a man make way,
He shall find no life but the sea-wind's, restless
      Night and day.

The dense hard passage is blind and stifled
   That crawls by a track none turn to climb
To the strait waste place that the years have rifled
   Of all but the thorns that are touched not of time.
The thorns he spares when the rose is taken;
   The rocks are left when he wastes the plain.

The wind that wanders, the weeds wind-shaken,
These remain.

Not a flower to be pressed of the foot that falls not;
As the heart of a dead man the seed-plots are dry;
From the thicket of thorns whence the nightingale calls not,
Could she call, there were never a rose to reply.
Over the meadows that blossom and wither
Rings but the note of a sea-bird's song;
Only the sun and the rain come hither
All year long.

The sun burns sere and the rain dishevels
One gaunt bleak blossom of scentless breath.
Only the wind here hovers and revels
In a round where life seems barren as death.
Here there was laughing of old, there was weeping,
Haply, of lovers none ever will know,
Whose eyes went seaward a hundred sleeping
Years ago.

Heart handfast in heart as they stood, "Look thither,"
Did he whisper? "look forth from the flowers to the sea;
For the foam-flowers endure when the rose-blossoms wither,
And men that love lightly may die—but we?"
And the same wind sang and the same waves whitened,
And or ever the garden's last petals were shed,
In the lips that had whispered, the eyes that had lightened,
Love was dead.

Or they loved their life through, and then went whither?
And were one to the end—but what end who knows?
Love deep as the sea as a rose must wither,
As the rose-red seaweed that mocks the rose.
Shall the dead take thought for the dead to love them?
What love was ever as deep as a grave?
They are loveless now as the grass above them
Or the wave.

All are at one now, roses and lovers,
   Not known of the cliffs and the fields and the sea.
Not a breath of the time that has been hovers
   In the air now soft with a summer to be.
Not a breath shall there sweeten the seasons hereafter
   Of the flowers or the lovers that laugh now or weep,
When as they that are free now of weeping and laughter
         We shall sleep.

Here death may deal not again for ever;
   Here change may come not till all change end.
From the graves they have made they shall rise up never,
   Who have left nought living to ravage and rend.
Earth, stones, and thorns of the wild ground growing,
   While the sun and the rain live, these shall be;
Till a last wind's breath upon all these blowing
         Roll the sea.

Till the slow sea rise and the sheer cliff crumble,
   Till terrace and meadow the deep gulfs drink,
Till the strength of the waves of the high tides humble
   The fields that lessen, the rocks that shrink,
Here now in his triumph where all things falter,
   Stretched out on the spoils that his own hand spread,
As a god self-slain on his own strange altar,
         Death lies dead.

A Wasted Vigil

I

Couldst thou not watch with me one hour? Behold,
Dawn skims the sea with flying feet of gold,
With sudden feet that graze the gradual sea;
      Couldst thou not watch with me?

II

What, not one hour? for star by star the night
Falls, and her thousands world by world take flight;
They die, and day survives, and what of thee?
    Couldst thou not watch with me?

III

Lo, far in heaven the web of night undone,
And on the sudden sea the gradual sun;
Wave to wave answers, tree responds to tree;
    Couldst thou not watch with me?

IV

Sunbeam by sunbeam creeps from line to line,
Foam by foam quickens on the brightening brine;
Sail by sail passes, flower by flower gets free;
    Couldst thou not watch with me?

V

Last year, a brief while since, an age ago,
A whole year past, with bud and bloom and snow,
O moon that wast in heaven, what friends were we!
    Couldst thou not watch with me?

VI

Old moons, and last year's flowers, and last year's snows!
Who now saith to thee, moon? or who saith, rose?
O dust and ashes, once found fair to see!
    Couldst thou not watch with me?

VII

O dust and ashes, once thought sweet to smell!
With me it is not, is it with thee well?
O sea-drift blown from windward back to lee!
    Couldst thou not watch with me?

VIII

The old year's dead hands are full of their dead flowers.
The old days are full of dead old loves of ours,
Born as a rose, and briefer born than she;
    Couldst thou not watch with me?

IX

Could two days live again of that dead year,
One would say, seeking us and passing here,
Where is she? and one answering, *Where is he?*
    Couldst thou not watch with me?

X

Nay, those two lovers are not anywhere;
If we were they, none knows us what we were,
Nor aught of all their barren grief and glee.
    Couldst thou not watch with me?

XI

Half false, half fair, all feeble, be my verse
Upon thee not for blessing nor for curse;
For some must stand, and some must fall or flee;
    Couldst thou not watch with me?

XII

As a new moon above spent stars thou wast;
But stars endure after the moon is past.
Couldst thou not watch one hour, though I watch three?
    Couldst thou not watch with me?

XIII

What of the night? The night is full, the tide
Storms inland, the most ancient rocks divide;
Yet some endure, and bow nor head nor knee;
    Couldst thou not watch with me?

XIV

Since thou art not as these are, go thy ways;
Thou hast no part in all my nights and days.
Lie still, sleep on, be glad—as such things be;
    Thou couldst not watch with me.

The Complaint of Lisa

(Double Sestina)

DECAMERON, X. 7

There is no woman living that draws breath
So sad as I, though all things sadden her.
There is not one upon life's weariest way
Who is weary as I am weary of all but death.
Toward whom I look as looks the sunflower
All day with all his whole soul toward the sun;
While in the sun's sight I make moan all day,

And all night on my sleepless maiden bed
Weep and call out on death, O Love, and thee,
That thou or he would take me to the dead,
And know not what thing evil I have done
That life should lay such heavy hand on me.

Alas, Love, what is this thou wouldst with me?
What honour shall thou have to quench my breath,
Or what shall my heart broken profit thee?
O Love, O great god Love, what have I done,
That thou shouldst hunger so after my death?
My heart is harmless as my life's first day:
Seek out some false fair woman, and plague her
Till her tears even as my tears fill her bed:
I am the least flower in thy flowery way,
But till my time be come that I be dead
Let me live out my flower-time in the sun
Though my leaves shut before the sunflower.

O Love, Love, Love, the kingly sunflower!
Shall he the sun hath looked on look on me,
That live down here in shade, out of the sun,
Here living in the sorrow and shadow of death?
Shall he that feeds his heart full of the day
Care to give mine eyes light, or my lips breath?
Because she loves him shall my lord love her
Who is as a worm in my lord's kingly way?
I shall not see him or know him alive or dead;
But thou, I know thee, O Love, and pray to thee
That in brief while my brief life-days be done,
And the worm quickly make my marriage-bed.

For underground there is no sleepless bed:
But here since I beheld my sunflower
These eyes have slept not, seeing all night and day
His sunlike eyes, and face fronting the sun.
Wherefore if anywhere be any death,
I would fain find and fold him fast to me,

That I may sleep with the world's eldest dead,
With her that died seven centuries since, and her
That went last night down the night-wandering way.
For this is sleep indeed, when labour is done,
Without love, without dreams, and without breath,
And without thought, O name unnamed! of thee.

Ah, but, forgetting all things, shall I thee?
Wilt thou not be as now about my bed
There underground as here before the sun?
Shall not thy vision vex me alive and dead,
Thy moving vision without form or breath?
I read long since the bitter tale of her
Who read the tale of Launcelot on a day,
And died, and had no quiet after death,
But was moved ever along a weary way,
Lost with her love in the underworld; ah me,
O my king, O my lordly sunflower,
Would God to me too such a thing were done!

But if such sweet and bitter things be done,
Then, flying from life, I shall not fly from thee.
For in that living world without a sun
Thy vision will lay hold upon me dead,
And meet and mock me, and mar my peace in death.
Yet if being wroth God had such pity on her,
Who was a sinner and foolish in her day,
That even in hell they twain should breathe one breath,
Why should he not in some wise pity me?
So if I sleep not in my soft strait bed
I may look up and see my sunflower
As he the sun, in some divine strange way.

O poor my heart, well knowest thou in what way
This sore sweet evil unto us was done.
For on a holy and a heavy day
I was arisen out of my still small bed
To see the knights tilt, and one said to me

"The king," and seeing him, somewhat stopped my breath,
And if the girl spake more, I heard not her,
For only I saw what I shall see when dead,
A kingly flower of knights, a sunflower,
That shone against the sunlight like the sun,
And like a fire, O heart, consuming thee,
The fire of love that lights the pyre of death.

Howbeit I shall not die an evil death
Who have loved in such a sad and sinless way,
That this my love, lord, was no shame to thee.
So when mine eyes are shut against the sun,
O my soul's sun, O the world's sunflower,
Thou nor no man will quite despise me dead.
And dying I pray with all my low last breath
That thy whole life may be as was that day,
That feast-day that made trothplight death and me,
Giving the world light of thy great deeds done;
And that fair face brightening thy bridal bed,
That God be good as God hath been to her.

That all things goodly and glad remain with her,
All things that make glad life and goodly death;
That as a bee sucks from a sunflower
Honey, when summer draws delighted breath,
Her soul may drink of thy soul in like way,
And love make life a fruitful marriage-bed
Where day may bring forth fruits of joy to day
And night to night till days and nights be dead.
And as she gives light of her love to thee,
Give thou to her the old glory of days long done;
And either give some heat of light to me,
To warm me where I sleep without the sun.

O sunflower made drunken with the sun,
O knight whose lady's heart draws thine to her,
Great king, glad lover, I have a word to thee.
There is a weed lives out of the sun's way,

Hid from the heat deep in the meadow's bed,
That swoons and whitens at the wind's least breath,
A flower star-shaped, that all a summer day
Will gaze her soul out on the sunflower
For very love till twilight finds her dead.
But the great sunflower heeds not her poor death,
Knows not when all her loving life is done;
And so much knows my lord the king of me.

Aye, all day long he has no eye for me;
With golden eye following the golden sun
From rose-coloured to purple-pillowed bed,
From birthplace to the flame-lit place of death,
From eastern end to western of his way.
So mine eye follows thee, my sunflower,
So the white star-flower turns and yearns to thee,
The sick weak weed, not well alive or dead,
Trod underfoot if any pass by her,
Pale, without colour of summer or summer breath
In the shrunk shuddering petals, that have done
No work but love, and die before the day.

But thou, to-day, to-morrow, and every day,
Be glad and great, O love whose love slays me.
Thy fervent flower made fruitful from the sun
Shall drop its golden seed in the world's way,
That all men thereof nourished shall praise thee
For grain and flower and fruit of works well done;
Till thy shed seed, O shining sunflower,
Bring forth such growth of the world's garden-bed
As like the sun shall outlive age and death.
And yet I would thine heart had heed of her
Who loves thee alive; but not till she be dead.
Come, Love, then, quickly, and take her utmost breath.

Song, speak for me who am dumb as are the dead;
From my sad bed of tears I send forth thee,
To fly all day from sun's birth to sun's death

Down the sun's way after the flying sun,
For love of her that gave thee wings and breath,
Ere day be done, to seek the sunflower.

Ave Atque Vale

IN MEMORY OF CHARLES BAUDELAIRE

> Nous devrions pourtant lui porter quelques fleurs;
> Les morts, les pauvres morts, ont de grandes douleurs,
> Et quand Octobre souffle, émondeur des vieux arbres,
> Son vent mélancolique à l'entour de leurs marbres,
> Certe, ils doivent trouver les vivants bien ingrats.
>
> *Les Fleurs du Mal.*

I

Shall I strew on thee rose or rue or laurel,
  Brother, on this that was the veil of thee?
  Or quiet sea-flower moulded by the sea,
Or simplest growth of meadow-sweet or sorrel,
  Such as the summer-sleepy Dryads weave,
  Waked up by snow-soft sudden rains at eve?
Or wilt thou rather, as on earth before,
  Half-faded fiery blossoms, pale with heat
  And full of bitter summer, but more sweet
To thee than gleanings of a northern shore
  Trod by no tropic feet?

II

For always thee the fervid languid glories
  Allured of heavier suns in mightier skies;
  Thine ears knew all the wandering watery sighs
Where the sea sobs round Lesbian promontories,

The barren kiss of piteous wave to wave
That knows not where is that Leucadian grave
Which hides too deep the supreme head of song.
Ah, salt and sterile as her kisses were,
The wild sea winds her and the green gulfs bear
Hither and thither, and vex and work her wrong,
Blind gods that cannot spare.

III

Thou sawest, in thine old singing season, brother,
Secrets and sorrows unbeheld of us:
Fierce loves, and lovely leaf-buds poisonous,
Bare to thy subtler eye, but for none other
Blowing by night in some unbreathed-in clime;
The hidden harvest of luxurious time,
Sin without shape, and pleasure without speech;
And where strange dreams in a tumultuous sleep
Make the shut eyes of stricken spirits weep;
And with each face thou sawest the shadow on each,
Seeing as men sow men reap.

IV

O sleepless heart and sombre soul unsleeping,
That were athirst for sleep and no more life
And no more love, for peace and no more strife!
Now the dim gods of death have in their keeping
Spirit and body and all the springs of song,
Is it well now where love can do no wrong,
Where stingless pleasure has no foam or fang
Behind the unopening closure of her lips?
Is it not well where soul from body slips
And flesh from bone divides without a pang
As dew from flower-bell drips?

V

It is enough; the end and the beginning
  Are one thing to thee, who art past the end.
  O hand unclasped of unbeholden friend,
For thee no fruits to pluck, no palms for winning,
  No triumph and no labour and no lust,
  Only dead yew-leaves and a little dust.
O quiet eyes wherein the light saith nought,
  Whereto the day is dumb, nor any night
  With obscure finger silences your sight,
Nor in your speech the sudden soul speaks thought,
  Sleep, and have sleep for light.

VI

Now all strange hours and all strange loves are over,
  Dreams and desires and sombre songs and sweet,
  Hast thou found place at the great knees and feet
Of some pale Titan-woman like a lover,
  Such as thy vision here solicited,
  Under the shadow of her fair vast head,
The deep division of prodigious breasts,
  The solemn slope of mighty limbs asleep,
  The weight of awful tresses that still keep
The savour and shade of old-world pine-forests
  Where the wet hill-winds weep?

VII

Hast thou found any likeness for thy vision?
  O gardener of strange flowers, what bud, what bloom,
  Hast thou found sown, what gathered in the gloom?
What of despair, of rapture, of derision,
  What of life is there, what of ill or good?
  Are the fruits grey like dust or bright like blood?

Does the dim ground grow any seed of ours,
  The faint fields quicken any terrene root,
  In low lands where the sun and moon are mute
And all the stars keep silence? Are there flowers
  At all, or any fruit?

VIII

Alas, but though my flying song flies after,
  O sweet strange elder singer, thy more fleet
  Singing, and footprints of thy fleeter feet,
Some dim derision of mysterious laughter
  From the blind tongueless warders of the dead,
  Some gainless glimpse of Proserpine's veiled head,
Some little sound of unregarded tears
  Wept by effaced unprofitable eyes,
  And from pale mouths some cadence of dead sighs—
These only, these the hearkening spirit hears,
  Sees only such things rise.

IX

Thou art far too far for wings of words to follow,
  Far too far off for thought or any prayer.
  What ails us with thee, who art wind and air?
What ails us gazing where all seen is hollow?
  Yet with some fancy, yet with some desire,
  Dreams pursue death as winds a flying fire,
Our dreams pursue our dead and do not find.
  Still, and more swift than they, the thin flame flies,
  The low light fails us in elusive skies,
Still the foiled earnest ear is deaf, and blind
  Are still the eluded eyes.

X

Not thee, O never thee, in all time's changes,
  Not thee, but this the sound of thy sad soul,
  The shadow of thy swift spirit, this shut scroll
I lay my hand on, and not death estranges
  My spirit from communion of thy song—
  These memories and these melodies that throng
Veiled porches of a Muse funereal—
  These I salute, these touch, these clasp and fold
  As though a hand were in my hand to hold,
Or through mine ears a mourning musical
  Of many mourners rolled.

XI

I among these, I also, in such station
  As when the pyre was charred, and piled the sods,
  And offering to the dead made, and their gods,
The old mourners had, standing to make libation,
  I stand, and to the gods and to the dead
  Do reverence without prayer or praise, and shed
Offering to these unknown, the gods of gloom,
  And what of honey and spice my seedlands bear,
  And what I may of fruits in this chilled air,
And lay, Orestes-like, across the tomb
  A curl of severed hair.

XII

But by no hand nor any treason stricken,
  Not like the low-lying head of Him, the King,
  The flame that made of Troy a ruinous thing,
Thou liest, and on this dust no tears could quicken
  There fall no tears like theirs that all men hear
  Fall tear by sweet imperishable tear

Down the opening leaves of holy poets' pages.
Thee not Orestes, not Electra mourns;
But bending us-ward with memorial urns
The most high Muses that fulfil all ages
Weep, and our God's heart yearns.

XIII

For, sparing of his sacred strength, not often
Among us darkling here the lord of light
Makes manifest his music and his might
In hearts that open and in lips that soften
With the soft flame and heat of songs that shine.
Thy lips indeed he touched with bitter wine,
And nourished them indeed with bitter bread;
Yet surely from his hand thy soul's food came,
The fire that scarred thy spirit at his flame
Was lighted, and thine hungering heart he fed
Who feeds our hearts with fame.

XIV

Therefore he too now at thy soul's sunsetting,
God of all suns and songs, he too bends down
To mix his laurel with thy cypress crown,
And save thy dust from blame and from forgetting.
Therefore he too, seeing all thou wert and art,
Compassionate, with sad and sacred heart,
Mourns thee of many his children the last dead,
And hallows with strange tears and alien sighs
Thine unmelodious mouth and sunless eyes,
And over thine irrevocable head
Sheds light from the under skies.

XV

And one weeps with him in the ways Lethean,
And stains with tears her changing bosom chill:
That obscure Venus of the hollow hill,
That thing transformed which was the Cytherean,
With lips that lost their Grecian laugh divine
Long since, and face no more called Erycine;
A ghost, a bitter and luxurious god.
Thee also with fair flesh and singing spell
Did she, a sad and second prey, compel
Into the footless places once more trod,
And shadows hot from hell.

XVI

And now no sacred staff shall break in blossom,
No choral salutation lure to light
A spirit sick with perfume and sweet night
And love's tired eyes and hands and barren bosom.
There is no help for these things; none to mend
And none to mar; not all our songs, O friend,
Will make death clear or make life durable.
Howbeit with rose and ivy and wild vine
And with wild notes about this dust of thine
At least I fill the place where white dreams dwell
And wreathe an unseen shrine.

XVII

Sleep; and if life was bitter to thee, pardon,
If sweet, give thanks; thou hast no more to live;
And to give thanks is good, and to forgive.
Out of the mystic and the mournful garden
Where all day through thine hands in barren braid
Wove the sick flowers of secrecy and shade,

Green buds of sorrow and sin, and remnants grey,
Sweet-smelling, pale with poison, sanguine-hearted,
Passions that sprang from sleep and thoughts that started,
Shall death not bring us all as thee one day
Among the days departed?

XVIII

For thee, O now a silent soul, my brother,
Take at my hands this garland, and farewell.
Thin is the leaf, and chill the wintry smell,
And chill the solemn earth, a fatal mother,
With sadder than the Niobean womb,
And in the hollow of her breasts a tomb.
Content thee, howsoe'er, whose days are done;
There lies not any troublous thing before,
Nor sight nor sound to war against thee more,
For whom all winds are quiet as the sun,
All waters as the shore.

A Ballad of Dreamland

I hid my heart in a nest of roses,
Out of the sun's way, hidden apart;
In a softer bed than the soft white snow's is,
Under the roses I hid my heart.
Why would it sleep not? why should it start,
When never a leaf of the rose-tree stirred?
What made sleep flutter his wings and part?
Only the song of a secret bird.

Lie still, I said, for the wind's wing closes,
And mild leaves muffle the keen sun's dart;

Lie still, for the wind on the warm sea dozes,
  And the wind is unquieter yet than thou art.
  Does a thought in thee still as a thorn's wound smart?
Does the fang still fret thee of hope deferred?
  What bids the lids of thy sleep dispart?
Only the song of a secret bird.

The green land's name that a charm encloses,
  It never was writ in the traveller's chart,
And sweet on its trees as the fruit that grows is,
  It never was sold in the merchant's mart.
  The swallows of dreams through its dim fields dart,
And sleep's are the tunes in its tree-tops heard;
  No hound's note wakens the wildwood hart,
Only the song of a secret bird.

ENVOI

In the world of dreams I have chosen my part,
  To sleep for a season and hear no word
Of true love's truth or of light love's art,
  Only the song of a secret bird.

Before Sunset

In the lower lands of day
  On the hither side of night,
There is nothing that will stay,
  There are all things soft to sight;
  Lighted shade and shadowy light
In the wayside and the way,
  Hours the sun has spared to smite,
Flowers the rain has left to play.

Shall these hours run down and say
  No good thing of thee and me?
Time that made us and will slay
  Laughs at love in me and thee;
  But if here the flowers may see
One whole hour of amorous breath,
  Time shall die, and love shall be
Lord as time was over death.

Triads

I

I

The word of the sun to the sky,
 The word of the wind to the sea,
  The word of the moon to the night,
   What may it be?

II

The sense to the flower of the fly,
 The sense of the bird to the tree,
  The sense to the cloud of the light,
   Who can tell me?

III

The song of the fields to the kye,
 The song of the lime to the bee,

The song of the depth to the height,
Who knows all three?

II

I

The message of April to May
That May sends on into June
And June gives out to July
For birthday boon;

II

The delight of the dawn in the day,
The delight of the day in the noon,
The delight of a song in a sigh
That breaks the tune;

III

The secret of passing away,
The cost of the change of the moon,
None knows it with ear or with eye,
But all will soon.

III

I

The live wave's love for the shore,
 The shore's for the wave as it dies,
  The love of the thunder-fire
   That sears the skies,

II

We shall know not though life wax hoar,
 Till all life, spent into sighs,
  Burn out as consumed with desire
   Of death's strange eyes;

III

Till the secret be secret no more
 In the light of one hour as it flies,
  Be the hour as of suns that expire
   Or suns that rise.

The Complaint of the Fair Armouress

I

Meseemeth I heard cry and groan
  That sweet who was the armourer's maid;
For her young years she made sore moan,
  And right upon this wise she said;
  "Ah fierce old age with foul bald head,
To spoil fair things thou art over fain;
  Who holdeth me? who? would God I were dead!
Would God I were well dead and slain!

II

"Lo, thou hast broken the sweet yoke
  That my high beauty held above
All priests and clerks and merchant-folk;
  There was not one but for my love
  Would give me gold and gold enough,
Though sorrow his very heart had riven,
  To win from me such wage thereof
As now no thief would take if given.

III

"I was right chary of the same,
  God wot it was my great folly,
For love of one sly knave of them,
  Good store of that same sweet had he;

For all my subtle wiles, perdie,
God wot I loved him well enow;
Right evilly he handled me,
But he loved well my gold, I trow.

IV

"Though I gat bruises green and black,
I loved him never the less a jot;
Though he bound burdens on my back,
If he said 'Kiss me and heed it not'
Right little pain I felt, God wot,
When that foul thief's mouth, found so sweet,
Kissed me—Much good thereof I got!
I keep the sin and the shame of it.

V

"And he died thirty year agone.
I am old now, no sweet thing to see;
By God, though, when I think thereon,
And of that good glad time, woe's me,
And stare upon my changed body
Stark naked, that has been so sweet,
Lean, wizen, like a small dry tree,
I am nigh mad with the pain of it.

VI

"Where is my faultless forehead's white,
The lifted eyebrows, soft gold hair,
Eyes wide apart and keen of sight,
With subtle skill in the amorous air;
The straight nose, great nor small, but fair,
The small carved ears of shapeliest growth,

Chin dimpling, colour good to wear,
And sweet red splendid kissing mouth?

VII

"The shapely slender shoulders small,
Long arms, hands wrought in glorious wise,
Round little breasts, the hips withal
High, full of flesh, not scant of size,
Fit for all amorous masteries;
The large loins, and the flower that was
Planted above my strong round thighs
In a small garden of soft grass.

VIII

"A writhled forehead, hair gone grey,
Fallen eyebrows, eyes gone blind and red,
Their laughs and looks all fled away,
Yea, all that smote men's hearts are fled;
The bowed nose, fallen from goodlihead;
Foul flapping ears like water-flags;
Peaked chin, and cheeks all waste and dead,
And lips that are two skinny rags:

IX

"Thus endeth all the beauty of us.
The arms made short, the hands made lean,
The shoulders bowed and ruinous,
The breasts, alack! all fallen in;
The flanks too, like the breasts, grown thin;
As for the sweet place, out on it!
For the lank thighs, no thighs but skin,
They are specked with spots like sausage-meat.

X

"So we make moan for the old sweet days,
  Poor old light women, two or three
Squatting above the straw-fire's blaze,
  The bosom crushed against the knee,
  Like faggots on a heap we be,
Round fires soon lit, soon quenched and done;
  And we were once so sweet, even we!
Thus fareth many and many an one."

Fragment on Death

And Paris be it or Helen dying,
  Who dies soever, dies with pain.
He that lacks breath and wind for sighing,
  His gall bursts on his heart; and then
  He sweats, God knows what sweat!—again,
No man may ease him of his grief;
  Child, brother, sister, none were fain
To bail him thence for his relief.

Death makes him shudder, swoon, wax pale,
  Nose bend, veins stretch, and breath surrender,
Neck swell, flesh soften, joints that fail
  Crack their strained nerves and arteries slender.
  O woman's body found so tender,
Smooth, sweet, so precious in men's eyes,
  Must thou too bear such count to render?
Yes; or pass quick into the skies.

Ballad against the Enemies of France

May he fall in with beasts that scatter fire,
Like Jason, when he sought the fleece of gold,
Or change from man to beast three years entire,
As King Nebuchadnezzar did of old;
Or else have times as shameful and as bad
As Trojan folk for ravished Helen had;
Or gulfed with Proserpine and Tantalus
Let hell's deep fen devour him dolorous,
With worse to bear than Job's worst sufferance,
Bound in his prison-maze with Dædalus,
Who could wish evil to the state of France!

May he four months, like bitterns in the mire,
Howl with head downmost in the lake-springs cold,
Or to bear harness like strong bulls for hire
To the Great Turk for money down be sold;
Or thirty years like Magdalen live sad,
With neither wool nor web of linen clad;
Drown like Narciss', or swing down pendulous
Like Absalom with locks luxurious,
Or liker Judas fallen to reprobance;
Or find such death as Simon sorcerous,
Who could wish evil to the state of France!

May the old times come of fierce Octavian's ire,
And in his belly molten coin be told;
May he like Victor in the mill expire,
Crushed between moving millstones on him rolled,
Or in deep sea drenched breathless, more adrad
Than in the whale's bulk Jonas, when God bade:
From Phoebus' light, from Juno's treasure-house
Driven, and from joys of Venus amorous,
And cursed of God most high to the utterance,
As was the Syrian king Antiochus,
Who could wish evil to the state of France!

Prince, may the bright-winged brood of Æolus
To sea-king Glaucus' wild wood cavernous
  Bear him bereft of peace and hope's least glance,
For worthless is he to get good of us,
  Who could wish evil to the state of France.

The Dispute of the Heart and the Body of François Villon

Who is this I hear?—Lo, this is I, thine heart,
  That holds on merely now by a slender string.
Strength fails me, shape and sense are rent apart,
  The blood in me is turned to a bitter thing,
  Seeing thee skulk here like a dog shivering.—
Yea, and for what?—For that thy sense found sweet.—
What irks it thee?—I feel the sting of it.—
  Leave me at peace.—Why?—Nay now, leave me at peace;
I will repent when I grow ripe in wit.—
  I say no more.—I care not though thou cease.—

What art thou, trow?—A man worth praise, perfay.—
  This is thy thirtieth year of wayfaring.—
'Tis a mule's age.—Art thou a boy still?—Nay.—
  Is it hot lust that spurs thee with its sting,
  Grasping thy throat? Know'st thou not anything?—
Yea, black and white, when milk is specked with flies,
I can make out.—No more?—Nay, in no wise.
  Shall I begin again the count of these?——
Thou art undone.—I will make shift to rise.—
  I say no more.—I care not though thou cease.—

I have the sorrow of it, and thou the smart.
  Wert thou a poor mad fool or weak of wit,
Then might'st thou plead this pretext with thine heart;
  But if thou know not good from evil a whit,

Either thy head is hard as stone to hit,
Or shame, not honour, gives thee most content.
What canst thou answer to this argument?—
When I am dead I shall be well at ease.—
God! what good hope!—Thou art over eloquent.—
I say no more.—I care not though thou cease.—

Whence is this ill?—From sorrow and not from sin.
When Saturn packed my wallet up for me
I well believe he put these ills therein.—
Fool, wilt thou make thy servant lord of thee?
Hear now the wise king's counsel; thus saith he:
All power upon the stars a wise man hath;
There is no planet that shall do him scathe.—
Nay, as they made me I grow and I decrease.—
What say'st thou?—Truly this is all my faith.—
I say no more.—I care not though thou cease.—

Wouldst thou live still?—God help me that I may!—
Then thou must—What? turn penitent and pray?—
Read always—What?—Grave words and good to say;
Leave off the ways of fools, lest they displease.—
Good; I will do it.—Wilt thou remember?—Yea.—
Abide not till there come an evil day.
I say no more.—I care not though thou cease.

Epistle in form of a Ballad to his Friends

Have pity, pity, friends, have pity on me,
Thus much at least, may it please you, of your grace!
I lie not under hazel or hawthorn-tree
Down in this dungeon ditch, mine exile's place
By leave of God and fortune's foul disgrace.
Girls, lovers, glad young folk and newly wed,

Jumpers and jugglers, tumbling heel o'er head,
  Swift as a dart, and sharp as needle-ware,
Throats clear as bells that ring the kine to shed,
  Your poor old friend, what, will you leave him there?

Singers that sing at pleasure, lawlessly,
  Light, laughing, gay of word and deed, that race
And run like folk light-witted as ye be
  And have in hand nor current coin nor base,
  Ye wait too long, for now he's dying apace.
Rhymers of lays and roundels sung and read,
Ye'll brew him broth too late when he lies dead.
  Nor wind nor lightning, sunbeam nor fresh air,
May pierce the thick wall's bound where lies his bed;
  Your poor old friend, what, will you leave him there?

O noble folk from tithes and taxes free,
  Come and behold him in this piteous case,
Ye that nor king nor emperor holds in fee,
  But only God in heaven; behold his face
  Who needs must fast, Sundays and holidays,
Which makes his teeth like rakes; and when he hath fed
With never a cake for banquet but dry bread,
  Must drench his bowels with much cold watery fare,
With board nor stool, but low on earth instead;
  Your poor old friend, what, will you leave him there?

Princes afore-named, old and young foresaid,
Get me the king's seal and my pardon sped,
  And hoist me in some basket up with care:
So swine will help each other ill bested,
For where one squeaks they run in heaps ahead.
  Your poor old friend, what, will you leave him there?

The Epitaph in form of a Ballad

which Villon made for himself and his comrades, expecting to be hanged along with them

Men, brother men, that after us yet live,
  Let not your hearts too hard against us be;
For if some pity of us poor men ye give,
  The sooner God shall take of you pity.
  Here are we five or six strung up, you see,
And here the flesh that all too well we fed
Bit by bit eaten and rotten, rent and shred,
  And we the bones grow dust and ash withal;
Let no man laugh at us discomforted,
  But pray to God that he forgive us all.

If we call on you, brothers, to forgive,
  Ye should not hold our prayer in scorn, though we
Were slain by law; ye know that all alive
  Have not wit alway to walk righteously;
  Make therefore intercession heartily
With him that of a virgin's womb was bred,
That his grace be not as a dry well-head
  For us, nor let hell's thunder on us fall;
We are dead, let no man harry or vex us dead,
  But pray to God that he forgive us all.

The rain has washed and laundered us all five,
  And the sun dried and blackened; yea, perdie,
Ravens and pies with beaks that rend and rive
  Have dug our eyes out, and plucked off for fee
  Our beards and eyebrows; never are we free,
Not once, to rest; but here and there still sped,
Drive at its wild will by the wind's change led,
  More pecked of birds than fruits on garden-wall;
Men, for God's love, let no gibe here be said,
  But pray to God that he forgive us all.

Prince Jesus, that of all art lord and head,
Keep us, that hell be not our bitter bed;
  We have nought to do in such a master's hall.
Be not ye therefore of our fellowhead,
  But pray to God that he forgive us all.

From STUDIES IN SONG (1880)

From *By the North Sea*

I

1

A land that is lonelier than ruin;
   A sea that is stranger than death:
Far fields that a rose never blew in,
   Wan waste where the winds lack breath;
Waste endless and boundless and flowerless
   But of marsh-blossoms fruitless as free:
Where earth lies exhausted, as powerless
      To strive with the sea.

2

Far flickers the flight of the swallows,
   Far flutters the weft of the grass
Spun dense over desolate hollows
   More pale than the clouds as they pass:
Thick woven as the weft of a witch is
   Round the heart of a thrall that hath sinned,
Whose youth and the wrecks of its riches
      Are waifs on the wind.

3

The pastures are herdless and sheepless,
No pasture or shelter for herds:
The wind is relentless and sleepless,
And restless and songless the birds;
Their cries from afar fall breathless,
Their wings are as lightnings that flee;
For the land has two lords that are deathless:
Death's self, and the sea.

4

These twain, as a king with his fellow,
Hold converse of desolate speech:
And her waters are haggard and yellow
And crass with the scurf of the beach:
And his garments are grey as the hoary
Wan sky where the day lies dim;
And his power is to her, and his glory,
As hers unto him.

5

In the pride of his power she rejoices,
In her glory he glows and is glad:
In her darkness the sound of his voice is,
With his breath she dilates and is mad:
"If thou slay me, O death, and outlive me,
Yet thy love hath fulfilled me of thee."
"Shall I give thee not back if thou give me,
O sister, O sea?"

6

And year upon year dawns living,
   And age upon age drops dead:
And his hand is not weary of giving,
   And the thirst of her heart is not fed:
And the hunger that moans in her passion,
   And the rage in her hunger that roars,
As a wolf's that the winter lays lash on,
      Still calls and implores.

7

Her walls have no granite for girder,
   No fortalice fronting her stands:
But reefs the bloodguiltiest of murder
   Are less than the banks of her sands:
These number their slain by the thousand;
   For the ship hath no surety to be,
When the bank is abreast of her bows and
      Aflush with the sea.

8

No surety to stand, and no shelter
   To dawn out of darkness but one,
Out of waters that hurtle and welter
   No succour to dawn with the sun,
But a rest from the wind as it passes,
   Where, hardly redeemed from the waves,
Lie thick as the blades of the grasses
      The dead in their graves.

9

A multitude noteless of numbers,
As wild weeds cast on an heap:
And sounder than sleep are their slumbers,
And softer than song is their sleep;
And sweeter than all things and stranger
The sense, if perchance it may be,
That the wind is divested of danger
And scatheless the sea.

10

That the roar of the banks they breasted
Is hurtless as bellowing of herds,
And the strength of his wings that invested
The wind, as the strength of a bird's;
As the sea-mew's might or the swallow's
That cry to him back if he cries,
As over the graves and their hollows
Days darken and rise.

11

As the souls of the dead men disburdened
And clean of the sins that they sinned,
With a lovelier than man's life guerdoned
And delight as a wave's in the wind,
And delight as the wind's in the billow,
Birds pass, and deride with their glee
The flesh that has dust for its pillow
As wrecks have the sea.

12

When the ways of the sun wax dimmer,
  Wings flash through the dusk like beams;
As the clouds in the lit sky glimmer,
  The bird in the graveyard gleams;
As the cloud at its wing's edge whitens
  When the clarions of sunrise are heard,
The graves that the bird's note brightens
    Grow bright for the bird.

13

As the waves of the numberless waters
  That the wind cannot number who guides
Are the sons of the shore and the daughters
  Here lulled by the chime of the tides:
And here in the press of them standing
  We know not if these or if we
Live truliest, or anchored to landing
    Or drifted to sea.

14

In the valley he named of decision
  No denser were multitudes met
When the soul of the seer in her vision
  Saw nations for doom of them set;
Saw darkness in dawn, and the splendour
  Of judgment, the sword and the rod;
But the doom here of death is more tender
    And gentler the god.

15

And gentler the wind from the dreary
Sea-banks by the waves overlapped,
Being weary, speaks peace to the weary
From slopes that the tide-stream hath sapped;
And sweeter than all that we call so
The seal of their slumber shall be
Till the graves that embosom them also
Be sapped of the sea.

III

1

Miles, and miles, and miles of desolation!
Leagues on leagues on leagues without a change!
Sign or token of some eldest nation
Here would make the strange land not so strange.
Time-forgotten, yea since time's creation,
Seem these borders where the sea-birds range.

2

Slowly, gladly, full of peace and wonder
Grows his heart who journeys here alone.
Earth and all its thoughts of earth sink under
Deep as deep in water sinks a stone.
Hardly knows it if the rollers thunder,
Hardly whence the lonely wind is blown.

3

Tall the plumage of the rush-flower tosses,
  Sharp and soft in many a curve and line
Gleam and glow the sea-coloured marsh-mosses,
  Salt and splendid from the circling brine.
Streak on streak of glimmering seashine crosses
  All the land sea-saturate as with wine.

4

Far, and far between, in divers orders,
  Clear grey steeples cleave the low grey sky;
Fast and firm as time-unshaken warders,
  Hearts made sure by faith, by hope made high.
These alone in all the wild sea-borders
  Fear no blast of days and nights that die.

5

All the land is like as one man's face is,
  Pale and troubled still with change of cares.
Doubt and death pervade her clouded spaces:
  Strength and length of life and peace are theirs;
Theirs alone amid these weary places,
  Seeing not how the wild world frets and fares.

6

Firm and fast where all is cloud that changes
  Cloud-clogged sunlight, cloud by sunlight thinned,
Stern and sweet, above the sand-hill ranges
  Watch the towers and tombs of men that sinned
Once, now calm as earth whose only change is
  Wind, and light, and wind, and cloud, and wind.

[…]

V

1

For the sea too seeks and rejoices,
  Gains and loses and gains,
And the joy of her heart's own choice is
  As ours, and as ours are her pains:
As the thoughts of our hearts are her voices,
  And as hers is the pulse of our veins.

2

Her fields that know not of dearth
  Nor lie for their fruit's sake fallow
Laugh large in the depth of their mirth:
  But inshore here in the shallow,
Embroiled with encumbrance of earth,
  Their skirts are turbid and yellow.

3

The grime of her greed is upon her,
  The sign of her deed is her soil;
As the earth's is her own dishonour,
  And corruption the crown of her toil:
She hath spoiled and devoured, and her honour
  Is this, to be shamed by her spoil.

4

But afar where pollution is none,
   Nor ensign of strife nor endeavour,
Where her heart and the sun's are one,
   And the soil of her sin comes never,
She is pure as the wind and the sun,
   And her sweetness endureth for ever.

From TRISTRAM OF LYONESSE (1882)

From Book 1

Iseult of Ireland aboard the Swallow, bound for Cornwall.

And sighing, she looked from wave to cloud about,
And even with that the full-grown feet of day
Sprang upright on the quivering water-way,
And his face burned against her meeting face
Most like a lover's thrilled with great love's grace
Whose glance takes fire and gives; the quick sea shone
And shivered like spread wings of angels blown
By the sun's breath before him; and a low
Sweet gale shook all the foam-flowers of thin snow
As into rainfall of sea-roses shed
Leaf by wild leaf on that green garden-bed
Which tempests till and sea-winds turn and plough:
For rosy and fiery round the running prow
Fluttered the flakes and feathers of the spray,
And bloomed like blossoms cast by God away
To waste on the ardent water; swift the moon
Withered to westward as a face in swoon
Death-stricken by glad tidings: and the height
Throbbed and the centre quivered with delight
And the depth quailed with passion as of love,
Till like the heart of some new-mated dove
Air, light, and wave seemed full of burning rest,
With motion as of one God's beating breast.

And her heart sprang in Iseult, and she drew
With all her spirit and life the sunrise through
And through her lips the keen triumphant air
Sea-scented, sweeter than land-roses were,
And through her eyes the whole rejoicing east
Sun-satisfied, and all the heaven at feast
Spread for the morning; and the imperious mirth
Of wind and light that moved upon the earth,
Making the spring, and all the fruitful might
And strong regeneration of delight
That swells the seedling leaf and sapling man,
Since the first life in the first world began
To burn and burgeon through void limbs and veins,
And the first love with sharp sweet procreant pains
To pierce and bring forth roses; yea, she felt
Through her own soul the sovereign morning melt,
And all the sacred passion of the sun;
And as the young clouds flamed and were undone
About him coming, touched and burnt away
In rosy ruin and yellow spoil of day,
The sweet veil of her body and corporal sense
Felt the dawn also cleave it, and incense
With light from inward and with effluent heat
The kindling soul through fleshly hands and feet.
And as the august great blossom of the dawn
Burst, and the full sun scarce from sea withdrawn
Seemed on the fiery water a flower afloat,
So as a fire the mighty morning smote
Throughout her, and incensed with the influent hour
Her whole soul's one great mystical red flower
Burst, and the bud of her sweet spirit broke
Rose-fashion, and the strong spring at a stroke
Thrilled, and was cloven, and from the full sheath came
The whole rose of the woman red as flame:
And all her Mayday blood as from a swoon
Flushed, and May rose up in her and was June.
So for a space her heart as heavenward burned:
Then with half summer in her eyes she turned,

And on her lips was April yet, and smiled,
As though the spirit and sense unreconciled
Shrank laughing back, and would not ere its hour
Let life put forth the irrevocable flower.

From Book 2

Iseult of Ireland is abducted by Sir Palamede and rescued by Sir Tristram.

And the king waking saw beside his head
That face yet passion-coloured, amorous red
From lips not his, and all that strange hair shed
Across the tissued pillows, fold on fold,
Innumerable, incomparable, all gold,
To fire men's eyes with wonder, and with love
Men's hearts; so shone its flowering crown above
The brows enwound with that imperial wreath,
And framed with fragrant radiance round the face beneath.
    And the king marvelled, seeing with sudden start
Her very glory, and said out of his heart;
"What have I done of good for God to bless
That all this he should give me, tress on tress,
All this great wealth and wondrous? Was it this
That in mine arms I had all night to kiss,
And mix with me this beauty? this that seems
More fair than heaven doth in some tired saint's dreams,
Being part of that same heaven? yea, more, for he,
Though loved of God so, yet but seems to see,
But to me sinful such great grace is given
That in mine hands I hold this part of heaven,
Not to mine eyes lent merely. Doth God make
Such things so godlike for man's mortal sake?
Have I not sinned, that in this fleshly life

Have made of her a mere man's very wife?"
    So the king mused and murmured; and she heard
The faint sound trembling of each breathless word,
And laughed into the covering of her hair.
    And many a day for many a month as fair
Slid over them like music; and as bright
Burned with love's offerings many a secret night.
And many a dawn and many a fiery noon
Blew prelude, when the horn's heart-kindling tune
Lit the live woods with sovereign sound of mirth
Before the mightiest huntsman hailed on earth
Lord of its lordliest pleasure, where he rode
Hard by her rein whose peerless presence glowed
Not as that white queen's of the virgin hunt
Once, whose crown-crescent braves the night-wind's brunt,
But with the sun for frontlet of a queenlier front.
For where the flashing of her face was turned
As lightning was the fiery light that burned
From eyes and brows enkindled more with speed
And rapture of the rushing of her steed
That once with only beauty; and her mouth
Was as a rose athirst that pants for drouth
Even while it laughs for pleasure of desire,
And all her heart was as a leaping fire.
Yet once more joy they took of woodland ways
Than came of all those flushed and fiery days
When the loud air was mad with life and sound,
Through many a dense green mile, of horn and hound
Before the king's hunt going along the wind,
And ere the timely leaves were changed or thinned,
Even in mid maze of summer. For the knight
Forth was once ridden toward some frontier fight
Against the lewd folk of the Christless lands
That warred with wild and intermittent hands
Against the king's north border; and there came
A knight unchristened yet of unknown name,
Swart Palamede, upon a secret quest,
To high Tintagel, and abode as guest

In likeness of a minstrel with the king.
Nor was there man could sound so sweet a string,
Save Tristram only, of all held best on earth.
And one loud eve, being full of wine and mirth,
Ere sunset left the walls and waters dark,
To that strange minstrel strongly swore King Mark,
By all that makes a knight's faith firm and strong,
That he for guerdon of his harp and song
Might crave and have his liking. Straight there came
Up the swart cheek a flash of swarthier flame
And the deep eyes fulfilled of glittering night
Laughed out in lightnings of triumphant light
As the grim harper spake: "O king, I crave
No gift of man that king may give to slave,
But this thy crowned queen only, this thy wife,
Whom yet unseen I loved, and set my life
On this poor chance to compass, even as here,
Being fairer famed than all save Guenevere."
Then as the noise of seaward storm that mocks
With roaring laughter from reverberate rocks
The cry from ships near shipwreck, harsh and high
Rose all the wrath and wonder in one cry
Through all the long roof's hollow depth and length
That hearts of strong men kindled in their strength
May speak in laughter lion-like, and cease,
Being wearied: only two men held their peace
And each glared hard on other: but King Mark
Spake first of these: "Man, though thy craft be dark
And thy mind evil that begat this thing,
Yet stands the word once plighted of a king
Fast: and albeit less evil it were for me
To give my life up than my wife, or be
A landless man crowned only with a curse,
Yet this in God's and all men's sight were worse,
To live soul-shamed a man of broken troth,
Abhorred of men as I abhor mine oath
Which yet I may forswear not." And he bowed
His head, and wept: and all men wept aloud,

Save one, that heard him weeping: but the queen
Wept not: and statelier yet than eyes had seen
That ever looked upon her queenly state
She rose, and in her eyes her heart was great
And full of wrath seen manifest and scorn
More strong than anguish to go thence forlorn
Of all men's comfort and her natural right.
And they went forth into the dawn of night.
Long by wild ways and clouded light they rode,
Silent; and fear less keen at heart abode
With Iseult than with Palamede: for awe
Constrained him, and the might of love's high law,
That can make lewd men loyal; and his heart
Yearned on her, if perchance with amourous art
And soothfast skill of very love he might
For courtesy find favour in her sight
And comfort of her mercies: for he wist
More grace might come of that sweet mouth unkissed
Than joy for violence done it, that should make
His name abhorred for shame's disloyal sake.
And in the stormy starlight clouds were thinned
And thickened by short gusts of changing wind
That panted like a sick man's fitful breath:
And like a moan of lions hurt to death
Came the sea's hollow noise along the night.
But ere its gloom from aught but foam had light
They halted, being aweary: and the knight
As reverently forbore her where she lay
As one that watched his sister's sleep till day.
Nor durst he kiss or touch her hand or hair
For love and shamefast pity, seeing how fair
She slept, and fenceless from the fitful air.
And shame at heart stung nigh to death desire,
But grief at heart burned in him like a fire
For hers and his own sorrowing sake, that had
Such grace for guerdon as makes glad men sad,
To have their will and want it. And the day
Sprang: and afar along the wild waste way

They heard the pulse and press of hurrying horse hoofs play:
And like the rushing of a ravenous flame
Whose wings make tempest of the darkness, came
Upon them headlong as in thunder borne
Forth of the darkness of the labouring morn
Tristram: and up forthright upon his steed
Leapt, as one blithe of battle, Palamede,
And mightily with shock of horse and man
They lashed together: and fair that fight began
As fair came up that sunrise: to and fro,
With knees nigh staggered and stout heads bent low
From each quick shock of spears on either side,
Reeled the strong steeds heavily, haggard-eyed
And heartened high with passion of their pride
As sheer the stout spears shocked again, and flew
Sharp-splintering: then, his sword as each knight drew,
They flashed and foined full royally, so long
That but to see so fair a strife and strong
A man might well have given out of his life
One year's void space forlorn of love or strife.
As when a bright north-easter, great of heart,
Scattering the strengths of squadrons, hurls apart
Ship from ship labouring violently, in such toil
As earns but ruin—with even so strong recoil
Back were the steeds hurled from the spear-shock, fain
And foiled of triumph: then with tightened rein
And stroke of spur, inveterate, either knight
Bore in again upon his foe with might,
Heart-hungry for the hot-mouthed feast of fight
And all athirst of mastery: but full soon
The jarring notes of that tempestuous tune
Fell, and its mighty music made of hands
Contending, clamorous through the loud waste lands,
Broke at once off; and shattered from his steed
Fell, as a mainmast ruining, Palamede,
Stunned: and those lovers left him where he lay,
And lightly through green lawns they rode away.
    There was a bower beyond man's eye more fair

Than ever summer dews and sunniest air
Fed full with rest and radiance till the boughs
Had wrought a roof as for a holier house
Than aught save love might breathe in; fairer far
Than keeps the sweet light back of moon and star
From high king's chambers: there might love and sleep
Divide for joy the darkling hours, and keep
With amorous alternation of sweet strife
The soft and secret ways of death and life
Made smooth for pleasure's feet to rest and run
Even from the moondawn to the kindling sun,
Made bright for passion's feet to run and rest
Between the midnight's and the morning's breast,
Where hardly though her happy head lie down
It may forget the hour that wove its crown;
Where hardly though her joyous limbs be laid
They may forget the mirth that midnight made.
And thither, ere sweet night had slain sweet day,
Iseult and Tristram took their wandering way,
And rested, and refreshed their hearts with cheer
In hunters' fashion of the woods; and here
More sweet it seemed, while this might be, to dwell
And take of all world's weariness farewell
Than reign of all world's lordship queen and king.
Nor here would time for three moon's changes bring
Sorrow nor thought of sorrow; but sweet earth
Fostered them like her babes of eldest birth,
Reared warm in pathless woods and cherished well.
And the sun sprang above the sea and fell,
And the stars rose and sank upon the sea;
And outlaw-like, in forest wise and free,
The rising and the setting of their lights
Found those twain dwelling all those days and nights.
And under change of sun and star and moon
Flourished and fell the chaplets woven of June,
And fair through fervours of the deepening sky
Panted and passed the hours that lit July,
And each day blessed them out of heaven above,

And each night crowned them with the crown of love.
Nor till the might of August overhead
Weighed on the world was yet one roseleaf shed
Of all their joy's warm coronal, nor aught
Touched them in passing ever with a thought
That ever this might end on any day
Or any night not love them where they lay;
But like a babbling tale of barren breath
Seemed all report and rumour held of death,
And a false bruit the legend tear-impearled
That such a thing as change was in the world.
And each bright song upon his lips that came,
Mocking the powers of change and death by name,
Blasphemed their bitter godhead, and defied
Time, though clothed round with ruin as kings with pride,
To blot the glad life out of love: and she
Drank lightly deep of his philosophy
In that warm wine of amorous words which is
Sweet with all truths of all philosophies.
For well he wist all subtle ways of song,
And in his soul the secret eye was strong
That burns in meditation, till bright words
Break flamelike forth as notes from fledgeling birds
That feel the soul speak through them of the spring.
So fared they night and day as queen and king
Crowned of a kingdom wide as day and night.
Nor ever cloudlet swept or swam in sight
Across the darkling depths of their delight
Whose stars no skill might number, nor man's art
Sound the deep stories of its heavenly heart.
Till, even for wonder that such life should live,
Desires and dreams of what death's self might give
Would touch with tears and laughter and wild speech
The lips and eyes of passion, fain to reach,
Beyond all bourne of time or trembling sense,
The verge of love's last possible eminence.
Out of the heaven that storm nor shadow mars,
Deep from the starry depth beyond the stars,

A yearning ardour without scope or name
Fell on them, and the bright night's breath of flame
Shot fire into their kisses; and like fire
The lit dews lightened on the leaves, as higher
Night's heart beat on toward midnight. Far and fain
Somewhiles the soft rush of rejoicing rain
Solaced the darkness, and from steep to steep
Of heaven they saw the sweet sheet lightning leap
And laugh its heart out in a thousand smiles,
When the clear sea for miles on glimmering miles
Burned as though dawn were strewn abroad astray,
Or, showering out of heaven, all heaven's array
Had paven instead the waters: fain and far
Somewhiles the burning love of star for star
Spake words that love might wellnigh seem to hear
In such deep hours as turn delight to fear
Sweet as delight's self ever. So they lay
Tranced once, nor watched along the fiery bay
The shine of summer darkness palpitate and play.
She had nor sight nor voice; her swooning eyes
Knew not if night or light were in the skies;
Across her beauty sheer the moondawn shed
Its light as on a thing as white and dead;
Only with stress of soft fierce hands she prest
Between the throbbing blossoms of her breast
His ardent face, and through his hair her breath
Went quivering as when life is hard on death;
And with strong trembling fingers she strained fast
His head into her bosom; till at last
Satiate with sweetness of that burning bed,
His eyes afire with tears, he raised his head
And laughed into her lips; and all his heart
Filled hers; then face from face fell, and apart
Each hung on each with panting lips, and felt
Sense into sense and spirit in spirit melt.
"Hast thou no sword? I would not live till day;
O love, this night and we must pass away,
It must die soon, and let not us die late."

"Take then my sword and slay me; nay, but wait
Till day be risen; what, wouldst thou think to die
Before the light take hold upon the sky?"
"Yea, love; for how shall we have twice, being twain,
This very night of love's most rapturous reign?
Live thou and have thy day, and year by year
Be great, but what shall I be? Slay me here;
Let me die not when love lies dead, but now
Strike through my heart: nay, sweet, what heart hast thou?
Is it so much I ask thee, and spend my breath
In asking? nay, thou knowest it is but death.
Hadst thou true heart to love me, thou wouldst give
This: but for hate's sake thou wilt let me live."
Here he caught up her lips with his, and made
The wild prayer silent in her heart that prayed,
And strained her to him till all her faint breath sank
And her bright light limbs palpitated and shrank
And rose and fluctuated as flowers in rain
That bends them and they tremble and rise again
And heave and straighten and quiver all through with bliss
And turn afresh their mouths up for a kiss,
Amorous, athirst of that sweet influent love;
So, hungering towards his hovering lips above,
Her red-rose mouth yearned silent, and her eyes
Closed, and flashed after, as through June's darkest skies
The divine heartbeats of the deep live light
Make open and shut the gates of the outer night.
Long lay they still, subdued with love, nor knew
If cloud or light changed colour as it grew,
If star or moon beheld them; if above
The heaven of night waxed fiery with their love,
Or earth beneath were moved at heart and root
To burn as they, to burn and bring forth fruit
Unseasonable for love's sake; if tall trees
Bowed, and close flowers yearned open, and the breeze
Failed and fell silent as a flame that fails:
And all that hour unheard the nightingales
Clamoured, and all the woodland soul was stirred,

And depth and height were one great song unheard,
As though the world caught music and took fire
From the instant heart alone of their desire.
    So sped their night of nights between them: so,
For all fears past and shadows, shine and snow,
That one pure hour all-golden where they lay
Made their life perfect and their darkness day.
And warmer waved its harvest yet to reap,
Till in the lovely fight of love and sleep
At length had sleep the mastery; and the dark
Was lit with soft live gleams they might not mark,
Fleet butterflies, each like a dead flower's ghost,
White, blue, and sere leaf-coloured; but the most
White as the sparkle of snow-flowers in the sun
Ere with his breath they lie at noon undone
Whose kiss devours their tender beauty, and leaves
But raindrops on the grass and sere thin leaves
That were engraven with traceries of the snow
Flowerwise ere any flower of earth's would blow;
So swift they sprang and sank, so sweet and light
They swam the deep dim breathless air of night.
Now on her rose-white amorous breast half bare,
Now on her slumberous love-dishevelled hair,
The white wings lit and vanished, and afresh
Lit soft as snow lights on her snow-soft flesh,
On hand or throat or shoulder; and she stirred
Sleeping, and spake some tremulous bright word,
And laughed upon some dream too sweet for truth,
Yet not so sweet as very love and youth
That there had charmed her eyes to sleep at last.
Nor woke they till the perfect night was past,
And the soft sea thrilled with blind hope of light.
But ere the dusk had well the sun in sight
He turned and kissed her eyes awake and said,
Seeing earth and water neither quick nor dead
And twilight hungering toward the day to be,
"As the dawn loves the sunlight I love thee."
And even as rays with cloudlets in the skies

Confused in brief love's bright contentious wise,
Sleep strove with sense rekindling in her eyes;
And as the flush of birth scarce overcame
The pale pure pearl of unborn light with flame
Soft as may touch the rose's heart with shame
To break not all reluctant out of bud,
Stole up her sleeping cheek her waking blood;
And with the lovely laugh of love that takes
The whole soul prisoner ere the whole sense wakes,
Her lips for love's sake bade love's will be done.
And all the sea lay subject to the sun.

From Book 3

Sir Tristram, exiled in Brittany, encounters Iseult of the Fair Hands.

And now that after many a season spent
In barren ways and works of banishment,
Toil of strange fights and many a fruitless field,
Ventures of quest and vigils under shield,
He came back to the strait of sundering sea
That parts green Cornwall from grey Brittany,
Where dwelt the high king's daughter of the lands,
Iseult, named alway from her fair white hands,
She looked on him and loved him; but being young
Made shamefastness a seal upon her tongue,
And on her heart, that none might hear its cry,
Set the sweet signet of humility.
Yet when he came a stranger in her sight,
A banished man and weary, no such knight
As when the Swallow dipped her bows in foam
Steered singing that imperial Iseult home,
This maiden with her sinless sixteen years
Full of sweet thoughts and hopes that played at fears

Cast her eyes on him but in courteous wise,
And lo, the man's face burned upon her eyes
As though she had turned them on the naked sun:
And through her limbs she felt sweet passion run
As fire that flowed down from her face, and beat
Soft through stirred veins on even to her hands and feet
As all her body were one heart on flame,
Athrob with love and wonder and sweet shame.
And when he spake there sounded in her ears
As 'twere a song out of the graves of years
Heard, and again forgotten, and again
Remembered with a rapturous pulse of pain.
But as the maiden mountain snow sublime
Takes the first sense of April's trembling time
Soft on a brow that burns not though it blush
To feel the sunrise hardly half aflush,
So took her soul the sense of change, nor thought
That more than maiden love was more than nought.
Her eyes went hardly after him, her cheek
Grew scarce a goodlier flower to hear him speak,
Her bright mouth no more trembled than a rose
May for the least wind's breathless sake that blows
Too soft to sue save for a sister's kiss,
And if she sighed in sleep she knew not this.
Yet in her heart hovered the thoughts of things
Past, that with lighter or with heavier wings
Beat round about her memory, till it burned
With grief that brightened and with hope that yearned,
Seeing him so great and sad, not knowing what fate
Had bowed and crowned a head so sad and great.
Nor might she guess but little, first or last,
Though all her heart so hung upon his past,
Of what so bowed him for what sorrow's sake:
For scarce of aught at any time he spake
That from his own land oversea had sent
His lordly life to barren banishment.
Yet still or soft or keen remembrance clung
Close round her of the least word from his tongue

That fell by chance of courtesy, to greet
With grace of tender thanks to her pity, sweet
As running streams to men's way-wearied feet.
And when between strange words her name would fall,
Suddenly straightway to that lure's recall
Back would his heart bound as the falconer's bird,
And tremble and bow down before the word.
"Iseult"——and all the cloudlike world grew flame,
And all his heart flashed lightning at her name;
"Iseult"——and all the wan waste weary skies
Shone as his queen's own love-enkindled eyes.
And seeing the bright blood in his face leap up
As red wine mantling in a royal cup
To hear the sudden sweetness of the sound
Ring, but ere well his heart had time to bound
His cheek would change, and grief bowed down his head,
"Haply," the girl's heart, though she spake not, said,
"This name of mine was worn of one long dead,
Some sister that he loved:" and therewithal
Would pity bring her heart more deep in thrall.
But once, when winds about the world made mirth,
And March held revel hard on April's birth
Till air and sea were jubilant as earth,
Delight and doubt in sense and soul began,
And yearning of the maiden toward the man,
Harping on high before her: for his word
Was fire that kindled in her heart that heard,
And alway through the rhymes reverberate came
The virginal soft burden of her name.
And ere the full song failed upon her ear
Joy strove within her till it cast out fear,
And all her heart was as his harp, and rang
Swift music, made of hope whose birthnote sprang
Bright in the blood that kindled as he sang.

"Stars know not how we call them, nor may flowers
Know by what happy name the hovering hours
  Baptize their new-born heads with dew and flame:

And Love, adored of all time as of ours,
Iseult, knew nought for ages of his name.

"With many tongues men called on him, but he
Wist not which word of all might worthiest be
To sound for ever in his ear the same,
Till heart of man might hear and soul might see,
Iseult, the radiance ringing from thy name.

"By many names men called him, as the night
By many a name calls many a starry light,
Her several sovereigns of dividual fame;
But day by one name only calls aright,
Iseult, the sun that bids men praise his name.

"In many a name of man his name soared high
And song shone round it soaring, till the sky
Rang rapture, and the world's fast-founded frame
Trembled with sense of triumph, even as I,
Iseult, with sense of worship at thy name.

"In many a name of woman smiled his power
Incarnate, as all summer in a flower,
Till winter bring forgetfulness or shame:
But thine, the keystone of his topless tower,
Iseult, is one with Love's own lordliest name.

"Iseult my love, Iseult my queen twice crowned,
In thee my death, in thee my life lies bound:
Names are there yet that all men's hearts acclaim,
But Love's own heart rings answer to the sound,
Iseult, that bids it bow before thy name."

There ceased his voice yearning upon the word,
Struck with strong passion dumb: but she that heard
Quailed to the heart, and trembled ere her eyes
Durst let the loving light within them rise,
And yearn on his for answer: yet at last,
Albeit not all her fear was overpast,
Hope, kindling even the frost of fear apace

With sweet fleet bloom and breath of gradual grace,
Flushed in the changing roses of her face.
And ere the strife took truce of white with red,
Or joy for soft shame's sake durst lift up head,
Something she would and would not fain have said,
And wist not what the fluttering word would be,
But rose and reached forth to him her hand: and he,
Heart-stricken, bowed his head and dropped his knee,
And on her fragrant hand his lips were fire;
And their two hearts were as one trembling lyre
Touched by the keen wind's kiss with brief desire
And music shuddering at its own delight.
So dawned the moonrise of their marriage night.

Book 5

Iseult at Tintagel.

But that same night in Cornwall oversea
Couched at Queen Iseult's hand, against her knee,
With keen kind eyes that read her whole heart's pain
Fast at wide watch lay Tristram's hound Hodain,
The goodliest and the mightiest born on earth,
That many a forest day of fiery mirth
Had plied his craft before them; and the queen
Cherished him, even for those dim years between,
More than of old in those bright months far flown
When ere a blast of Tristram's horn was blown
Each morning as the woods rekindled, ere
Day gat full empire of the glimmering air,
Delight of dawn would quicken him, and fire
Spring and pant in his breath with bright desire
To be among the dewy ways on quest:
But now perforce at restless-hearted rest

He chafed through days more barren than the sand,
Soothed hardly but soothed only with her hand,
Though fain to fawn thereon and follow, still
With all his heart and all his loving will
Desiring one divided from his sight,
For whose lost sake dawn was as dawn of night
And noon as night's noon in his eyes was dark.
But in the halls far under sat King Mark,
Feasting, and full of cheer, with heart uplift,
As on the night that harper gat his gift:
And music revelled on the fitful air,
And songs came floated up the festal stair,
And muffled roar of wassail, where the king
Took heart from wine-cups and the quiring string
Till all his cold thin veins rejoiced and ran
Strong as with lifeblood of a kinglier man.
But the queen shut from sound her wearied ears,
Shut her sad eyes from sense of aught save tears,
And wrung her hair with soft fierce hands, and prayed:
    "O God, God born of woman, of a maid,
Christ, once in flesh of thine own fashion clad;
O very love, so glad in heaven and sad
On earth for earth's sake alway; since thou art
Pure only, I only impure of spirit and heart,
Since thou for sin's sake and the bitter doom
Didst as a veil put on a virgin's womb,
I that am none, and cannot hear or see
Or shadow or likeness or a sound of thee
Far off, albeit with man's own speech and face
Thou shine yet and thou speak yet, showing forth grace—
Ah me! grace only shed on souls that are
Lit and led forth of shadow by thy star—
Alas! to these men only grace, to these,
Lord, whom thy love draws Godward, to thy knees—
I, can I draw thee me-ward, can I seek,
Who love thee not, to love me? seeing how weak,
Lord, all this little love I bear thee is,
And how much is my strong love more than this,

My love that I love man with, that I bear
Him sinning through me sinning? wilt thou care,
God, for this love, if love be any, alas,
In me to give thee, though long since there was,
How long, when I too, Lord, was clean, even I,
That now am unclean till the day I die—
Haply by burning, harlot-fashion, made
A horror in all hearts of wife and maid,
Hateful, not knowing if ever in these mine eyes
Shone any light of thine in any wise
Or this were love at all that I bore thee?"
    And the night spake, and thundered on the sea,
Ravening aloud for ruin of lives: and all
The bastions of the main cliff's northward wall
Rang response out from all their deepening length,
As the east wind girded up his godlike strength
And hurled in hard against that high-towered hold
The fleeces of the flock that knows no fold,
The rent white shreds of shattering storm: but she
Heard not nor heeded wind or storming sea,
Knew not if night were mild or mad with wind.
    "Yea, though deep lips and tender hair be thinned,
Though cheek wither, brow fade, and bosom wane,
Shall I change also from this heart again
To maidenhood of heart and holiness?
Shall I more love thee, Lord, or love him less—
Ah miserable! though spirit and heart be rent,
Shall I repent, Lord God? shall I repent?
Nay, though thou slay me! for herein I am blest,
That as I loved him yet I love him best—
More than mine own soul or thy love or thee,
Though thy love save and my love save not me.
Blest am I beyond women ever herein,
That beyond all born women is my sin,
And perfect my transgression: that above
All offerings of all others is my love,
Who have chosen it only, and put away for this
Thee, and my soul's hope, Saviour, of the kiss

Wherewith thy lips make welcome all thine own
When in them life and death are overthrown;
The sinless lips that seal the death of sin,
The kiss wherewith their dumb lips touched begin
Singing in heaven.
"Where we shall never, love,
Never stand up nor sing! for God above
Knows us, how too much more than God to me
Thy sweet love is, my poor love is to thee!
Dear, dost thou see now, dost thou hear to-night
Sleeping, my waste wild speech, my face worn white,
—Speech once heard soft by thee, face once kissed red!—
In such a dream as when men see their dead
And know not if they know if dead these be?
Ah love, are thy days my days, and to thee
Are all nights like as my nights? does the sun
Grieve thee? art thou soul-sick till day be done,
And weary till day rises? is thine heart
Full of dead things as mine is? Nay, thou art
Man, with man's strength and praise and pride of life,
No bondwoman, no queen, no loveless wife
That would be shamed albeit she had not sinned."
And swordlike was the sound of the iron wind,
And as a breaking battle was the sea.
"Nay, Lord, I pray thee let him love not me,
Love me not any more, nor like me die,
And be no more than such a thing as I.
Turn his heart from me, lest my love too lose
Thee as I lose thee, and his fair soul refuse
For my sake thy fair heaven, and as I fell
Fall, and be mixed with my soul and with hell.
Let me die rather, and only; let me be
Hated of him so he be loved of thee,
Lord: for I would not have him with me there
Out of thy light and love in the unlit air,
Out of thy sight in the unseen hell where I
Go gladly, going alone, so thou on high
Lift up his soul and love him—Ah, Lord, Lord,

Shalt thou love as I love him? she that poured
From the alabaster broken at thy feet
An ointment very precious, not so sweet
As that poured likewise forth before thee then
From the rehallowed heart of Magdalen,
From a heart broken, yearning like the dove,
An ointment very precious which is love—
Couldst thou being holy and God, and sinful she,
Love her indeed as surely she loved thee?
Nay, but if not, then as we sinners can
Let us love still in the old sad wise of man.
For with less love than my love, having had
Mine, though God love him he shall not be glad.
And with such love as my love, I wot well,
He shall not lie disconsolate in hell:
Sad only as souls for utter love's sake be
Here, and a little sad, perchance, for me—
Me happy, me more glad than God above,
In the utmost hell whose fires consume not love!
For in the waste ways emptied of the sun
He would say—'Dear, thy place is void, and one
Weeps among angels for thee, with his face
Veiled, saying, *O sister, how thy chosen place*
Stands desolate, that God made fair for thee!
Is heaven not sweeter, and we thy brethren, we
Fairer than love on earth and life in hell?'
And I—with me were all things then not well?
Should I not answer—'O love, be well content;
Look on me, and behold if I repent.'
This were more to me than an angel's wings.
Yea, many men pray God for many things,
But I pray that this only thing may be."
    And as a full field charging was the sea,
And as the cry of slain men was the wind.
    "Yea, since I surely loved him, and he sinned
Surely, though not as my sin his be black,
God, give him to me—God, God, give him back!
For now how should we live in twain or die?

I am he indeed, thou knowest, and he is I.
Not man and woman several as we were,
But one thing with one life and death to bear.
How should one love his own soul overmuch?
And time is long since last I felt the touch,
The sweet touch of my lover, hand and breath,
In such delight as puts delight to death,
Burn my soul through, till the spirit and soul and sense,
In the sharp grasp of the hour, with violence
Died, and again through pangs of violent birth
Lived, and laughed out with refluent might of mirth;
Laughed each on other and shuddered into one,
As a cloud shuddering dies into the sun.
Ah, sense is that or spirit, soul or flesh,
That only love lulls or awakes afresh?
Ah, sweet is that or bitter, evil or good,
That very love allays not as he would?
Nay, truth is this or vanity, that gives
No love assurance when love dies or lives?
This that my spirit is wrung withal, and yet
No surelier knows if haply thine forget,
Thou that my spirit is wrung for, nor can say
Love is not in thee dead as yesterday?
Dost thou feel, thou, this heartbeat whence my heart
Would send thee word what life is mine apart,
And know by keen response what life is thine?
Dost thou not hear one cry of all of mine?
O Tristram's heart, have I no part in thee?"
    And all her soul was as the breaking sea,
And all her heart anhungered as the wind.
    "Dost thou repent thee of the sin we sinned?
Dost thou repent thee of the days and nights
That kindled and that quenched for us their lights,
The months that feasted us with all their hours,
The ways that breathed of us in all their flowers,
The dells that sang of us with all their doves?
Dost thou repent thee of the wildwood loves?
Is thine heart changed, and hallowed? art thou grown

God's, and not mine? Yet, though my heart make moan,
Fain would my soul give thanks for thine, if thou
Be saved—yea, fain praise God, and knows not how.
How should it know thanksgiving? nay, or learn
Aught of the love wherewith thine own should burn,
God's that should cast out as an evil thing
Mine? yea, what hand or prayer have I to cling,
What heart to prophesy, what spirit of sight
To strain insensual eyes toward increate light,
Who look but back on life wherein I sinned?"
  And all their past came wailing in the wind,
And all their future thundered in the sea.
  "But if my soul might touch the time to be,
If hand might handle now or eye behold
My life and death ordained me from of old,
Life palpable, compact of blood and breath,
Visible, present, naked, very death,
Should I desire to know before the day
These that I know not, nor is man that may?
For haply, seeing, my heart would break for fear,
And my soul timeless cast its load off here,
Its load of life too bitter, love too sweet,
And fall down shamed and naked at thy feet,
God, who wouldst take no pity of it, nor give
One hour back, one of all its hours to live
Clothed with my mortal body, that once more,
Once, on this reach of barren beaten shore,
This stormy strand of life, ere sail were set,
Had haply felt love's arms about it yet—
Yea, ere death's bark put off to seaward, might
With many a grief have bought me one delight
That then should know me never. Ah, what years
Would I endure not, filled up full with tears,
Bitter like blood and dark as dread of death,
To win one amorous hour of mingling breath,
One fire-eyed hour and sunnier than the sun,
For all these nights and days like nights but one?
One hour of heaven born once, a stormless birth,

For all these windy, weary hours of earth?
One, but one hour from birth of joy to death,
For all these hungering hours of feverish breath?
And I should lose this, having died and sinned."
  And as a man's anguish clamouring cried the wind,
And as God's anger answering rang the sea.
  "And yet what life—Lord God, what life for me
Has thy strong wrath made ready? Dost thou think
How lips whose thirst hath only tears to drink
Grow grey for grief untimely? Dost thou know,
O happy God, how men wax weary of woe—
Yea, for their wrong's sake that thine hand hath done
Come even to hate thy semblance in the sun?
Turn back from dawn and noon and all thy light
To make their souls one with the soul of night?
Christ, if thou hear yet or have eyes to see,
Thou that hadst pity, and hast no pity on me,
Know'st thou no more, as in this life's sharp span,
What pain thou hadst on earth, what pain hath man?
Hast thou no care, that all we suffer yet?
What help is ours of thee if thou forget?
What profit have we though thy blood were given,
Not love but hate, thou bitter God and strange,
Whose heart as man's heart hath grown cold with change,
Not love but hate thou showest us that have sinned."
  And like a world's cry shuddering was the wind,
And like a God's voice threatening was the sea.
  "Nay, Lord, for thou wast gracious; nay, in thee
No change can come with time or varying fate,
No tongue bid thine be less compassionate,
No sterner eye rebuke for mercy thine,
No sin put out thy pity—no, not mine.
Thou knowest us, Lord, thou knowest us, all we are,
He, and the soul that hath his soul for star:
Thou knowest as I know, Lord, how much more worth
Than all souls clad and clasped about with earth,
But most of all, God, how much more than I,
Is this man's soul that surely shall not die.

What righteousness, what judgment, Lord most high,
Were this, to bend a brow of doom as grim
As threats me, the adulterous wife, on him?
There lies none other nightly by his side:
He hath not sought, he shall not seek a bride.
For as God sunders earth from heaven above,
So far was my love born beneath his love.
I loved him as the sea-wind loves the sea,
To rend and ruin it only and waste: but he,
As the sea loves a sea-bird loved he me,
To foster and uphold my tired life's wing,
And bounteously beneath me spread forth spring,
A springtide space whereon to float or fly,
A world of happy water, whence the sky
Glowed goodlier, lightening from so glad a glass,
Than with its own light only. Now, alas!
Cloud hath come down and clothed it round with storm,
And gusts and fits of eddying winds deform
The feature of its glory. Yet be thou,
God, merciful: nay, show but justice now,
And let the sin in him that scarce was his
Stand expiated with exile: and be this
The price for him, the atonement this, that I
With all the sin upon me live, and die
With all thy wrath on me that most have sinned."
    And like man's heart relenting sighed the wind,
And as God's wrath subsiding sank the sea.
    "But if such grace be possible—if it be
Not sin more strange than all sins past, and worse
Evil, that cries upon thee for a curse,
To pray such prayers from such a heart, do thou
Hear, and make wide thine hearing toward me now;
Let not my soul and his for ever dwell
Sundered: though doom keep always heaven and hell
Irreconcilable, infinitely apart,
Keep not in twain for ever heart and heart
That once, albeit by not thy law, were one;
Let this be not thy will, that this be done.

Let all else, all thou wilt of evil, be,
But no doom, none, dividing him and me."
    By this was heaven stirred eastward, and there came
Up the rough ripple a labouring light like flame;
And dawn, sore trembling still and grey with fear,
Looked hardly forth, a face of heavier cheer
Than one which grief or dread yet half enshrouds,
Wild-eyed and wan, across the cleaving clouds.
And Iseult, worn with watch long held on pain,
Turned, and her eye lit on the hound Hodain,
And all her heart went out in tears: and he
Laid his kind head along her bended knee,
Till round his neck her arms went hard, and all
The night past from her as a chain might fall:
But yet the heart within her, half undone,
Wailed, and was loth to let her see the sun.
    And ere full day brought heaven and earth to flower,
Far thence, a maiden in a marriage bower,
That moment, hard by Tristram, oversea,
Woke with glad eyes Iseult of Brittany.

From Book 9

Tristram, dying in Brittany, sends Ganhardine to bring Iseult of Ireland from Cornwall.

Three dim days through, three slumberless nights long,
Perplexed at dawn, oppressed at evensong,
The strong man's soul now sealed indeed with pain,
And all its springs half dried with drought, had lain
Prisoner within the fleshly dungeon-dress
Sore chafed and wasted with its weariness.
And fain it would have found the star, and fain
Made this funereal prison-house of pain

A watch-tower whence its eyes might sweep, and see
If any place for any hope might be
Beyond the hells and heavens of sleep and strife,
Or any light at all of any life
Beyond the dense false darkness woven above,
And could not, lacking grace to look on love,
And in the third night's dying hour he spake,
Seeing scarce the seals that bound the dayspring break
And scarce the daystar burn above the sea:
"O Ganhardine, my brother true to me,
I charge thee by those nights and days we knew
No great while since in England, by the dew
That bathed those nights with blessing, and the fire
That thrilled those days as music thrills a lyre,
Do now for me perchance the last good deed
That ever love may crave or life may need
Ere love lay life in ashes: take to thee
My ship that shows aloft against the sea
Carved on her stem the semblance of a swan,
And ere the waves at even again wax wan
Pass, if it may be, to my lady's land,
And give this ring into her secret hand,
And bid her think how hard on death I lie,
And fain would look upon her face and die.
But as a merchant's laden be the bark
With royal ware for fraughtage, that King Mark
May take for toll thereof some costly thing;
And when this gift finds grace before the king,
Choose forth a cup, and put therein my ring
Where sureliest only of one it may be seen,
And bid her handmaid bear it to the queen
For earnest of thine homage: then shall she
Fear, and take counsel privily with thee,
To know what errand there is thine from me
And what my need in secret of her sight.
But make thee two sails, one like sea-foam white
To spread for signal if thou bring her back,
And if she come not see the sail be black,

That I may know or ever thou take land
If these my lips may die upon her hand
Or hers may never more be mixed with mine."
And his heart quailed for grief in Ganhardine,
Hearing; and all his brother bade he swore
Surely to do, and straight fare forth from shore.
But the white-handed Iseult hearkening heard
All, and her heart waxed hot, and every word
Thereon seemed graven and printed in her thought
As lines with fire and molten iron wrought.
And hard within her heavy heart she cursed
Both, and her life was turned to fiery thirst,
And all her soul was hunger, and its breath
Of hope and life a blast of raging death.
For only in hope of evil was her life.
So bitter burned within the unchilded wife
A virgin lust for vengeance, and such hate
Wrought in her now the fervent work of fate.
Then with a south-west wind the Swan set forth
And over wintering waters bore to north,
And round the wild land's windy westward end
Up the blown channel bade her bright way bend
East on toward high Tintagel: where at dark
Landing, fair welcome found they of King Mark,
And Ganhardine with Brangwain as of old
Spake, and she took the cup of chiselled gold
Wherein lay secret Tristram's trothplight ring,
And bare it unbeholden of the king
Even to her lady's hand, which hardly took
A gift whereon a queen's eyes well might look,
With grace forlorn of weary gentleness.
But, seeing, her life leapt in her, keen to guess
The secret of the symbol: and her face
Flushed bright with blood whence all its grief-worn grace
Took fire and kindled to the quivering hair.
And in the dark soft hour of starriest air
Thrilled through with sense of midnight, when the world
Feels the wide wings of sleep about it furled,

Down stole the queen, deep-muffled to her wan
Mute restless lips, and came where yet the Swan
Swung fast at anchor: whence by starlight she
Hoised snowbright sails, and took the glimmering sea.
But all the long night long more keen and sore
His wound's grief waxed in Tristram evermore,
And heavier always hung his heart asway
Between dim fear and clouded hope of day.
And still with face and heart at silent strife
Beside him watched the maiden called his wife,
Patient, and spake not save when scarce he spake,
Murmuring with sense distraught and spirit awake
Speech bitterer than the words thereof were sweet:
And hatred thrilled her to the hands and feet,
Listening: for alway back reiterate came
The passionate faint burden of her name.
Nor ever through the labouring lips astir
Came any word of any thought of her.
But the soul wandering struggled and clung hard
Only to dreams of joy in Joyous Gard
Or wildwood nights beside the Cornish strand,
Or Merlin's holier sleep here hard at hand
Wrapped round with deep soft spells in dim Broceliande.
And with such thirst as joy's drained wine-cup leaves
When fear to hope as hope to memory cleaves
His soul desired the dewy sense of leaves,
The soft green smell of thickets drenched with dawn.
The faint slot kindling on the fiery lawn
As day's first hour made keen the spirit again
That lured and spurred on quest his hound Hodain,
The breeze, the bloom, the splendour and the sound,
That stung like fire the hunter and the hound,
The pulse of wind, the passion of the sea,
The rapture of the woodland: then would he
Sigh, and as one that fain would all be dead
Heavily turn his heavy-laden head
Back, and close eyes for comfort, finding none.
And fain he would have died or seen the sun,

Being sick at heart of darkness: yet afresh
Began the long strong strife of spirit and flesh
And branching pangs of thought whose branches bear
The bloodred fruit whose core is black, despair.
And the wind slackened and again grew great,
Palpitant as men's pulses palpitate
Between the flowing and ebbing tides of fate
That wash their lifelong waifs of weal and woe
Through night and light and twilight to and fro.
Now as a pulse of hope its heartbeat throbbed,
Now like one stricken shrank and sank and sobbed,
Then, yearning as with child of death, put forth
A wail that filled the night up south and north
With woful sound of waters: and he said,
"So might the wind wail if the world were dead
And its wings wandered over nought but sea.
I would I knew she would not come to me,
For surely she will come not: then should I,
Once knowing I shall not look upon her, die.
I knew not life could so long breathe such breath
As I do. Nay, what grief were this, if death,
The sole sure friend of whom the whole world saith
He lies not, nor hath ever this been said,
That death would heal not grief—if death were dead
And all ways closed whence grief might pass with life!"
    Then softly spake his watching virgin wife
Out of her heart, deep down below her breath:
"Fear not but death shall come—and after death
Judgment." And he that heard not answered her,
Saying—"Ah, but one there was, if truth not err,
For true men's trustful tongues have said it—one
Whom these mine eyes knew living while the sun
Looked yet upon him, and mine own ears heard
The deep sweet sound once of his godlike word—
Who sleeps and dies not, but with soft live breath
Takes always all the deep delight of death,
Through love's gift of a woman: but for me
Love's hand is not the hand of Nimue,

Love's word no still smooth murmur of the dove,
No kiss of peace for me the kiss of love.
Nor, whatsoe'er thy life's love ever give,
Dear, shall it ever bid me sleep or live;
Nor from thy brows and lips and living breast
As from his Nimue's shall my soul take rest;
Not rest but unrest hath our long love given—
Unrest on earth that wins not rest in heaven.
What rest may we take ever? what have we
Had ever more of peace than has the sea?
Has not our life been as a wind that blows
Through lonelier lands than rear the wild white rose
That each year sees requickened, but for us
Time once and twice hath here or there done thus
And left the next year following empty and bare?
What rose hath our last year's rose left for heir,
What wine our last year's vintage? and to me
More were one fleet forbidden sense of thee,
One perfume of thy present grace, one thought
Made truth one hour, ere all mine hours be nought,
One very word, breath, look, sign, touch of hand,
Than all the green leaves in Broceliande
Full of sweet sound, full of sweet wind and sun;
O God, thou knowest I would no more but one,
I would no more but once more ere I die
Find thus much mercy. Nay, but then were I
Happier than he whom there thy grace hath found,
For thine it must be, this that wraps him round,
Thine only, albeit a fiend's force gave him birth,
Thine that has given him heritage on earth
Of slumber-sweet eternity to keep
Fast in soft hold of everliving sleep.
Happier were I, more sinful man, than he,
Whom one love-worthier then than Nimue
Should with a breath make blest among the dead."
　And the wan wedded maiden answering said,
Soft as hate speaks within itself apart:
"Surely ye shall not, ye that rent mine heart,

Being one in sin, in punishment be twain."
And the great knight that heard not spake again
And sighed, but sweet thought of sweet things gone by
Kindled with fire of joy the very sigh
And touched it through with rapture: "Ay, this were
How much more than the sun and sunbright air,
How much more than the springtide, how much more
Than sweet strong sea-wind quickening wave and shore
With one divine pulse of continuous breath,
If she might kiss me with the kiss of death,
And make the light of life by death's look dim!"
And the white wedded virgin answered him,
Inwardly, wan with hurt no herb makes whole:
"Yea, surely, ye whose sin hath slain my soul,
Surely your own souls shall have peace in death
And pass with benediction in their breath
And blessing given of mine their sin hath slain."
And Tristram with sore yearning spake again,
Saying: "Yea, might this thing once be, how should I,
With all my soul made one thanksgiving, die,
And pass before what judgment-seat may be,
And cry, 'Lord, now do all thou wilt with me,
Take all thy fill of justice, work thy will;
Though all thy heart of wrath have all its fill,
My heart of suffering shall endure, and say,
For that thou gavest me living yesterday
I bless thee though thou curse me.' Ay, and well
Might one cast down into the gulf of hell,
Remembering this, take heart and thank his fate—
That God, whose doom now scourges him with hate,
Once, in the wild and whirling world above,
Bade mercy kiss his dying lips with love.
But if this come not, then he doth me wrong.
For what hath love done, all this long life long
That death should trample down his poor last prayer
Who prays not for forgiveness? Though love were
Sin dark as hate, have we not here that sinned
Suffered? has that been less than wintry wind

Wherewith our love lies blasted? O mine own,
O mine and no man's yet save mine alone,
Iseult! what ails thee that I lack so long
All of thee, all things thine for which I long?
For more than watersprings to shadeless sands,
More to me were the comfort of her hands
Touched once, and more than rays that set and rise
The glittering arrows of her glorious eyes,
More to my sense than fire to dead cold air
The wind and light and odour of her hair,
More to my soul than summer's to the south
The mute clear music of her amorous mouth,
And to my heart's heart more than heaven's great rest
The fullness of the fragrance of her breast.
Iseult, Iseult, what grace hath life to give
More than we twain have had of life, and live?
Iseult, Iseult, what grace may death not keep
As sweet for us to win of death, and sleep?
Come therefore, let us twain pass hence and try
If it be better not to live but die,
With love for lamp to light us out of life."
    And on that word his wedded maiden wife,
Pale as the moon in star-forsaken skies
Ere the sun fill them, rose with set strange eyes
And gazed on him that saw not: and her heart
Heaved as a man's death-smitten with a dart
That smites him sleeping, warm and full of life:
So toward her lord that was not looked his wife,
His wife that was not: and her heart within
Burnt bitter like an aftertaste of sin
To one whose memory drinks and loathes the lee
Of shame or sorrow deeper than the sea:
And no fear touched him of her eyes above
And ears that hoarded each poor word whence love
Made sweet the broken music of his breath.
"Iseult, my life that wast and art my death,
My life in life that hast been, and that art
Death in my death, sole wound that cleaves mine heart,

Mine heart that else, how spent soe'er, were whole,
Breath of my spirit and anguish of my soul,
How can this be that hence thou canst not hear,
Being but by space divided? One is here,
But one of twain I looked at once to see;
Shall death keep time and thou not keep with me?"
    And the white married maiden laughed at heart,
Hearing, and scarce with lips at all apart
Spake, and as fire between them was her breath;
"Yea, now thou liest not: yea, for I am death."
    By this might eyes that watched without behold
Deep in the gulfs of aching air acold
The roses of the dawning heaven that strew
The low soft sun's way ere his power shine through
And burn them up with fire: but far to west
Had sunk the dead moon on the live sea's breast,
Slain as with bitter fear to see the sun:
And eastward was a strong bright wind begun
Between the clouds and waters: and he said,
Seeing hardly through dark dawn her doubtful head,
"Iseult?" and like a death-bell faint and clear
The virgin voice rang answer—"I am here."
And his heart sprang, and sank again: and she
Spake, saying, "What would my knightly lord with me?"
And Tristram: "Hath my lady watched all night
Beside me, and I knew not? God requite
Her love for comfort shown a man nigh dead."
    "Yea, God shall surely guerdon it," she said,
"Who hath kept me all my days through to this hour."
    And Tristram: "God alone hath grace and power
To pay such grace toward one unworthier shown
Than ever durst, save only of God alone,
Crave pardon yet and comfort, as I would
Crave now for charity if my heart were good,
But as a coward's it fails me, even for shame."
    Then seemed her face a pale funereal flame
That burns down slow by midnight, as she said:
"Speak, and albeit thy bidding spake me dead,

God's love renounce me if it were not done."
    And Tristram: "When the sea-line takes the sun
That now should be not far off sight from far,
Look if there come not with the morning star
My ship bound hither from the northward back,
And if the sail be white thereof or black."
    And knowing the soothfast sense of his desire
So sore the heart within her raged like fire
She could not wring forth of her lips a word,
But bowing made sign how humbly had she heard.
And the sign given made light his heart; and she
Set her face hard against the yearning sea
Now all athirst with trembling trust of hope
To see the sudden gates of sunrise ope;
But thirstier yearned the heart whose fiery gate
Lay wide that vengeance might come in to hate.
And Tristram lay at thankful rest, and thought
Now surely life nor death could grieve him aught,
Since past was now life's anguish as a breath,
And surely past the bitterness of death.
For seeing he had found at these her hands this grace,
It could not be but yet some breathing-space
Might leave him life to look again on love's own face.
"Since if for death's sake," in his heart he said,
"Even she take pity upon me quick or dead,
How shall not even from God's hand be compassion shed?
For night bears dawn, how weak soe'er and wan,
And sweet ere death, men fable, sings the swan.
So seems the Swan my signal from the sea
To sound a song that sweetens death to me
Clasped round about with radiance from above
Of dawn, and closer clasped on earth by love.
Shall all things brighten, and this my sign be dark?"
    And high from heaven suddenly rang the lark,
Triumphant; and the far first refluent ray
Filled all the hollow darkness full with day.
And on the deep sky's verge a fluctuant light
Gleamed, grew, shone, strengthened into perfect sight,

As bowed and dipped and rose again the sail's clear white.
And swift and steadfast as a sea-mew's wing
It neared before the wind, as fain to bring
Comfort, and shorten yet its narrowing track.
And she that saw looked hardly toward him back,
Saying, "Ah, the ship comes surely; but her sail is black."
And fain he would have sprung upright, and seen,
And spoken: but strong death struck sheer between,
And darkness closed as iron round his head:
And smitten through the heart lay Tristram dead.
    And scarce the word had flown abroad, and wail
Risen, ere to shoreward came the snowbright sail,
And lightly forth leapt Ganhardine on land,
And led from ship with swift and reverent hand
Iseult: and round them up from all the crowd
Broke the great wail for Tristram out aloud.
And ere her ear might hear her heart had heard,
Nor sought she sign for witness of the word;
But came and stood above him newly dead,
And felt his death upon her: and her head
Bowed, as to reach the spring that slakes all drouth;
And their four lips became one silent mouth.

So came their hour on them that were in life
Tristram and Iseult: so from love and strife
The stroke of love's own hand felt last and best
Gave them deliverance to perpetual rest.
So, crownless of the wreaths that life had wound,
They slept, with flower of tenderer comfort crowned;
From bondage and the fear of time set free,
And all the yoke of space on earth and sea
Cast as a curb for ever: nor might now
Fear and desire bid soar their souls or bow,
Lift up their hearts or break them: doubt nor grief
More now might move them, dread nor disbelief
Touch them with shadowy cold or fiery sting,
Nor sleepless languor with its weary wing,
Nor harsh estrangement, born of time's vain breath,

Nor change, a darkness deeper far than death.
And round the sleep that fell around them then
Earth lies not wrapped, nor records wrought of men
Rise up for timeless token: but their sleep
Hath round it like a raiment all the deep;
No change or gleam or gloom of sun and rain,
But all time long the might of all the main
Spread round them as round earth soft heaven is spread,
And peace more strong than death round all the dead.
For death is of an hour, and after death
Peace: nor for aught that fear or fancy saith,
Nor even for very love's own sake, shall strife
Perplex again that perfect peace with life.
And if, as men that mourn may deem or dream,
Rest haply here than there might sweeter seem,
And sleep, that lays one hand on all, more good
By some sweet grave's grace given of wold or wood
Or clear high glen or sunbright wind-worn down
Than where life thunders through the trampling town
With daylong feet and nightlong overhead,
What grave may cast such grace round any dead,
What so sublime sweet sepulchre may be
For all that life leaves mortal, as the sea?
And these, rapt forth perforce from earthly ground,
These twain the deep sea guards, and girdles round
Their sleep more deep than any sea's gulf lies,
Though changeless with the change in shifting skies,
Nor mutable with seasons: for the grave
That held them once, being weaker than a wave,
The waves long since have buried: though their tomb
Was royal that by ruth's relenting doom
Men gave them in Tintagel: for the word
Took wing which thrilled all piteous hearts that heard
The word wherethrough their lifelong lot stood shown,
And when the long sealed springs of fate were known,
The blind bright innocence of lips that quaffed
Love, and the marvel of the mastering draught,
And all the fraughtage of the fateful bark,

Loud like a child upon them wept King Mark,
Seeing round the sword's hilt which long since had fought
For Cornwall's love a scroll of writing wrought,
A scripture writ of Tristram's hand, wherein
Lay bare the sinless source of all their sin,
No choice of will, but chance and sorcerous art,
With prayer of him for pardon: and his heart
Was molten in him, wailing as he kissed
Each with the kiss of kinship—"Had I wist,
Ye had never sinned nor died thus, nor had I
Borne in this doom that bade you sin and die
So sore a part of sorrow." And the king
Built for their tomb a chapel bright like spring
With flower-soft wealth of branching tracery made
Fair as the frondage each fleet year sees fade,
That should not fall till many a year were done.
There slept they wedded under moon and sun
And change of stars: and through the casements came
Midnight and noon girt round with shadow and flame
To illume their grave or veil it; till at last
On these things too was doom as darkness cast:
For the strong sea hath swallowed wall and tower,
And where their limbs were laid in woful hour
For many a fathom gleams and moves and moans
The tide that sweeps above their coffined bones
In the wrecked chancel by the shivered shrine:
Nor where they sleep shall moon or sunlight shine
Nor man look down for ever: none shall say,
Here once, or here, Tristram and Iseult lay:
But peace they have that none may gain who live,
And rest about them that no love can give,
And over them, while death and life shall be,
The light and sound and darkness of the sea.

From A CENTURY OF ROUNDELS (1883)

The Way of the Wind

The wind's way in the deep sky's hollow
None may measure, as none can say
How the heart in her shows the swallow
    The wind's way.

Hope nor fear can avail to stay
Waves that whiten on wrecks that wallow,
Times and seasons that wane and slay.

Life and love, till the strong night swallow
Thought and hope and the red last ray,
Swim the waters of years that follow
    The wind's way.

A Dialogue

I

Death, if thou wilt, fain would I plead with thee:
Canst thou not spare, of all our hopes have built,
One shelter where our spirits fain would be,
    Death, if thou wilt?

No dome with suns and dews impearled and gilt,
Imperial: but some roof of wildwood tree,
Too mean for sceptre's heft or swordblade's hilt.

Some low sweet roof where love might live, set free
From change and fear and dreams of grief or guilt;
Canst thou not leave life even thus much to see,
    Death, if thou wilt?

II

Man, what art thou to speak and plead with me?
What knowest thou of my workings, where and how
What things I fashion? Nay, behold and see,
    Man, what art thou?

Thy fruits of life, and blossoms of thy bough,
What are they but my seedlings? Earth and sea
Bear nought but when I breathe on it must bow.

Bow thou too down before me: though thou be
Great, all the pride shall fade from off thy brow,
When Time and strong Oblivion ask of thee,
    Man, what art thou?

III

Death, if thou be or be not, as was said,
Immortal; if thou make us nought, or we
Survive: thy power is made but of our dread,
    Death, if thou be.

Thy might is made out of our fear of thee:
Who fears thee not, hath plucked from off thine head
The crown of cloud that darkens earth and sea.

Earth, sea, and sky, as rain or vapour shed,
Shall vanish; all the shows of them shall flee:
Then shall we know full surely, quick or dead,
    Death, if thou be.

Change

But now life's face beholden
    Seemed bright as heaven's bare brow
With hope of gifts withholden
    But now.

    From time's full-flowering bough
Each bud spake bloom to embolden
    Love's heart, and seal his vow.

Joy's eyes grew deep with olden
    Dreams, born he wist not how;
Thought's meanest garb was golden;
    But now!

From *Three Faces*

III.—Venice

Out of the dark pure twilight, where the stream
Flows glimmering, streaked by many a birdlike bark
That skims the gloom whence towers and bridges gleam
    Out of the dark,

Once more a face no glance might choose but mark
Shone pale and bright, with eyes whose deep slow beam
Made quick the twilight, lifeless else and stark.

The same it seemed, or mystery made it seem,
As those before beholden; but St. Mark
Ruled here the ways that showed it like a dream
    Out of the dark.

From A MIDSUMMER HOLIDAY AND OTHER POEMS (1884)

From *A Midsummer Holiday*

VI

The Cliffside Path

Seaward goes the sun, and homeward by the down
We, before the night upon his grave be sealed.
Low behind us lies the bright steep murmuring town,
High before us heaves the steep rough silent field.
Breach by ghastlier breach, the cliffs collapsing yield:
Half the path is broken, half the banks divide;
Flawed and crumbled, riven and rent, they cleave and slide
Toward the ridged and wrinkled waste of girdling sand
Deep beneath, whose furrows tell how far and wide
Wind is lord and change is sovereign of the strand.

Star by star on the unsunned waters twiring down,
Golden spear-points glance against a silver shield.
Over banks and bents, across the headland's crown,
As by pulse of gradual plumes through twilight wheeled,
Soft as sleep, the waking wind awakes the weald.
Moor and copse and fallow, near or far descried,
Feel the mild wings move, and gladden where they glide:
Silence, uttering love that all things understand,
Bids the quiet fields forget that hard beside
Wind is lord and change is sovereign of the strand.

Yet may sight, ere all the hoar soft shade grow brown,
Hardly reckon half the rifts and rents unhealed
Where the scarred cliffs downward sundering drive and drown,
Hewn as if with stroke of swords in tempest steeled,
Wielded as the night's will and the wind's may wield.
Crowned and zoned in vain with flowers of autumn-tide,
Soon the blasts shall break them, soon the waters hide;
Soon, where late we stood, shall no man ever stand.
Life and love seek harbourage on the landward side:
Wind is lord and change is sovereign of the strand.

Friend, though man be less than these, for all his pride,
Yet, for all his weakness, shall not hope abide?
Wind and change can wreck but life and waste but land:
Truth and trust are sure, though here till all subside
Wind is lord and change is sovereign of the strand.

A Double Ballad of August

(1884)

All Afric, winged with death and fire,
Pants in our pleasant English air.
Each blade of grass is tense as wire,
And all the wood's loose trembling hair
Stark in the broad and breathless glare
Of hours whose touch wastes herb and tree.
This bright sharp death shines everywhere;
Life yearns for solace toward the sea.

Earth seems a corpse upon the pyre;
The sun, a scourge for slaves to bear.
All power to fear, all keen desire,
Lies dead as dreams of days that were
Before the new-born world lay bare

In heaven's wide eye, whereunder we
Lie breathless till the season spare:
Life yearns for solace toward the sea.

Fierce hours, with ravening fangs that tire
On spirit and sense, divide and share
The throbs of thoughts that scarce respire,
The throes of dreams that scarce forbear
One mute immitigable prayer
For cold perpetual sleep to be
Shed snowlike on the sense of care.
Life yearns for solace toward the sea.

The dust of ways where men suspire
Seems even the dust of death's dim lair.
But though the feverish days be dire
The sea-wind rears and cheers its fair
Blithe broods of babes that here and there
Make the sands laugh and glow for glee
With gladder flowers than gardens wear.
Life yearns for solace toward the sea.

The music dies not off the lyre
That lets no soul alive despair.
Sleep strikes not dumb the breathless choir
Of waves whose note bids sorrow spare.
As glad they sound, as fast they fare,
As when fate's word first set them free
And gave them light and night to wear.
Life yearns for solace toward the sea.

For there, though night and day conspire
To compass round with toil and snare
And changeless whirl of change, whose gyre
Draws all things deathwards unaware,
The spirit of life they scourge and scare,
Wild waves that follow on waves that flee
Laugh, knowing that yet, though earth despair,
Life yearns for solace toward the sea.

A Solitude

Sea beyond sea, sand after sweep of sand,
  Here ivory smooth, here cloven and ridged with flow
  Of channelled waters soft as rain or snow,
Stretch their lone length at ease beneath the bland
Grey gleam of skies whose smile on wave and strand
  Shines weary like a man's who smiles to know
  That now no dream can mock his faith with show,
Nor cloud for him seem living sea or land.

Is there an end at all of all this waste,
These crumbling cliffs defeatured and defaced,
These ruinous heights of sea-sapped walls that slide
  Seaward with all their banks of bleak blown flowers
Glad yet of life, ere yet their hope subside
  Beneath the coil of dull dense waves and hours?

From POEMS AND BALLADS, THIRD SERIES (1889)

Night

I

FROM THE ITALIAN OF GIOVANNI STROZZI

Night, whom in shape so sweet thou here may'st see
 Sleeping, was by an Angel sculptured thus
 In marble, and since she sleeps hath life like us:
Thou doubt'st? Awake her: she will speak to thee.

II

FROM THE ITALIAN OF MICHELANGELO BUONARROTI

Sleep likes me well, and better yet to know
 I am but stone. While shame and grief must be,
 Good hap is mine, to feel not, nor to see:
Take heed, then, lest thou wake me: ah, speak low.

In Time of Mourning

"Return," we dare not as we fain
    Would cry from hearts that yearn:
Love dares not bid our dead again
    Return.

    O hearts that strain and burn
As fires fast fettered burn and strain!
    Bow down, lie still, and learn.

The heart that healed all hearts of pain
    No funeral rites inurn:
Its echoes, while the stars remain,
    Return.

May 1885

From ASTROPHEL AND OTHER POEMS (1894)

A Nympholept

Summer, and noon, and a splendour of silence, felt,
  Seen, and heard of the spirit within the sense.
Soft through the frondage the shades of the sunbeams melt,
  Sharp through the foliage the shafts of them, keen and dense,
  Cleave, as discharged from the string of the God's bow,
    tense
As a war-steed's girth, and bright as a warrior's belt.
  Ah, why should an hour that is heaven for an hour pass hence?

I dare not sleep for delight of the perfect hour,
  Lest God be wroth that his gift should be scorned of man.
The face of the warm bright world is the face of a flower,
  The word of the wind and the leaves that the light winds fan
  As the word that quickened at first into flame, and ran,
Creative and subtle and fierce with invasive power,
  Through darkness and cloud, from the breath of the one
    God, Pan.

The perfume of earth possessed by the sun pervades
  The chaster air that he soothes but with sense of sleep.
Soft, imminent, strong as desire that prevails and fades,
  The passing noon that beholds not a cloudlet weep
  Imbues and impregnates life with delight more deep
Than dawn or sunset or moonrise on lawns or glades
  Can shed from the skies that receive it and may not keep.

The skies may hold not the splendour of sundown fast;
   It wanes into twilight as dawn dies down into day.
And the moon, triumphant when twilight is overpast,
   Takes pride but awhile in the hours of her stately sway.
   But the might of the noon, though the light of it pass away,
Leaves earth fulfilled of desires and of dreams that last;
   But if any there be that hath sense of them none can say.

For if any there be that hath sight of them, sense, or trust
   Made strong by the might of a vision, the strength of a
      dream,
His lips shall straiten and close as a dead man's must,
   His heart shall be sealed as the voice of a frost-bound stream.
   For the deep mid mystery of light and of heat that seem
To clasp and pierce dark earth, and enkindle dust,
   Shall a man's faith say what it is? or a man's guess deem?

Sleep lies not heavier on eyes that have watched all night
   Than hangs the heat of the noon on the hills and trees.
Why now should the haze not open, and yield to sight
   A fairer secret than hope or than slumber sees?
   I seek not heaven with submission of lips and knees,
With worship and prayer for a sign till it leap to light:
   I gaze on the gods about me, and call on these.

I call on the gods hard by, the divine dim powers
   Whose likeness is here at hand, in the breathless air,
In the pulseless peace of the fervid and silent flowers,
   In the faint sweet speech of the waters that whisper there.
   Ah, what should darkness do in a world so fair?
The bent-grass heaves not, the couch-grass quails not or cowers;
   The wind's kiss frets not the rowan's or aspen's hair.

But the silence trembles with passion of sound suppressed,
   And the twilight quivers and yearns to the sunward, wrung
With love as with pain; and the wide wood's motionless breast
   Is thrilled with a dumb desire that would fain find tongue
   And palpitates, tongueless as she whom a man-snake stung,

Whose heart now heaves in the nightingale, never at rest
  Nor satiated ever with song till her last be sung.

Is it rapture or terror that circles me round, and invades
  Each vein of my life with hope—if it be not fear?
Each pulse that awakens my blood into rapture fades,
  Each pulse that subsides into dread of a strange thing near
  Requickens with sense of a terror less dread than dear.
Is peace not one with light in the deep green glades
  Where summer at noonday slumbers? Is peace not here?

The tall thin stems of the firs, and the roof sublime
  That screens from the sun the floor of the steep still wood,
Deep, silent, splendid, and perfect and calm as time,
  Stand fast as ever in sight of the night they stood,
  When night gave all that moonlight and dewfall could.
The dense ferns deepen, the moss glows warm as the thyme:
  The wild heath quivers about me: the world is good.

Is it Pan's breath, fierce in the tremulous maidenhair,
  That bids fear creep as a snake through the woodlands, felt
In the leaves that it stirs not yet, in the mute bright air,
  In the stress of the sun? For here has the great God dwelt:
  For hence were the shafts of his love or his anger dealt.
For here has his wrath been fierce as his love was fair,
  When each was as fire to the darkness its breath bade melt.

Is it love, is it dread, that enkindles the trembling noon,
  That yearns, reluctant in rapture that fear has fed,
As man for woman, as woman for man? Full soon,
  If I live, and the life that may look on him drop not dead,
  Shall the ear that hears not a leaf quake hear his tread,
The sense that knows not the sound of the deep day's tune
  Receive the God, be it love that he brings or dread.

The naked noon is upon me: the fierce dumb spell,
  The fearful charm of the strong sun's imminent might,
Unmerciful, steadfast, deeper than seas that swell,

Pervades, invades, appals me with loveless light,
With harsher awe than breathes in the breath of night.
Have mercy, God who art all! For I know thee well,
How sharp is thine eye to lighten, thine hand to smite.

The whole wood feels thee, the whole air fears thee: but fear
So deep, so dim, so sacred, is wellnigh sweet.
For the light that hangs and broods on the woodlands here,
Intense, invasive, intolerant, imperious, and meet
To lighten the works of thine hands and the ways of thy feet,
Is hot with the fire of the breath of thy life, and dear
As hope that shrivels or shrinks not for frost or heat.

Thee, thee the supreme dim godhead, approved afar,
Perceived of the soul and conceived of the sense of man,
We scarce dare love, and we dare not fear: the star
We call the sun, that lit us when life began
To brood on the world that is thine by his grace for a span,
Conceals and reveals in the semblance of things that are
Thine immanent presence, the pulse of thy heart's life, Pan.

The fierce mid noon that wakens and warms the snake
Conceals thy mercy, reveals thy wrath: and again
The dew-bright hour that assuages the twilight brake
Conceals thy wrath and reveals thy mercy: then
Thou art fearful only for evil souls of men
That feel with nightfall the serpent within them wake,
And hate the holy darkness on glade and glen.

Yea, then we know not and dream not if ill things be,
Or if aught of the work of the wrong of the world be thine.
We hear not the footfall of terror that treads the sea,
We hear not the moan of winds that assail the pine:
We see not if shipwreck reign in the storm's dim shrine;
If death do service and doom bear witness to thee
We see not,—know not if blood for thy lips be wine.

But in all things evil and fearful that fear may scan,
As in all things good, as in all things fair that fall,
We know thee present and latent, the lord of man;
In the murmuring of doves, in the clamouring of winds that call
And wolves that howl for their prey; in the midnight's pall,
In the naked and nymph-like feet of the dawn, O Pan,
And in each life living, O thou the God who art all.

Smiling and singing, wailing and wringing of hands,
Laughing and weeping, watching and sleeping, still
Proclaim but and prove but thee, as the shifted sands
Speak forth and show but the strength of the sea's wild will
That sifts and grinds them as grain in the storm-wind's mill.
In thee is the doom that falls and the doom that stands:
The tempests utter thy word, and the stars fulfil.

Where Etna shudders with passion and pain volcanic
That rend her heart as with anguish that rends a man's,
Where Typho labours, and finds not his thews Titanic,
In breathless torment that ever the flame's breath fans,
Men felt and feared thee of old, whose pastoral clans
Were given to the charge of thy keeping; and soundless panic
Held fast the woodland whose depths and whose heights were Pan's.

And here, though fear be less than delight, and awe
Be one with desire and with worship of earth and thee,
So mild seems now thy secret and speechless law,
So fair and fearless and faithful and godlike she,
So soft the spell of thy whisper on stream and sea,
Yet man should fear lest he see what of old men saw
And withered: yet shall I quail if thy breath smite me.

Lord God of life and of light and of all things fair,
Lord God of ravin and ruin and all things dim,
Death seals up life, and darkness the sunbright air,
And the stars that watch blind earth in the deep night swim
Laugh, saying, "What God is your God, that ye call on him?

What is man, that the God who is guide of our way should care
  If day for a man be golden, or night be grim?"

But thou, dost thou hear? Stars too but abide for a span,
  Gods too but endure for a season; but thou, if thou be
God, more than shadows conceived and adored of man,
  Kind Gods and fierce, that bound him or made him free,
  The skies that scorn us are less in thy sight than we,
Whose souls have strength to conceive and perceive thee, Pan,
  With sense more subtle than senses that hear and see.

Yet may not it say, though it seek thee and think to find
  One soul of sense in the fire and the frost-bound clod,
What heart is this, what spirit alive or blind,
  That moves thee: only we know that the ways we trod
  We tread, with hands unguided, with feet unshod,
With eyes unlightened; and yet, if with steadfast mind,
  Perchance may we find thee and know thee at last for God.

Yet then should God be dark as the dawn is bright,
  And bright as the night is dark on the world—no more.
Light slays not darkness, and darkness absorbs not light;
  And the labour of evil and good from the years of yore
  Is even as the labour of waves on a sunless shore.
And he who is first and last, who is depth and height,
  Keeps silence now, as the sun when the woods wax hoar.

The dark dumb godhead innate in the fair world's life
  Imbues the rapture of dawn and of noon with dread,
Infects the peace of the star-shod night with strife,
  Informs with terror the sorrow that guards the dead.
  No service of bended knee or of humbled head
May soothe or subdue the God who has change to wife:
  And life with death is as morning with evening wed.

And yet, if the light and the life in the light that here
  Seem soft and splendid and fervid as sleep may seem
Be more than the shine of a smile or the flash of a tear,

Sleep, change, and death are less than a spell-struck dream,
And fear than the fall of a leaf on a starlit stream.
And yet, if the hope that hath said it absorb not fear,
What helps it man that the stars and the waters gleam?

What helps it man, that the noon be indeed intense,
The night be indeed worth worship? Fear and pain
Were lords and masters yet of the secret sense,
Which now dares deem not that light is as darkness, fain
Though dark dreams be to declare it, crying in vain.
For whence, thou God of the light and the darkness, whence
Dawns now this vision that bids not the sunbeams wane?

What light, what shadow, diviner than dawn or night,
Draws near, makes pause, and again—or I dream—draws near?
More soft than shadow, more strong than the strong sun's light,
More pure than moonbeams—yea, but the rays run sheer
As fire from the sun through the dusk of the pinewood, clear
And constant; yea, but the shadow itself is bright
That the light clothes round with love that is one with fear.

Above and behind it the noon and the woodland lie,
Terrible, radiant with mystery, superb and subdued,
Triumphant in silence; and hardly the sacred sky
Seems free from the tyrannous weight of the dumb fierce mood
Which rules as with fire and invasion of beams that brood
The breathless rapture of earth till its hour pass by
And leave her spirit released and her peace renewed.

I sleep not: never in sleep has a man beholden
This. From the shadow that trembles and yearns with light
Suppressed and elate and reluctant—obscure and golden
As water kindled with presage of dawn or night—
A form, a face, a wonder to sense and sight,
Grows great as the moon through the month; and her eyes embolden
Fear, till it change to desire, and desire to delight.

I sleep not: sleep would die of a dream so strange;
A dream so sweet would die as a rainbow dies,
As a sunbow laughs and is lost on the waves that range
And reck not of light that flickers or spray that flies.
But the sun withdraws not, the woodland shrinks not or sighs,
No sweet thing sickens with sense or with fear of change;
Light wounds not, darkness blinds not, my steadfast eyes.

Only the soul in my sense that receives the soul
Whence now my spirit is kindled with breathless bliss
Knows well if the light that wounds it with love makes whole,
If hopes that carol be louder than fears that hiss,
If truth be spoken of flowers and of waves that kiss,
Of clouds and stars that contend for a sunbright goal.
And yet may I dream that I dream not indeed of this?

An earth-born dreamer, constrained by the bonds of birth,
Held fast by the flesh, compelled by his veins that beat
And kindle to rapture or wrath, to desire or to mirth,
May hear not surely the fall of immortal feet,
May feel not surely if heaven upon earth be sweet;
And here is my sense fulfilled of the joys of earth,
Light, silence, bloom, shade, murmur of leaves that meet.

Bloom, fervour, and perfume of grasses and flowers aglow,
Breathe and brighten about me: the darkness gleams,
The sweet light shivers and laughs on the slopes below,
Made soft by leaves that lighten and change like dreams;
The silence thrills with the whisper of secret streams
That well from the heart of the woodland: these I know:
Earth bore them, heaven sustained them with showers and beams.

I lean my face to the heather, and drink the sun
Whose flame-lit odour satiates the flowers: mine eyes
Close, and the goal of delight and of life is one:
No more I crave of earth or her kindred skies.

No more? But the joy that springs from them smiles and flies:
The sweet work wrought of them surely, the good work done,
If the mind and the face of the season be loveless, dies.

Thee, therefore, thee would I come to, cleave to, cling,
If haply thy heart be kind and thy gifts be good,
Unknown sweet spirit, whose vesture is soft in spring,
In summer splendid, in autumn pale as the wood
That shudders and wanes and shrinks as a shamed thing should,
In winter bright as the mail of a war-worn king
Who stands where foes fled far from the face of him stood.

My spirit or thine is it, breath of thy life or of mine,
Which fills my sense with a rapture that casts out fear?
Pan's dim frown wanes, and his wild eyes brighten as thine,
Transformed as night or as day by the kindling year.
Earth-born, or mine eye were withered that sees, mine ear
That hears were stricken to death by the sense divine,
Earth-born I know thee: but heaven is about me here.

The terror that whispers in darkness and flames in light,
The doubt that speaks in the silence of earth and sea,
The sense, more fearful at noon than in midmost night,
Of wrath scarce hushed and of imminent ill to be,
Where are they? Heaven is as earth, and as heaven to me
Earth: for the shadows that sundered them here take flight;
And nought is all, as am I, but a dream of thee.

From *Loch Torridon*

All night long, in the world of sleep,
Skies and waters were soft and deep:
Shadow clothed them, and silence made
Soundless music of dream and shade:
All above us, the livelong night,
Shadow, kindled with sense of light;
All around us, the brief night long,
Silence, laden with sense of song.
Stars and mountains without, we knew,
Watched and waited, the soft night through:
All unseen, but divined and dear,
Thrilled the touch of the sea's breath near:
All unheard, but alive like sound,
Throbbed the sense of the sea's life round:
Round us, near us, in depth and height,
Soft as darkness and keen as light.

From A CHANNEL PASSAGE AND OTHER POEMS (1904)

The Lake of Gaube

The sun is lord and god, sublime, serene,
  And sovereign on the mountains: earth and air
Lie prone in passion, blind with bliss unseen
  By force of sight and might of rapture, fair
  As dreams that die and know not what they were.
The lawns, the gorges, and the peaks, are one
Glad glory, thrilled with sense of unison
In strong compulsive silence of the sun.

Flowers dense and keen as midnight stars aflame
  And living things of light like flames in flower
That glance and flash as though no hand might tame
  Lightnings whose life outshone their stormlit hour
  And played and laughed on earth, with all their power
Gone, and with all their joy of life made long
And harmless as the lightning life of song,
Shine sweet like stars when darkness feels them strong.

The deep mild purple flaked with moonbright gold
  That makes the scales seem flowers of hardened light,
The flamelike tongue, the feet that noon leaves cold,
  The kindly trust in man, when once the sight
  Grew less than strange, and faith bade fear take flight,
Outlive the little harmless life that shone

And gladdened eyes that loved it, and was gone
Ere love might fear that fear had looked thereon.

Fear held the bright thing hateful, even as fear,
  Whose name is one with hate and horror, saith
That heaven, the dark deep heaven of water near,
  Is deadly deep as hell and dark as death.
  The rapturous plunge that quickens blood and breath
With pause more sweet than passion, ere they strive
To raise again the limbs that yet would dive
Deeper, should there have slain the soul alive.

As the bright salamander in fire of the noonshine exults and is glad of his day,
The spirit that quickens my body rejoices to pass from the sunlight away,
To pass from the glow of the mountainous flowerage, the high multitudinous bloom,
Far down through the fathomless night of the water, the gladness of silence and gloom.
Death-dark and delicious as death in the dream of a lover and dreamer may be,
It clasps and encompasses body and soul with delight to be living and free:
Free utterly now, though the freedom endure but the space of a perilous breath,
And living, though girdled about with the darkness and coldness and strangeness of death:
Each limb and each pulse of the body rejoicing, each nerve of the spirit at rest,
All sense of the soul's life rapture, a passionate peace in its blindness blest.
So plunges the downward swimmer, embraced of the water unfathomed of man,
The darkness unplummeted, icier than seas in midwinter, for blessing or ban;
And swiftly and sweetly, when strength and breath fall short, and the dive is done,

Shoots up as a shaft from the dark depth shot, sped straight into sight of the sun;
And sheer through the snow-soft water, more dark than the roof of the pines above,
Strikes forth, and is glad as a bird whose flight is impelled and sustained of love.
As a sea-mew's love of the sea-wind breasted and ridden for rapture's sake
Is the love of his body and soul for the darkling delight of the soundless lake:
As the silent speed of a dream too living to live for a thought's space more
Is the flight of his limbs through the still strong chill of the darkness from shore to shore.
Might life be as this is and death be as life that casts off time as a robe,
The likeness of infinite heaven were a symbol revealed of the lake of Gaube.

Whose thought has fathomed and measured
The darkness of life and of death,
The secret within them treasured,
The spirit that is not breath?
Whose vision has yet beholden
The splendour of death and of life?
Though sunset as dawn be golden,
Is the word of them peace, not strife?
Deep silence answers: the glory
We dream of may be but a dream,
And the sun of the soul wax hoary
As ashes that show not a gleam.
But well shall it be with us ever
Who drive through the darkness here,
If the soul that we live by never,
For aught that a lie saith, fear.

Roundel

FROM THE FRENCH OF VILLON

Death, I would plead against thy wrong,
  Who hast reft me of my love, my wife,
  And art not satiate yet with strife,
But needs wilt hold me lingering long.
No strength since then has kept me strong:
  But what could hurt thee in her life,
    Death?

Twain we were, and our hearts one song,
  One heart: if that be dead, thy knife
  Hath cut me off alive from life,
Dead as the carver's figured throng,
    Death!

Introductory Notes to the Longer Works

Atalanta in Calydon

Though not his first publication, it was *Atalanta in Calydon* that brought the young Swinburne to sudden fame in 1865, a year before the first *Poems and Ballads*. The verse drama of *Atalanta* was his first attempt to compose a tragedy after the Greek model, and its startling idiosyncrasies provoked extreme reactions. It could not escape notice that the play was saturated with antitheistic sentiments far beyond anything to be discovered in the authentic Greek precedents, and Swinburne's habitual allusions to a singular 'God', together with a recurrent preoccupation with 'sin', looked like the signs of a barely concealed personal bugbear, and a dangerous sentiment. At the same time, the beauties of the versification, especially in the choral odes, was widely acknowledged: the drama contained Swinburne's first widely read exercises in lyric. Its first choral ode, 'When the hounds of spring are on winter's traces', which begins this selection, has remained perhaps the one passage in Swinburne's oeuvre most often quoted, collected, and praised. The second choral song, 'Before the beginning of years', is also one of Swinburne's best remembered passages, and also given here. His characteristic prosody, judiciously interweaving anapaests in continually various rhythms, with his exaggerated use of alliteration, rhyme and repetition, are all fully present in both songs.

But the rest of *Atalanta* is much less often read than these egregious parts, and to many readers the sections of blank-verse dialogue are unfamiliar. I have extracted some of the finest passages, which show the lyrical impulse of the poetry even outside of the songs. Meleager's description of the landing at Colchis, when he sights the white spray flying in the wind on the craggy shore, is just one of this play's remarkable set-pieces which are too often overlooked; Althaea's final speech, and the Herald's report of the hunting, are excellent examples of Swinburne's purple melodrama; and the stunning bathetic anticlimax of Meleager's death is wonderfully achieved.

The story of Atalanta and Meleager was taken, of course, from Greek mythology. The following summary of the plot, dressed in the idiom of sixteenth-century prose, was prefixed to the play:

> THE ARGUMENT. *Althaea, daughter of Thestius and Eurythemis, queen of Calydon, being with child of Meleager her first-born son, dreamed that she brought forth a brand burning; and upon his birth came the three Fates and prophesied of him three things, namely these; that he should have great strength of his hands, and good fortune in this life, and that he should live no longer when the brand then in the fire were consumed: wherefore his mother plucked it forth and kept it by her. And the child being a man grown sailed with Jason after the fleece of gold, and won himself great praise of all men living; and when the tribes of the north and west made war upon Aetolia, he fought against their army and scattered it. But Artemis, having at the first stirred up these tribes to war against Oeneus king of Calydon, because he had offered sacrifice to all the gods saving her alone, but her he had forgotten to honour, was yet more wroth because of the destruction of this army, and sent upon the land of Calydon a wild boar which slew many and wasted all their increase, but him could none slay, and many went against him and perished. Then were all the chief men of Greece gathered together, and among them Atalanta daughter of Iasius the Arcadian, a virgin, for whose sake Artemis let slay the boar, seeing she favoured the maiden greatly; and Meleager having despatched it gave the spoil thereof to Atalanta, as one beyond measure enamoured of her; but the brethren of Althaea his mother, Toxeus and Plexippus, with such others as misliked that she only should bear off the praise whereas many had borne the labour, laid wait for her to take away her spoil; but Meleager fought against them and slew them: whom when Althaea their sister beheld and knew to be slain of her son, she waxed for wrath and sorrow like as one mad, and taking the brand whereby the measure of her son's life was meted to him, she cast it upon a fire; and with the wasting thereof his life likewise wasted away, that being brought back to his father's house he died in a brief space, and his mother also endured not long after for very sorrow; and this was his end, and the end of that hunting.*

The drama is permeated by a pessimistic suspicion of language itself. This is closely connected with its antitheism. Speech is dangerous because the consequences of words are *unconscious*:

> ALTH. What if they [the gods] give us poisonous drinks for wine?

CHO. They have their will; much talking mends it not.
ALTH. And gall for milk, and cursing for a prayer?

[lines 153–55].

There is a kind of cosmic, dramatic irony rooted perniciously in words. The act of speaking, in itself, functions like an adverse god—becomes an object with the power to mock, to goad, ultimately to doom the speaker. The Chorus delves into this deep unease in the brilliant fourth choral song 'Who hath given man speech?', which is given here in full. Our inmost thoughts are so terrible that they must not be formulated in words. The gods are against us, and mortals are poor, contemptible things. So the Chorus rails against the indifferent gods, who are beyond 'change or sleep'; for even sleep is a weakness, a cruel limitation. Althaea says as much, in the passage included here under the title 'Althaea's Scorn of Prayer'. All of these sentiments would be repeated in *Poems and Ballads*.

Chastelard and Bothwell

Chastelard, also published in 1865, had been begun in Swinburne's undergraduate days, some time before *Atalanta*, and it has often been judged a less mature work. Certainly it has fared less well over the years. Critics of the time complained that it was grotesque, morbid and self-indulgent, and although the blank verse found some praise, the form of the five-act play (this time a pastiche of Jacobean tragedy) made much less room for Swinburne's lyrical genius. Nevertheless, the verse is, once again, frequently lyrical in texture, and Swinburne seems wholly at home in the style, so that there is a sense of authenticity and commitment here as much as in *Atalanta*.

Swinburne had been fascinated by Mary Stuart since boyhood, when he had become convinced that one of his ancestors, Thomas Swinburne of Capheaton, had been one of her most ardent supporters and admirers. *Chastelard* treats a minor episode in the histories of her life. Pierre de Boscosel de Chastelard was a French poet who found a place in Mary's retinue when she returned from the French court to Scotland in 1561. The various accounts of his fatal passion for the queen leave the true events and motivations dubious, but the facts are these: that he was discovered on two occasions in her bedchamber by night, and that in 1562 he was executed for the offence, either by hanging or (as in the play) beheading. Swinburne himself calls Chastelard 'the first of all her voluntary victims'. The phrase comes from the entry on Mary Queen of Scots that Swinburne contributed to the *Encyclopedia Britannica* in 1883.

Swinburne follows some of the early historical sources in imagining a mutual dalliance between Mary and Chastelard. He departs, however, from all sources by bringing into the play the queen's marriage to Darnley, which, as Swinburne well knew, did not really occur until two years after Chastelard's death. It is implied that Mary's impulsive decision to marry Darnley is precipitated by her jealous displeasure with Chastelard, following the revelation of a tryst with one of the ladies-in-waiting whom he momentarily mistakes for the queen. Chastelard's obsession swells, until he resolves to steal into the royal bedchamber on the night of the wedding, expecting to be gloriously slain before her eyes, a sacrifice to his doomed love.

The scene between them in the chamber, given here in full, does not end in the climax he desires. He is imprisoned, and the drama then turns upon Mary's state of mind as she debates the best course of action, and tries to manipulate those around her. The brilliance of Swinburne's portrayal is in the subtlety with which he allows Mary to talk herself around, to elide altruism with self-interest, to calculate and insinuate without ever quite acknowledging what she means. To pardon might incriminate herself; to condemn would lead to a potentially embarrassing trial. In a wonderful scene, she does her best to persuade her brother Murray to murder Chastelard at once, but studiously avoids giving the explicit instruction, and so taking responsibility for the act. The plain-speaking Murray is disinclined to be played upon, and forces the queen into desperate euphemisms, all to no avail. After much indecision—including the issue of a reprieve which has already been torn up by the martyr Chastelard before she has time to revoke it—she determines to have him executed without trial. The play ends with a marvellous moment of pathetically banal anticlimax, or rather mis-timed climax, comparable with that which ends *Atalanta*.

Chastelard is a dark play, certainly influenced by continental Romanticism, but also savouring strongly of the more extreme forms of Jacobean tragedy. Chastelard's insane passion is indeed the stuff of rousing romance, but I think we are also allowed to find his behaviour silly. In fact, the particular kind of pathos Swinburne evokes for his protagonist is partly reliant upon our recognition of the egomaniacal ridiculousness of his death-wish. The ambiguous relationship between the two central characters, as illustrated by the passages selected in this edition, is perceptively delineated, and the queen is not, as one might very reasonably have feared, a typical *femme fatale*, but a character uncomfortable with her own emotions—and with her want of emotion—faced with genuine difficulties. Her vacillations are truly dramatic, since they provide narrative tension at the same time as they show psychological depth: it is not only a question of our trying to second-guess her plots and intentions, but of *her* struggles to come to terms with the contents and inclinations of her own mind.

Chastelard was written for the page, not the stage. The same is certainly true of *Bothwell*, Swinburne's second play about the life of Mary Stuart. It is three times the length of its predecessor and spans more than two years of Mary's life. It is really not so much a play as an historical epic composed in dramatic form—like Chapman's *Charles Duke of Byron* (which Swinburne called 'a small epic in ten books or acts')[1] mixed with Sir Walter Scott. Yet, however far from the stage they may be, both plays have real dramatic tension, subtle characterisation, and lucid structure. They do not fail in their purposes, nor are their idiosyncrasies owing to inexperience in dramatic construction. Whether to regard them as poems or plays is a profitless question, but their banishment from the canon of Swinburne's 'poetry' inevitably leads to their being thought of, when at all, as unimportant side-projects attempted by an author whose vocation lay elsewhere—like the plays of Tennyson. But Tennyson's plays are not among the few very best

1 Swinburne, *George Chapman: A Critical Essay* (London, 1875), p. 92.

things that he did, and that really *is* the status of *Chastelard* and particularly *Bothwell.*

Bothwell, published in 1874, depicts a more eventful period in Mary's life, the years 1566 to 1568. It takes in the murder of Rizzio, the birth of James, and the murder of Darnley; the 'abduction' of Mary by Bothwell, and their subsequent marriage; the revolt of those nobles opposed to Bothwell's ascendancy, and the consequent skirmish at Carberry Hill, precipitating the flight of Bothwell, who disappears into exile; Mary's imprisonment at Loch Leven and her forced abdication in favour of her son, James, under the regency of Murray; her escape, and defeat at the Battle of Langside; and finally her fateful departure for England at Solway Firth. The scope of the play being so much grander than that of *Chastelard*, and the action so much more various, *Bothwell* smacks a little less of overheated adolescent fantasy. It was an ambitious undertaking, and an unlikely success, which, taken whole, reads like nothing else in English literature. Although given to morbid Websterian extravagances here and there, Swinburne in this play seldom seems to be far in thought from Shakespeare. *Antony and Cleopatra* comes to mind again and again in the scenes between the clever queen and her gruff, impulsive soldier of a lover, so that his flight from Carberry Hill becomes an ironic inversion of Cleopatra's desertion at Actium. But *Bothwell* is haunted even more tenaciously by the memory of *Macbeth*, which gives another associative aspect to the central relationship. One can see the resemblance clearly in the extracts which present Bothwell in nervy soliloquy, readying himself for the murder of Darnley.

John Knox ('the only man able to withstand her', according to Swinburne) is a prophetic figure in the background of Mary's life in this play, and his mixture of moralistic opprobrium and humane generosity gives *Bothwell* a more serious moral content than sceptics of Swinburne's 'decadence' might expect: not simply because Knox is 'right', but because he provides counterpoint and perspective, functioning as an intermediary between the queen and the populace. Swinburne neither vindicates the *femme fatale* nor straightforwardly sides with Knox; it is a real drama, and 'negative capability' is the rule. The scene in which

Mary grants audience to Knox is the first example of what will become one of the keenest effects in the play: the really affecting pathos elicited by Mary's stung pride, even when we know she is in the wrong. The intricacies of Mary's bad faith are so sympathetically imagined, and so dextrously veiled and revealed, that the reader is made to feel the genuine hurt and helplessness that underlie all her passions and feignings, calculations and contradictions. Some of the most memorable passages included here produce their tension from the volatile oscillations of the queen's thinking, as she swings between stoicism and vitriol, calm self-pity and the thirst for revenge, while the line between performance and sincerity is always unclear.

Tristram of Lyonesse

Tristram of Lyonesse, published in 1882, is the great masterpiece of the Putney years, although some parts of it had been started as early as 1869. Swinburne's Arthurian epyllion was conceived in deliberate contrast with Tennyson's ongoing Arthurian narratives, the *Idylls of the King*, of which the first parts had been published in 1859. The *Idylls* did not much suit the tastes of the aesthetic Rossetti set. A young Edward Burne-Jones in 1858 had passionately implored Tennyson not to use the name 'Nimuë' for the malicious character in his version of the story of Merlin's demise. Tennyson, acknowledging the changes he had wrought to the character, agreed to change the name to 'Vivien'.[2] Swinburne was less polite, and later referred to the *Idylls* as the 'Morte d'Albert', not only because they were dedicated to Prince Albert, but because he found them so offensively Victorian in spirit.[3] In his critical essay *Under the Microscope* (1872), he spoke of the inhuman 'vulgarity' of Tennyson's 'repulsive' Vivien. It was not the case that Swinburne or Burne-Jones, his close friend in the 1860s and dedicatee of

2 The story was recorded by Valentine Prinsep and retold by Georgiana Burne-Jones ('E B-J') in *Memorials of Edward Burne-Jones* (London, 1904), ch. X.

3 The derisive tag was used in *Under the Microscope* and in Swinburne's correspondence.

the first *Poems and Ballads*, simply scoffed at Tennyson; both held him in high regard, and had been zealous admirers in youth. But their own ideas of the Arthurian legends, about which they could sympathise profoundly, were wholly different. Their Aesthetic Arthurianism had no room for banal modern sentiments or crass moralizing—as it seemed to them. Burne-Jones' two famous paintings of Merlin and Nimuë are worlds away from Tennyson's 'Merlin and Vivien': their oblique emotionality comes from a complete submission to the moral ambiguities of the medieval sources.

The story of Merlin and Nimuë is told in *Tristram of Lyonesse*, too, and it is with Burne-Jones that Swinburne sides. There is more than a hint of Marlowe's *Hero and Leander* about Swinburne's poem, though it is unmistakably post-Shelleyan; and Swinburne goes much futher than Burne-Jones ever would in the direction of promoting—not excusing—the 'sinful' aspects of erotic impulse and transgression. The whole story of Tristram and Iseult is turned into a celebration of the beautiful sins and glorious damnation of the adulterous couple, heroes of forbidden love like Dante's Paolo and Francesca. And Swinburne set out to make the sensual scenes as titillating as possible. To D. G. Rossetti he wrote on 12 February 1870: 'I hope to make the copulative passages of the poem more warm and provocative of sinful appetite than anything my chaste Muse has yet attempted'.

Swinburne does not follow Malory, whose relation of the tale was best known to English readers. Like Burne-Jones, with whom he corresponded about the sources, he was conversant with various Arthurian romances in medieval French as well as English, and his narrative is a composite from various versions. Sir Tristram is sent across the Irish Sea to escort Iseult of Ireland, the intended bride of King Mark of Cornwall, from her home to the Cornish court. Swinburne's narrative begins at sea on the return journey. My extract from this first canto depicts Iseult's rapt contemplation of the waves, and represents Swinburne's passion for the sea at its most ravishing. Whilst still on board the 'Swallow', Tristram and Iseult unwittingly drink a love-potion intended for the royal couple, and when the wedding night comes, Iseult's handmaid Brangwain contrives to swap places with her:

Iseult, therefore, visits Tristram instead. They carry on their affair at Tintagel until the arrival of the minstrel-knight Sir Palamede, who takes advantage of a rash oath of the king's, and claims Iseult as the promised reward for his song. Tristram pursues and kills the abductor, and there follows a vividly imagined erotic encounter in a woodland bower. All this is given in the second extract here.

The lovers are disovered by King Mark, and, by diving from a clifftop into the sea, Tristram narrowly escapes execution. Washed up on the Breton shore, he is nursed by Iseult of the White Hands, whom he eventually marries; for her name reminds him of his true love, and when he sings love-songs to 'Iseult', the girl mistakes them for addresses to herself (see the third extract here). On their wedding night, which Tristram is unable to consummate, the narrative turns back to Cornwall, where Iseult of Ireland delivers an impassioned soliloquy, given here in full. When Tristram returns to Tintagel and flees with Iseult of Ireland to the sanctuary of Joyous Gard, the castle of Sir Launcelot, Iseult of Brittany, the abandoned wife, vows to take revenge. But now Tristram is charged by King Arthur to quell a troublesome giant, and Iseult of Ireland returns to Tintagel. Tristram succeeds in his mission, but afterwards sets off for Brittany, not Cornwall; and when he arrives, he is fatally injured in a chance combat. The healing hands of Iseult of Ireland are his only hope of survival, and he sends his brother-in-law, Ganhardine, to fetch her from Cornwall. It is agreed that Ganhardine will hoist a white sail if he returns with Iseult, or a black sail if he comes alone. As the ship approaches (with Iseult of Ireland on board), Iseult of the White Hands takes her revenge by telling Tristram, in his sick-bed, that the sail is black. Tristram dies before his love arrives, whereupon she too dies in an agony of grief. This, with the honours finally done the lovers by King Mark, constitutes the final extract.

Although *Tristram* is uneven, it is a magnificent poem and a unique achievement. In it, Swinburne consciously honed and perfected the prosodic style or 'scheme' of heroic couplet that he had first developed in 'Anactoria'. Although the verse often feels anapaestic (to this reader, at least), nevertheless it is overwhelmingly formed of disyllabic feet, and the effect of quickening is achieved not by tripping into triple-time, but rather by an unusual number of metrical inversions, trochee for iamb, which keeps the rhythm shifting and unstable without (in most cases) actually adding syllables to the decasyllabic base. Enjambment is deftly handled, carefully built up, and then allowed to career impetuously in the most thrilling passages; the cadence is always varied, not only in rhythm but also in the pitch it demands, and always seems to run on a strong musical instinct.

Explanatory Notes

The following notes are neither critical nor biographical, nor do they discuss sources, manuscript variants or concerns of that nature. Such notes for some of the poems may be found in the Yale edition by McGann and Sligh; and for the whole of *Atalanta* and the 1866 *Poems and Ballads*, see especially the extensive critical notes to the Penguin edition by Kenneth Haynes (cf. 'Further Reading'). The notes provided in the present instance are minimal by comparison. They are meant only to explain certain references, to gloss unusual vocabulary, to translate from all languages other than English, and—without dispelling intended mysteries—to offer thoughts on the interpretation of passages in which the syntax may cause difficulty.

ATALANTA IN CALYDON

For a summary of the plot, see the Introductory Notes to the Longer Works.

The First Choral Song

69ff. *And the brown bright nightingale amorous / Is half assuaged for Itylus.* A reference to the story of Philomela, Procne and Itys. Philomela is raped by her brother-in-law, Tereus, who cuts out her tongue to prevent her from revealing the crime. She reveals it to her sister, Procne (the wife of Tereus), through her needlework; Procne, in revenge, kills her own young son Itys, and serves his flesh to his father as a meal. When this is discovered by Tereus, he pursues the sisters murderously, and they, fleeing, pray to the gods to change them into birds. In most versions (e.g. Ovid, *Met.* VI), Procne becomes a nightingale and Philomela a swallow. See Swinburne's poem 'Itylus', from *Poems and Ballads*, 1866.

108 *The Maenad and the Bassarid.* Both are names for the Bacchantes, the followers of the wine-god Dionysus. Their behaviour was crazed;

the word 'maenad' is derived from the verb 'to be mad' (*mainomai*), and 'bassarid' from the long robes (*bassara*) which they wore.

[Meleager rejects his Mother's Counsel concerning Atalanta]

584ff. … *but chiefly when the sail / First caught between stretched ropes the roaring west [etc.].* Meleager was one of Jason's crew on the Argo; here he remembers the journey to Colchis, the quest for the Golden Fleece, and the abduction of Medea.

593 *Nereid.* Ocean nymph; one of the daughters of the sea-god Poseidon.

599 *Irremeable.* Admitting of no return. *Symplegades*: a perilous narrow strait where the Bosphorus joins the Black Sea. The high rocks on either side were said to crash together, destroying unlucky ships as they passed.

613 *Euxine.* The Black Sea.

[The Herald reports the Slaying of the Boar]

1266 *Plexippus.* Brother of Toxeus and Althaea.

1284 *Speed it as I send it for thy sake, / Goddess.* Atalanta addresses Artemis, the virginal goddess of the hunt.

1296/98, 1304–06 *Hyleus, Peleus, Eurytion, Amphiaraus.* Members of the hunting party, with Meleager and Atalanta.

[Althaea's Final Words, having Burnt the Brand]

1943–44 *My name is gone, / My name that was a healing.* In Greek, *Althaia* (which also refers to the medicinal marsh mallow) is derived from the verb *althainein*, 'to heal'.

CHASTELARD

For a summary of the plot, see the Introductory Notes to the Longer Works. The numbering of lines begins in each extract as a new series, since the whole of *Chastelard* was never printed with line numbers.

A Ballad of Life

76 *Borgia.* Lucrezia Borgia, the paradigmatic Renaissance *femme fatale.*

A Ballad of Death

41 *Upon her raiment of dyed sendaline.* Sendaline (sendal): a type of delicate silk used in clothing.

Laus Veneris

The poem is based on the legend of Tannhäuser, the thirteenth-century German poet who was said to have discovered the 'Venusberg', the hill under which Venus had been residing since the coming of Christianity and the consequent end of her worship. Tannhäuser lives there, worshipping the goddess, for some time. Eventually he departs and makes pilgrimage to Rome, where he asks the Pope for absolution. The Pope replies that his wooden staff would sooner blossom again than God would forgive Tannhäuser's sins. The staff does blossom, but only after Tannhäuser has already returned in despair to the Venusberg.

[Title]. 'The Praise of Venus' (Latin).

[Epigraph]. This is of Swinburne's own invention, written in pastiche Renaissance French. The following translation has been provided by Arabella Milbank:

> Then said he all in tears; Alas, too too unhappy man and curséd sinner, never will I know the clemency and mercy of God. Now will I go forth and hide myself in Mount Horsel, appealing for favour and loving pity to my sweet Lady Venus, for it is for love of her that I will be damned forever to Hell. Thus end all my feats of arms and all my lovely songs. Alas, too lovely were the face and the eyes of my lady, how evil the day wherein I beheld these things. So, groaning, he left and returned to her, and lived sadly there in great love close to his lady. It came to pass afterwards that one day the Pope saw burst from his rod many lovely red and white flowers, and many buds,

and so he saw the whole bark flourish green again. He was greatly afeared by this, and much moved, and had great pity of this knight who had departed without hope, as a man miserable and damned. Therefore he sent many messengers to him to bring him back, saying that he would have from God grace and full absolution from his great sin of love. But never more did he see him, for this poor knight remained ever close to Venus, the high and mighty goddess, between the flanks of love's mount.

25 *Inside the Horsel here the air is hot.* Mount Horsel is the Venusberg. See Swinburne's epigraph, above.

193–96 *I see the marvellous mouth whereby there fell / Cities and people whom the gods loved well.* The reference is to Helen and the Trojan War.

197–98 *And softer than the Egyptian lote-leaf is, / The queen whose face was worth the world to kiss.* The reference is to Cleopatra. 'Worth the world' refers to the neglect and loss of the Roman Empire by Marc Antony through his love-alliance with the Egyptian queen; Swinburne probably has in mind several passages from Shakespeare's *Antony and Cleopatra.*

199–204 *And large pale lips of strong Semiramis.* Semiramis: a legendary ancient Assyrian queen associated with sensual excesses; she appears, for instance, in the fifth canto of the *Inferno* of Dante.

252 *Teen.* Pain, grief.

257 *An one that hath a plague-mark on his brows.* i.e. 'like one who hath...' ('an' being used in the archaic sense 'as though').

267 *Slotwise.* From 'slot', meaning the track of an animal.

271–72 *And lo, one springe and you are fast in hell, / Fast as the gin's grip of a wayfarer.* 'Gin' and 'springe': snares.

[Latin]. *EXPLICIT LAUS VENERIS.* 'Here endeth the Praise of Venus'. Swinburne imitates the medieval habit of closing texts with formulaic Latin markers.

The Triumph of Time

321–336 *There lived a singer in France of old … And so drew back, and the man was dead.* This alludes to the story of the troubadour poet Jaufré Rudel. According to the legendary account of his life, he joined the Second Crusade in order to see the fabled beauty of Hodierna of Jerusalem and Tripoli (wife of Raymond II of Tripoli). Taken ill on the way, he arrives at Tripoli on the verge of death; Hodierna hears of this, and comes down to see him, so that he dies in her arms. The French setting is Provence (the 'midland sea' is the Mediterranean), and the 'land of sand and ruin and gold' is the Levant.

Les Noyades

The poem alludes to the 'Noyades' (Drownings) of Nantes, a gruesome episode during the Revolutionary Reign of Terror in France. In 1793–94, Jean-Baptiste Carrier (mentioned by name in Swinburne's poem), in his function as Revolutionary representative to Nantes, ordered and supervised the mass execution in that town of several thousand supposed anti-revolutionaries by drowning in the Loire. There were reports of the stripping and binding together of male and female victims before drowning, a practice that became known as 'republican marriage'. It is this to which Swinburne refers.

Anactoria

The speaker in this poem is the ancient Greek lyric poet, Sappho of Lesbos, who addresses a female lover, Anactoria.

[Greek Epigraph]. 'From whom, through persuasion, have you recklessly (or vainly) caught up love?' This is Swinburne's own emendation of the lines from Sappho's 'Hymn to Aphrodite', texts of which differ significantly in their readings.

22 *Erotion or Erinna.* Names which occur in Sappho's poems. Erinna was another female poet in Lesbos; Erotion is a male name (see Swinburne's poem 'Erotion', from *Poems and Ballads*, 1866).

59–62 *Ah, take no thought for Love's sake … she forgives.* Sappho suggests that Anactoria is afraid of having incurred the wrath of Aphrodite because she has been unfaithful to Sappho in love; but Sappho claims to be on good terms with the goddess, who will therefore forgive the transgression.

63–64 *For I beheld in sleep the light that is / In her high place in Paphos.* Sappho describes a vision she has had of Aphrodite, at Paphos, one of the goddess's traditional seats.

86 *Shall not my songs assuage her at the heart? [etc.].* i.e. Venus will be appeased by Sappho's intercessions for Anactoria (in the form of her love songs), and so forgive her faithlessness for Sappho's sake.

121 *Yea, though their alien kisses do me wrong.* Refers to Anactoria's liaisons with lovers other than Sappho.

200 *High Pierian Flower.* i.e. the poet's wreath, awarded by the Muses (who reside at the Pierian Spring).

205 *That lordlier leaf.* The poet's bay or laurel leaf.

N.B. Cecil Y. Lang's critical notes to this poem in the second (revised) edition of his anthology, *The Pre-Raphaelites and Their Circle* (Chicago, 1975) are well worth consulting (pp. 522–24).

Hymn to Proserpine

In Greco-Roman mythology, Persephone (Proserpine in Latin) was the daughter of Zeus and Demeter. As a young girl she was abducted by the underworld god Hades (or Pluto) while she was gathering flowers (see Swinburne's dramatic monologue 'At Eleusis'). She becomes the wife of Hades/Pluto, and thus a goddess of death; but in Orphic tradition she was also a nature-goddess, maker and destroyer of all things. See also 'The Garden of Proserpine'.

[Subtitle]. *After the proclamation in Rome of the Christian faith.* i.e. in the reign (379–95 A.D.) of the Emperor Theodosius I (the Great), who made Christianity the state religion. Swinburne takes the pagan perspective.

[Latin Epigraph]. *Vicisti, Galilæe.* 'You have won, O Galilean' (compare Swinburne's line: 'Thou hast conquered, O pale Galilean' [l. 35]). The Galilean is, of course, Christ; and these were said to have been the dying words in 363 A.D. of the Roman Emperor Julian (the Apostate), who had turned his back on the dominant religion of Christianity and attempted to reinstate the pagan religious traditions of Rome. At his death, the empire reverted to Christian worship.

**** [Greek quotation].*** 'You are a little soul holding up a corpse'; from the Stoic philosopher Epictetus (55–135 A.D.).

Ilicet

[Title]. 'Let us go', or 'let us have done', or 'let us be hence' (Latin).

Hermaphroditus

As the postscript indicates, this poem is inspired by the late Hellenistic statue of the 'Sleeping Hermaphrodite', known to us through several Roman copies, of which the most famous Swinburne must have seen at the Louvre in Paris (presumably on the date given). In Greek myth, Hermaphroditus was a son of Hermes and Aphrodite. Salmacis (to whom the poem refers in l. **53**) was a nymph whose desire for the boy was not reciprocated. When, in desperation, she prays to the gods to unite them, her wish is miraculously fulfilled, and the two are joined into a single being with two sexes. The most familiar version of this story is provided by Ovid in *Metamorphoses*, Bk 4.

Fragoletta

[Title]. Refers to the French novel of this name (1829) by Henri de Latouche, in which Fragoletta is an hermaphrodite. Compare 'Hermaphroditus', also in *Poems and Ballads*, 1866 (above).

Satia Te Sanguine

[Title]. 'Satiate thee with blood' (Latin). When Cyrus the Great was killed by Thomyris, queen of the Massagetae, she is said to have thrown his severed head into a drinking bowl, with these words.

9–12 The ancient Greek poet Sappho, the most famous inhabitant of Lesbos, was said to have leapt to her death from a promontory on the island of Leucas (or Leucadia), in an agony of love for Phaon. Cf. 'Anactoria' (above) and 'Sapphics' (below).

Anima Anceps

[Title]. 'A divided soul' or 'a divided mind' (Latin). Compare with Clough's long, unfinished poem *Dipsychus* (the Greek title has a similar meaning). The phrase '*anima anceps*' comes from Victor Hugo's *Notre Dame de Paris*, a novel with which Swinburne was very familiar. The archdeacon, frustrated by the failure of his sexual advances, arranges for Esmerelda to be framed for murder. At her execution, the formula '*I* *nunc, anima anceps, et sit tibi Deus misericors!* ('Go now, divided soul, and may God have mercy upon you'), constitutes his final signal to the hangman (Bk 8, ch. 6).

N.B. Swinburne's poem closely shares the form—and the basic theme—of Byron's 'Stanzas' (*incipit* 'Could Love for ever').

In the Orchard

[Subtitle]. *Provençal Burden.* The poem is inspired by a Provençal *alba* (related to the *aubade*, a poem portraying the parting of lovers at dawn). This particular example would later be translated by Pound ('Alba Innominata', *Exultations*, 1909). The original, which has been often included in anthologies of troubadour verse, is the one beginning '*En un vergier, sotz folha d'albespi*'. The refrain is '*Oi Deus, oi Deus, de l'alba! tan tost ve*' ('Ah God, ah God, the dawn! how fast it comes'). Much of Swinburne's poem is, however, of his own invention and not a direct translation. 'Burden' refers to the use of a refrain at the end of the stanzas.

A Match

35–36 *We'd throw with leaves for hours / And draw for days with flowers.* These images are designed to evoke the throwing of dice and the drawing of cards.

Faustine

[Latin Epigraph]. *Ave Faustina Imperatrix, morituri te salutant.* 'Hail, Empress Faustina, those who are about to die salute you': a version of the traditional address of Roman gladiators to the imperial party. In *Notes on Poems and Reviews*, an embattled Swinburne called this poem 'the reverie of a man gazing on the bitter and vicious loveliness of a face as common and as cheap as the morality of reviewers, and dreaming of past lives in which this fair face may have held a nobler or fitter station'. In the same essay, Swinburne claimed that it had been Faustina the Elder, wife of Antoninus Pius, of whom he had originally thought. Yet her daughter, Faustina the Younger, wife of Marcus Aurelius, exceeded her mother in notoriety as a legendary *femme fatale* of sadistic inclinations, luxurious living and grotesque sensual appetites. Since the poem is underlain by a fantasy of reincarnation, it is not illogical that both mother and daughter appear to be invoked; and, indeed, that these Faustines are apparently elided also with the Empress Fausta (see note to ll. 83–84).

83–84 *Yea, even the bath's fierce reek and fume / That slew Faustine.* Neither the Elder nor the Younger Faustina was said to have died in a bath, but Flavia Maxima Fausta, the wife of Constantine the Great, was supposedly murdered in 326 A.D. by being suffocated in a steam bath. Taken together with the preceding stanzas, however, this image of the bath may also evoke the story recorded by Cassius Dio that Faustina the Younger once bathed in the blood of a gladiator for whom she had conceived a passion.

117–18 *Stray breaths of Sapphic song that blew / Through Mitylene.* An allusion to Sappho, who resided at Mitylene, on Lesbos.

130 *Epicene.* A person of ambiguous sex; androgyne.

146 *The Lampsacene.* The god Priapus, who was said to have been born at Lampsacus, a city on the eastern shore of the Hellespont.

The Leper

40 *For my sweet fault that scandals them.* The implication is that she has already consummated an illicit love-affair with the knight. That she will no longer need to fear rumours of her shame might suggest, further, the nature of the knight's words, which we do not hear.

43–44 *The third, / A sweeter thing than these, I said.* i.e. the third of the 'three thoughts' announced in l. 25; 'these' are the two thoughts (or memories) already described.

97–98 *Too sweet, for the least part in her, / To have shed life out by fragments.* i.e. for the clerk to have contracted leprosy for the lady's sake, which he would glady have suffered: this is *not* his regret.

119–20 *But that new shame could make love new / She saw not—yet her shame did make.* Although the poem suggests an erotic relationship between the clerk and the lady, these lines (and the previous stanza) suggest that the lady had no love for him. The last four words are deliberately ambiguous; but the lady is the subject of the verb, and shame the object.

[French Coda]. As in 'Laus Veneris', this feigned quotation is of Swinburne's invention. The following translation is offered by Arabella Milbank:

At that time there were in the land a great number of white and black lepers, which greatly displeased the King, since by this it appeared that God must be very grievously angered. One day it happened that a noble damsel named Yolande of Sallières was stricken and ravaged by this evil malady. All her friends and relations, having before their eyes the fear of God, sent her out from their homes, never again wishing to receive or give comfort to her, a thing accursed of God and stinking and abominable before all men. This lady had been very lovely and graceful in form, and her body was ample and formed by a lustful life. However none of the lovers who had many times embraced and kissed her most tenderly wanted now to shelter such an ugly woman and such a hideous sinner. One clerk only, who had in early days been her lackey and her go-between in matters of love, took her in and stowed her in a little hut. There the girl died in great misery and deathly agony. And after her died also the aforesaid clerk, who out of great love had for a space of six months cared for her, washed, dressed and undressed her each day with his own hands. It is even said that this evil man and cursed clerk, recalling the great beauty, now past and ravaged, of this lady, delighted many times in kissing her foul and leprous mouth and embracing her softly with loving hands. Thus he died of this same abominable sickness. This occurred near Fontainebellant in Gastinois. And when King Philip heard this history he marvelled greatly at it.

A Ballad of Burdens

For 'burden', see note to 'In the Orchard' (above); but here it also carries the sense of 'heavy fate'.

Rondel

The 'rondel' is a lyric form with a repeated refrain, as here, though the precise structure varies; it is related to the medieval French lyric form of the 'rondeau', which also varies in scheme. Swinburne later developed his own fixed version of this type of scheme, the 'roundel' (see below, *A Century of Roundels*).

Before the Mirror

[Subtitle]. *Verses written under a picture: Inscribed to J. A. Whistler.* This poem was inspired by Whistler's famous painting *The Little White Girl*, later surtitled *Symphony in White No. 2*. Stanzas 4 and 6 were printed in the exhibition catalogue of the Royal Academy in 1865 to complement the painting, whose original frame displayed the text of the entire poem.

Dolores

[Title]. The female name 'Dolores' is derived from the Latin *dolor* (sorrow, grief).

[Subtitle]. *Notre-Dame des Sept Douleurs.* 'Our Lady of the Seven Sorrows'. In Roman Catholicism, the Virgin Mary has seven joys and seven sorrows, upon which worshippers may meditate while praying the rosary. They are also remembered in various Marian hymns and litanies, the idiom of which Swinburne here parodies. Iconographically, the Virgin of the Seven Sorrows appears stabbed by seven daggers. 'Dolores' is a burlesque sado-masochistic version of the Mother of God in this guise, but she is also recurrently identified with Venus-Aphrodite.

51–52 *Libitina thy mother, Priapus / Thy father, a Tuscan and Greek.* Libitina: an ancient Italian divinity associated with fertility and gardens, sometimes identified with Venus; also associated with death. Priapus: a Greek god of fertility, sexuality and gardens, associated with the image of the phallus; he was the son of Aphrodite by Dionysus. Swinburne imagines his 'Dolores' as the offspring of Libitina and Priapus, but this, of course, is pure fancy with no mythological basis or analogy.

223–24 *And they hailed thee re-risen, O Thalassian, / Foam-white, from the foam.* The 'Thalassian' (an epithet derived from the Greek *thalassa*, 'the sea') is Aphrodite, who was born out of the Ocean. Swinburne evokes the image of 'Venus Anadyomene', the goddess seen rising from the waves.

249–56 This stanza depicts the Emperor Nero, who was said to have played on his lyre while Rome burned.

299ff. *Was it Alciphron once or Arisbe, / Male ringlets or feminine gold, / That thy lips met with under the statue [etc.].* Alciphron was a Greek author of fictitious epistles; Arisbe could refer to several mythological figures, but McGann and Sligh (2004) consider it most likely that Swinburne had in mind the daughter of Macareus, who lived in Lesbos. It is possible, however, that both names are used here without specific referents, their function similar to that of 'Erotion' and 'Erinna' in 'Anactoria'. The 'statue' (possibly a herm) is either of Pan or of Priapus. This imaginary scenario does not seem to constitute a particular allusion.

326 *Ipsithilla.* A lover addressed in Catullus's poem 32, one of the lewdest of his poems. From his bed, where he is 'thrusting through tunic and cloak', he writes to her asking if she will invite him over to spend the afternoon in nine consecutive *fututiones.*

333–36 *From the midmost of Ida … Our Lady, / A goddess new-born.* 'Our Lady' refers to the ancient Phrygian goddess Cybele; Ida is a mountain in Phrygia associated with her. Cybele was a mother-goddess associated with fertility and sexuality; her worship was orgiastic, and her cult was observed by castrated priests known as *Galli.*

340 *And Catullus makes mouths at our speech.* Catullus: one of the most passionate, frank and racy of the Roman love poets. Swinburne held him in high regard. His poem 63 tells the story of the boy Attis, who becomes one of Cybele's eunuch followers.

345–48 *Out of Dindymus heavily laden … A queen over death and the dead.* Dindymus or Dindyma: a mountain in Phrygia sacred to Cybele. In these stanzas the attributes of Cybele are designed also to evoke the imagery of the Virgin Mary.

379–80 *Thy prophet, thy preacher, thy poet, / Sin's child by incestuous Death?* The reference is to the Marquis de Sade. The incest of Sin and Death recalls Milton's *Paradise Lost* (Bk II, 746–814).

405 *In Lampsacus fervent with faces.* Lampsacus: birthplace of Priapus and a centre of his worship.

406 *In Aphaca red from thy reign.* Aphaca was a town in ancient Syria famous for the excesses of its worship of Aphrodite Aphacitis, the local manifestation of Aphrodite (whose temple there was destroyed by Constantine). Her worship was strong in Aphaca because it was there that her lover Adonis was supposed to have died, and he was worshipped along with the goddess. The river was said to turn red each year with his blood.

409–10 *Cotytto or Venus, / Astarte or Ashtaroth.* Cotys or Cotytto: a Goddess of ancient Thrace, later worshipped in Athens and Corinth; her festivals were apparently orgiastic, and in this respect her cult was similar to that of Cybele. Astarte and Ashtaroth are variant names of an ancient Mesopotamian goddess of fertility and sexuality (and sometimes war), associated with the moon and with the evening star (Venus); hence she is closely related to the the Greco-Roman Aphrodite-Venus.

[Footnote]. **Nam te præcipuè in suis urbibus colit ora / Hellespontia, cæteris ostreosior oris.* [CATULL. *Carm.* xviii.]. 'For in its cities, the Hellespontian coast—richer in oysters than all other coasts—worships you in especial'. The address is to Priapus. The lines come from a fragment now no longer widely thought to be a genuine work of Catullus.

The Garden of Proserpine

Proserpine is a benign underworld divinity, and here stands for the comfort and peace of death. See notes to 'Hymn to Proserpine' (above) and 'At Eleusis' (below).

The Sundew

The sundew is a fleshy insectivorous flowering marsh plant which thrives in boggy coastal areas; Swinburne may have seen them near his family home on the Isle of Wight. Some doubt has been cast over the question of how much Swinburne would have known by 1866 about the sundew's carnivorous habits (which were apparently not widely known until later), but the poem seems evidently to take it for granted.

Félise

[French Epigraph]. *Mais où sont les neiges d'antan?* The refrain of one of the most celebrated *ballades* from Villon's *Testament*. This *ballade* was famously translated by D. G. Rossetti as the 'Ballad of Dead Ladies'. Rossetti renders the refrain: 'But where are the snows of yesteryear?'

Hendecasyllabics

Hendecasyllabics are eleven-syllable lines, and Swinburne is closely following the Latin hendecasyllabic metre (*phalaeceans*) closely associated with Catullus. The metrical pattern is the same in each line, but for a couple of minor permissable variations. In quantitative prosody (in Latin, that is), where '—' is long, 'u' is short and 'x' is an '*anceps*' (can be either long or short), the pattern is as follows:

x x — u u —   u — u — x

The standard form is:

— x — u u — u — u — —

(In Latin, the first two syllables in the latter *schema* may, however, be reversed.) Although the idea of prosodic 'length' is still, to a certain extent, relevant in Swinburne, nevertheless the easiest way to understand the matter is to consider Swinburne's hendecasyllabics as a stress-based equivalent of the Latin metre, where length becomes stress (and short becomes unstressed). Owing to the difficulty of reproducing successive stresses in English, Swinburne tends to scan thus (where '/' is stressed and 'u' unstressed):

/ u / u u / u / u / u

It has been suggested (see McGann and Sligh, 2004, p. 481) that Swinburne's poem recalls and significantly transforms Catullus 46.

Sapphics

On the prosodic principles, see the note foregoing; as in *Hendecasyllabics*, Swinburne substitutes stress for length. The sapphic stanza is made up of three hendecasyllabic lines (but of a different type from the *phalaecean*), followed by a shorter line at the end. The sapphic hendecasyllable runs thus:

— u — x — u u — u — —

In the Latin version of the sapphic hendecasyllable, the *anceps* here (fourth syllable) is usually and preferably long. This is not easy to achieve in English verse, and yet Swinburne—a devotee of Catullus as well as of Sappho—does show signs of an inclination toward this Latin use. Swinburne's lines therefore sometimes give the impression of beginning with two trochees, yet in many cases one can feel the attempt to make the fourth syllable emphatic, often through a combination of vocalic length and syntactic accent. For example, in line 1, '… night sleep came …' gives three successive stresses. After three of these hendecasyllabic lines, the final short line in each stanza scans thus:

— u u — —

This metre is (of course) associated with Sappho, but was also used in Latin by Catullus and Horace. Sappho's famous 'Hymn to Aphrodite' (*Lobel-Page* 1) is the major source of inspiration for this poem, or rather the object of Swinburne's celebratory pastiche, which puts Sappho into the role in which she herself had placed Aphrodite.

30 *Ah the tenth, the Lesbian! the nine were silent.* Sappho (of Lesbos) was traditionally hailed as 'the tenth muse'. 'Lesbian' here scans as two syllables, not three.

At Eleusis

The speaker of this dramatic monologue, which shows the influence of both Tennyson and Landor, is Demeter, the Greco-Roman goddess of the harvest and agriculture, whose daughter was the abducted Persephone (Proserpine: see notes to 'Hymn to Proserpine' and 'The Garden of Proserpine', above). According to myth, Demeter wandered for nine days searching for her daughter, and learnt of her fate on the tenth day from Hecate. Failing to solicit the help of Zeus, Demeter turned her back on Olympus and, taking mortal guise, went to Eleusis (a town in Attica), where she resided for some time. The poem is set during this period. It is partly inspired by the Homeric *Hymn to Demeter.*

28ff. *For as ill men by drugs or singing words / Shut the doors inward of the narrowed womb … Thus I shut up the body and sweet mouth / Of all soft pasture and the tender land.* Demeter refers to the magical practices by which women's fertility could be debilitated. As goddess of agriculture, she, by analogy, curses the land.

71 *For Hades and the sidelong will of Zeus.* Hades is the abductor of Persephone; Zeus her father, who refuses to order her return (although later he would change his mind).

115 *With competence of gold.* Competence = plenty.

146–47 *In care of this my choice, this child my choice, / Triptolemus, the king's selected son.* Grateful for her hospitable treatment at Eleusis, Demeter designs to take one of the sons of Celeus, King of Eleusis, under her care and turn him into a god. In order for this to be achieved, the child, Triptolemus, must be regularly burnt in a fire. He is unharmed by this, but his suspicious mother steals upon them one night, and screams, with the result that the baby becomes afraid and the whole process is immediately nullified. This, at least, is Swinburne's version of a myth with many variations.

209 *Sad-tressed and pleached.* Pleached = interlaced.

214–15 *This Celeus dead and swathed / Purple and pale for golden burial.* i.e. 'when King Celeus is dead—'. He will be succeeded by his son, Triptolemus, with whom Demeter is still intimate.

St. Dorothy

The poem retells the legend of St Dorothy of Caesarea, virgin and martyr of the fourth century A.D.

4 *Shawm-playing.* A shawm is a horn-shaped medieval woodwind instrument with a soft, oboe-like sound.

24 *They called it in their tongue lampadias.* Lampadias: Latin (from Greek): a comet resembling a torch.

29–31 *Waters Gaditane … (This was the place of sea-rocks under Spain / Called after the great praise of Hercules).* i.e. the sea along the coast of Gades (modern Cadiz) in southern Spain, near the 'Pillars of Hercules' at the Gibraltar Strait.

101–04 *For this soft wine that did such grace and good … Was new trans-shaped and mixed with Love's own blood, … That in the fighting Trojan time was bled; … For which came such a woe to Diomed.* In the *Iliad*, Diomedes (following the orders of Athene) pursues Aphrodite and wounds her. In *Iliad*, Bk V, 407–09, Dione comforts Aphrodite by implying that Diomedes will be punished, and will not return home to be welcomed by his children. Swinburne's conceit is that the spilt blood of Aphrodite ('Love') is mixed into the ritual wine, in a pagan parody of the Christian eucharist.

107 *Adonis' blood.* The spilt blood of Adonis, beloved of Aphrodite (Venus), when he received his death-wound from a wild boar. In many accounts, flowers sprang from his blood. See also the note concerning *Aphaca* in 'Dolores' (above).

185 *The house Janiculum.* Apparently the imperial palace. The Janiculum is a hill on the western side of Rome.

188 *Gabalus.* The Emperor Elagabalus (or Heliogabalus; reigned 218–22 A.D.), infamous for sexual, sadistic and religious excesses of all kinds.

191 *Beau sire, Dieu vous aide.* 'Good sir, God help you' (or 'God be with you'). It is of course absurd that French should be spoken in ancient Rome; this is part of Swinburne's archaistic style in the poem, which bears a strong Chaucerian influence.

283 *Such saws.* 'Saws' = words, sayings (a Middle English word).

292–93 *That is a noble scripture, well I weet, / That likens women to an empty can.* Refers to the proverb that says that empty vessels (or cans, barrels) make the loudest noise; and apparently, by extension, that women are noisy because vacuous. Like Theophilus' French greeting, this idiom is anachronistic, and part of the medieval-Renaissance pastiche rather than the Roman setting.

322–23 *Then cried King Gabalus upon his men / To have her forth and draw her with steel gins.* The emperor orders his men to subject Dorothy to the operation of mechanical devices of torture. ('Gins' = engines.)

328–29 *And in good time he gat an evil death / Out of his lewdness with his cursèd wives.* Elagabalus was assassinated at the age of eighteen by the Praetorian Guard (the imperial bodyguard corps). His depravity and corruption had roused the discontent that brought about his downfall; but Swinburne's talk of 'his lewdness with his cursèd wives' is (in the spirit of the pastiche) probably euphemistic: though Elagabalus married and divorced five times, Swinburne is probably alluding to the popular accounts of the emperor's prostituting himself (even in his own palace), and of his homosexual preferences.

382–83 *And on his brows a purfled purple hood, / They may not carry any golden thing.* 'Purfled' = decorated with an embroidered border. Death's brows can bear no golden crown.

435 *Sad and writhled in his face.* 'Writhled' = wrinkled.

The Two Dreams

[Subtitle]. *From Boccaccio.* The story of Andreuola and her lover Gabriotto (here unnamed) is taken from the sixth tale of the fourth day in Boccaccio's *Decameron.*

34 *Some roods away.* Rood = an old English unit of linear measurement, between 16.5 and 24 feet.

74 *The tune's impervious prevalence.* Prevalance = overmastering power.

78 *Turned evenwise with colours musical.* i.e. her face is 'musical' in its colouring in the same way ('evenwise') as the 'tune' with its sound.

124 *And flesh entoiled with mind.* 'Entoiled' = ensnared, captured, tangled together.

165 *Where the green shadow thickliest impleached.* Impleached = interlaced.

238 *Laughed with mere love.* i.e. pure love (from Latin *merus*, 'unmixed').

The King's Daughter

11ff. *May.* Maiden.

55 *And ye'll streek my brother at the side of me.* 'Streek' = stretch out, lay down (i.e. as a dead body in a grave). Scottish and Northern English dialect, to suit the form of the pastiche border ballad.

SONGS BEFORE SUNRISE

Prelude

102 *The tempest of the Thyiades.* Thyiades or Thyades: the orgiastic female worshippers of Dionysus, who went yearly to Mount Parnassus to celebrate his festival.

104 *The blood-feasts of the Bassarid.* See note to *Atalanta*, first choral ode.

117–18 *That called on Cotys by her name / Edonian.* For Cotys, see notes to 'Dolores'. The Edoni were a Thracian people (although the word was used poetically for the Thracians in general). They were also associated with Dionysus, and *edonis* in Roman poetry could refer to a female Bacchante. Cotys was a Thracian goddess, worshipped with revelry comparable with that of the cult of Dionysus.

Hertha

[Title]. 'Hertha' was a Germanic earth- and fertility-goddess.

63–64 *Prophet nor poet / Nor tripod nor throne.* The Delphic Oracle of Apollo delivered prophecies in poetic form from atop a 'tripod' seat.

99 *The life-tree am I.* A reference to the Tree of Life, Yggdrasil, which in Nordic mythology connects the earth with the heavens.

Before a Crucifix

48 *These that have not forsaken thee. / Thy faith [etc].* i.e. the priesthood, the Church: Swinburne's primary target here.

For a summary of the plot, see the Introductory Notes to the Longer Works. On the line numbering (which refers to the given extracts, not to the play as a whole), see note to *Chastelard*, above.

From Act 1, scene 3 [The Queen grants audience to John Knox].

[Dram. Pers.]. John Knox (1514–72): major Scottish Protestant reformer.

46–48 *And for him too, your husband, it may be / That as he spares not to dishonour God / For your delight, by service of the mass.* Knox refers to Henry Stuart, Lord Darnley, who had married Mary in 1565. He suggests that Darnley has been supporting and participating in Mary's Roman Catholic worship.

From Act 2, scene 1 [Escape from Holyrood].

Mary is to escape along with Darnley, whom she has, through skillful manipulation, persuaded to abandon the nobles who had murdered David Rizzio at his will (see note to 3.2, below). These, however, have control over Mary at the Palace of Holyrood.

52 *Lay hard hand on a woman weak with child.* Mary had been pregnant with the future James VI and I at the time of Rizzio's murder, when she had been manhandled by the assassins.

59 *Lo, here their aim was [etc.].* In the play, Mary had been threatened with a pistol during the murder of Rizzio.

71–74 *I purpose with the man's help—nay, what name / Shall his be now? [etc.].* i.e. Darnley.

From Act 2, scene 9 [The Queen's illness at Jedburgh].

Mary is ill after having ridden from Jedburgh to visit the wounded Bothwell at Hermitage Castle, and back again to Jedburgh—some considerable distance—in inclement weather. Both the notorious ride and the illness are historical, although the severity of the illness makes a causal relationship unlikely. By now her affair with Bothwell (James

Hepburn, fourth Earl) is well established.

9ff. *I know you who you are; / You were about me thus in our first days [etc.].* The queen's ladies in waiting, the 'three Maries'—Mary Beaton, Mary Seaton and Mary Carmichael—had been her companions and playmates in childhood.

163 *Enter* MURRAY. James Stuart, Earl of Murray (Moray), Mary's half-brother. He will later act as Regent in the infancy of James VI, following Mary's forced abdication in 1567.

From Act 2, scene 15 [Bothwell Meditates the Murder of Darnley (I)].

Darnley would be murdered, supposedly on the orders of Bothwell and Mary, at Kirk o' Field, Edinburgh, on 9 February 1567. There were two explosions near Darnley's quarters, but Darnley was apparently killed subsequently by other means.

From Act 2, scene 18 [Bothwell Meditates the Murder of Darnley (II)].

5 *Arthur's Seat.* The crest of a hill overlooking Edinburgh.

From Act 3, scene 2 [The Queen takes her leave of the murdered Darnley].

37 *By David whom he slew.* David Rizzio was Mary's private secretary, rumoured to be her lover, and famously murdered in her presence at Holyrood by a band of assassins, apparently on Darnley's instructions. This event had occurred in Act 1 of *Bothwell.*

From Act 5, scene 2 [The Queen incarcerated at Lochleven].

Mary's marriage to Bothwell, who was widely blamed for the murder of Darnley, had caused considerable discontent. A group of nobles confronted them at Carberry Hill (15 June 1567), where Mary's forces gradually deserted before battle could be joined. Bothwell fled into exile, and Mary was taken into custody. Thereafter she was imprisoned at Lochleven Castle (1567–68). It was here that she was forced to abdicate the Scottish throne. She would later escape.

From Act 5, scene 2 [The Queen is presented with a bond to sign].

This is the bond by which Mary was made to consent to her abdication in favour of her son, James VI, under the regency of her half-brother, Murray.

[Dram. Pers.]. *Lindsay and Ruthven.* Patrick Lindsay, sixth Lord Lindsay, and Patrick Ruthven, third Lord Ruthven. Both of these courtiers had been among the band of Darnley's supporters who had murdered David Rizzio (see note to 3.2). Ruthven was supposedly the leader of the attack. Mary has not seen them since the time of the murder.

15–16 *The place and name of regent through this realm / To the earl of Murray shall you here assign.* See above.

35–37 *Where my grandsire fell … was there none / That bore on Flodden, sirs, such names as yours.* At the Battle of Flodden in 1513, the Scottish army led by James IV (Mary's grandfather) had been defeated by the English forces, and James had been killed on the field. Mary mocks the disloyal Lindsay and Ruthven by suggesting that they are not worthy descendants of their ancestors who had made the heroic last stand in defence of James IV.

From Act 5, scene 4 [The Queen's conference with Murray, appointed Regent of Scotland].

11–12 *When your lord / Lay newly murdered.* i.e. Darnley.

14–16 *And yield up / That head to judgment which the whole world held / Blood-guilty.* i.e., Mary should have given up Bothwell for public trial after the murder of Darnley, for which he was generally held responsible. Her protection of him has turned the country against her.

20–22 *To put upon this loathing land / That great dishonour to behold and bear / The man your lover for its lord.* Murray refers to Mary's marriage to Bothwell, whose status as royal consort was unacceptable to the people of the 'land'.

44–47 *Ere that day had risen / Which gave the mockery of a ravished bride / To the false violence of his fraudful rape / That hardly she could feign to fear.* In April 1567, Bothwell and his militia 'abducted' Mary; their marriage followed in May. Murray suggests that the abduction was a pretence (which, in this play, indeed it is).

100–02 *But let your tears be rather as were hers / That wept upon the feet of God, and bought / With that poor price her pardon.* i.e. Mary Magdalene.

From Act 5, scene 11 [The Queen flees from the Battle of Langside].

After escaping from Lochleven and raising forces in her support, Mary met the forces of Murray at the Battle of Langside (13 May 1568). The battle was brief and Mary was easily defeated.

16ff. *O, thou that wast / My hate and husband [etc.].* An apostrophe to the shade of Darnley.

POEMS AND BALLADS, SECOND SERIES

The Complaint of Lisa

[Subtitle]. *Double Sestina.* An ordinary sestina is a poem in six stanzas each containing six lines, in which the words ending each line are repeated in every stanza, but in a different order each time; the poem then ends with a three-line *envoi* containing all six end-words. Swinburne's 'double sestina', a formal *tour de force*, doubles the number of lines in each stanza, and thus has twelve rotating end-words (all included in the *envoi*).

[Subtitle 2]. *Decameron, X. 7.* This dramatic monologue is very loosely based on an episode from the seventh tale of the tenth day in Boccaccio's *Decameron.*

54–69 *I read long since the bitter tale of her / Who read the tale of Launcelot on a day, / And died [etc.] … Yet if being wroth God had such pity on her, / Who was a sinner and foolish in her day, / That even in hell they twain should breathe one breath [etc.].* The reference is to Francesca da Rimini and her lover, Paolo, who begin their love-affair while reading the story of Lancelot and Guinevere. Eventually her husband catches them together and kills them both. In Hell, Dante finds the lovers burning in an eternal embrace (*Inferno* V), and Swinburne is recalling this famous episode from the *Commedia.*

Ave Atque Vale

[Title]. 'Hail and Farewell' (Latin); the final words from Catullus's elegy to his dead brother (poem 101).

[Subtitle]. *In memory of Charles Baudelaire.* Strangely enough, Baudelaire was not dead when Swinburne began this poem (in May

1867). Swinburne had heard a mistaken report. Baudelaire, however, only survived until August, and was dead by the time the poem first appeared in print, in the *Fortnightly Review* in January 1868. Swinburne never met Baudelaire, but had been a zealous enthusiast for his works since the early 1860s.

[French Epigraph]. 'But we should take some flowers to him. The dead, the poor dead, they know great sorrows; and when October, the stripper of old trees, blows its melancholic wind around their stones, they must surely find the living most ungrateful'. From Baudelaire's poem 'La Servante au Grand Coeur' (in which one should translate 'her' for 'him').

15–17 *Lesbian promontories … Leucadian grave.* See note (above) to 'Satia te Sanguine', ll. 9–12.

120–21 *And lay, Orestes-like, across the tomb / A curl of severed hair.* In Greek mythology, Orestes returns to Argos to avenge the death of his father, Agamemnon. At the very start of the *Choephoroi* of Aeschylus, Orestes arrives *incognito* and presents a lock of his hair to Agamemnon's tomb.

122–24 *But by no hand nor any treason stricken, / Not like the low-lying head of Him, the King, / The flame that made of Troy a ruinous thing.* The comparison is with Agamemnon, who was treacherously murdered by his wife, Clytemnestra, upon his return to Argos from the Trojan War in which he had been the commander of the Greeks.

129 *Thee not Orestes, not Electra mourns.* Orestes and Electra were the children of Agamemnon and Clytemnestra.

133–54 The 'lord of light' is Apollo.

157–60 *That obscure Venus of the hollow hill, / That thing transformed which was the Cytherean, … and face no more called Erycine.* Reference to the legend of the Venusberg (see notes, above, to 'Laus Veneris'). The 'Cytherean' is Aphrodite-Venus, who had one of her two most important cultic centres on the island of Cythera. She also took the epithet 'Erycina' after the mountain in Sicily named Eryx, on the summit of which was a famous temple to her. Baudelaire had published a pamphlet entitled *Richard Wagner et Tannhauser à Paris* (1861), which Swinburne praises in *Notes on Poems and Reviews* (1866), although he claims that he had not seen it until after the completion of his own 'Laus Veneris'.

166 *And now no sacred staff shall break in blossom.* See notes to 'Laus Veneris' (above).

192 *With sadder than the Niobean womb.* In Greek mythology, Niobe boasted of her fourteen children to the goddess Leto, who punished her for her pride by sending her own two children, Apollo and Artemis, to murder all of Niobe's seven sons and seven daughters, after which Niobe wept incessantly and was turned to stone.

TRANSLATIONS FROM THE FRENCH OF VILLON

François Villon, France's most famous poet of the late medieval period, flourished in Paris in the mid-fifteenth century. He received a degree from the University of Paris in 1449, but subsequently became involved with criminals and the Paris low-life—the world of thieves, brothels and taverns. His great long poem was the *Testament*. He was a great favourite with Swinburne, Rossetti and their circle, and would continue to be a canonical author in the English Aesthetic Movement and Decadence, as well as for the Modernists (especially Pound, Bunting and Wyndham Lewis).

The Complaint of the Fair Armouress

This lament of 'la Belle Heaulmière' is one of the most celebrated passages of the *Testament* (§§ 50–59).

N.B. Lines **54–56** and **70–72** were censored (replaced by asterisks) in the original text of 1878, and only lines **71–72** were restored in the 1904 *Poems*, which the present edition usually follows. The remaining lines were restored posthumously by T. J. Wise, and have been included here.

Ballad against the Enemies of France

1–2 *May he fall in with beasts that scatter fire, / Like Jason, when he sought the fleece of gold.* In Greek mythology (and especially in the *Argonautica* of Apollonius Rhodius), the *khalkotauroi* were enormous fire-breathing bulls. King Aeetes of Colchis promised to give Jason the Golden Fleece if he could plough a field with these bulls, and sow it with dragons' teeth.

3–4 *Or change from man to beast three years entire, / As King Nebuchadnezzar did of old.* Nebuchadnezzar II was humbled by God and lost his sanity for seven years, during which he lived like a wild beast (*Daniel* 4). It is unclear why Swinburne changes the number of years to three; Villon has seven.

9 *With worse to bear than Job's worst sufferance.* A general reference to the *Book of Job*.

18–19 *Or swing down pendulous / Like Absalom with locks luxurious.* In *2 Samuel*, Absalom, famous for his luxuriant hair, rebelled against his father David and, at the Battle of Ephraim's Wood, became caught by his head and hair in the high branches of a tree whilst riding beneath it. In this vulnerable position he was killed by Joab.

20 *Or liker Judas fallen to reprobance.* In the Bible, Judas Iscariot variously hanged himself (*Matthew* 27.3–10) or fell down and 'burst asunder' (*Acts* 1.18–19).

21 *Or find such death as Simon sorcerous.* Simon the Sorcerer (Simon Magus), who was traditionally said to have died whilst magically flying through the air; the prayers of St Peter interrupted the charm, and Simon fell to his death.

23–24 *May the old times come of fierce Octavian's ire, / And in his belly molten coin be told.* There are many stories from classical antiquity of execution by the pouring of molten gold down the throat; but in no case is Octavian (i.e. Augustus) responsible. Villon says only 'the *time* of Octavian', and does not refer to his 'ire'.

25–26 *May he like Victor in the mill expire, / Crushed between moving millstones on him rolled.* St Victor of Marseilles was martyred by being crushed by a millstone, or else (as Villon has it) ground between two millstones.

31–32 *And cursed of God most high to the utterance, / As was the Syrian king Antiochus.* The reference is to the Syrian king Antiochus IV Epiphanes, as recorded in *2 Maccabees*, 9: 'But the Lord Almighty, the God of Israel, smote him with an incurable and invisible plague' (9.5). Villon's original, however, refers instead to King Sardanapalus. Editors had suggested that Villon must have meant Antiochus (see the 1832 Paris edn by J. H. R. Prompsault, p. 337); but some texts have Villon referring (by name) to the god Mars, so that the reference to Sardanapalus—who is said to have been driven to such desperation in war that he burnt himself alive on a huge pyre along with his household—makes sense.

34–35 *May the bright-winged brood of Æolus / To sea-king Glaucus' wild wood cavernous [etc.].* In Greek mythology, Aeolus was the god and ruler of the winds; Glaucus, a sea-god.

The Epitaph in form of a Ballad which Villon made for himself and his comrades, expecting to be hanged along with them.

One of Villon's most famous independent poems. After brawling in the street, Villon was arrested in 1462, and with several earlier unexpiated crimes to his name, he was sentenced to death by hanging. The sentence was dropped later, but Villon was banished from Paris. This *ballade* had apparently been composed in the interim.

34 *Be not ye therefore of our fellowhead.* 'Fellowhead' is not in the *OED*, but its meaning is apparent from the context. The sense of the syntax is, however, less obvious. The penultimate line entails a shift of address, from Christ back to the people of Paris ('ye' is plural). The lines should probably be construed thus: 'Therefore let there be no-one among our own fellow men [in comparison with Christ] who does not pray to God that he forgive us all'.

STUDIES IN SONG

By the North Sea

The scene is along the Suffolk coast around Dunwich, a once-prosperous Anglo-Saxon town which had succumbed over the centuries to coastal erosion, so that many of its buildings (including the churchyard depicted in § 1) had been swept into or submerged under the encroaching sea.

105–12 *In the valley he named of decision [etc.].* See *Joel* 3, esp. ch. 14–16: 'Multitudes, multitudes in the valley of decision: for the day of the LORD is near in the valley of decision. The sun and the moon shall be darkened, and the stars shall withdraw their shining. The Lord also shall roar out of Zion, and utter his voice from Jerusalem; and the heavens and the earth shall shake: but the LORD will be the hope of His people, and the strength of the children of Israel'.

TRISTRAM OF LYONESSE

For a summary of the plot, see the Introductory Notes to the Longer Works.

From Book 2 [Iseult of Ireland is abducted by Sir Palamede and rescued by Sir Tristram].

106 *From lips not his.* King Mark has unwittingly spent the preceding night, his wedding-night, with Iseult's handmaid Brangwain (by her trickery), while Iseult has spent the night with Tristram.

141 *Not as that white queen's of the virgin hunt [etc.].* The reference is to Artemis (Diana).

158–59 *For the knight / Forth was once ridden toward some frontier fight [etc.].* This refers to Tristram, who is for this reason away from the Cornish court during Sir Palamede's sojourn.

From Book 3 [Sir Tristram, exiled in Brittany, encounters Iseult of the Fair Hands].

When Tristram sings his songs to 'Iseult' (meaning, of course, Iseult of Ireland), Iseult of the Fair Hands begins to imagine that he is singing to her.

Book 5: Iseult at Tintagel

N.B. Iseult of Ireland, the speaker in this canto, knows nothing of Tristram's marriage to Iseult of the White Hands, which is taking place at the same time in Brittany.

From Book 9 [Tristram, dying in Brittany, sends Ganhardine to bring Iseult of Ireland from Cornwall].

Ganhardine is the brother of Iseult of the Fair Hands, and hence Tristram's brother-in-law.

224–25ff. *Or Merlin's holier sleep here hard at hand / Wrapped round with deep soft spells in dim Broceliande [and references following].* The story of Merlin's knowing submission to the magical charms of his beloved, Nimue, to whom he has taught the secrets of his magic, is of recurrent importance in *Tristram*, and a favourite subject of Swinburne's friend, Edward Burne-Jones. Merlin is trapped eternally in a hawthorn tree in the Breton forest of Broceliande. See the Introductory Notes to the Longer Works.

305 *Nay, but then were I / Happier than he whom there thy grace hath found.* Another reference to Merlin, under Nimue's spell.

A CENTURY OF ROUNDELS

The 'roundel' is a fixed form which Swinburne set for himself as a variety of the 'rondeau' or 'rondel' (see note above to 'Rondel'). The metrical composition and length of line varies from poem to poem, but the rhyme-scheme is always the same.

A MIDSUMMER HOLIDAY AND OTHER POEMS

A Midsummer Holiday: VI. The Cliffside Path

11 *Twiring.* Rare word. To 'twire' is to sparkle, twinkle (as in Shakespeare's usage); perhaps also, with a different etymology, to twist, twirl: both meanings are germane here.

15 *Weald.* Woodland or forest.

POEMS AND BALLADS, THIRD SERIES

Night

Michelangelo's reclining allegorical figure of Night, part of the celebrated tomb of Giuliano de' Medici in the Medici Chapel in Florence, occasioned the admiring epigram by Giovanni Strozzi. The second epigram is the sculptor's own reply.

In Time of Mourning

[Date]. *May 1885.* The poem marks the death of one of Swinburne's greatest literary heroes, Victor Hugo.

A Nympholept

'There was a belief among Greeks and Romans … that the mortal who saw the nymph was bereft of his senses: hence the expression [*nympholeptos*] = frenzied' (William Smith, *A Classical Dictionary*, rev. G. E. Marindin, 1919, p. 611). A 'nympholept' is one 'seized', taken or possessed by the nymphs. In Swinburne's Dedicatory Epistle prefacing the collected edition of his *Poems* (1904), he spoke of 'the splendid opression of nature at noon which found utterance of old in words of such singular and everlasting significance as panic and nypholepsy' (p. xxiii). 'Panic', the experience of being seized by Pan, god of the woods and companion of the nymphs and satyrs, is a notion similar to nympholepsy; both are important in Swinburne's poem, which is a celebration of the ecstatic experience of nature. 'Pan' here is both the woodland god and the Great God Pan, an all-pervading nature god and symbol of paganism. He inspires in the speaker both veneration and 'panic'.

54–55 *Tongueless as she whom a man-snake stung, / Whose heart now heaves in the nightingale.* i.e. Philomela (see note to *Atalanta*, first choral ode).

136 *Where Typho labours.* Typhon (or Typhoneus): in Greek mythology, a primitive monster, the son of Gaia (Earth). He fought against Zeus in defence of the Titans, but was defeated and imprisoned in the earth (under Mount Etna, in many versions). Hence he was a manifestation of volcanic eruption and earthquake.

Loch Torridon

In the West Highlands of Scotland. Swinburne had visited Torridon on a tour of Scotland with the Oxford theologian and classicist Benjamin Jowett and a party of fellow Balliol men, in the summer of 1871. The memory of this time formed the basis of the much later poem, dedicated to Edwin Harrison, who had been a member of the touring party.

The Lake of Gaube

The Lac de Gaube is near Cauterets in the French Pyrenees, close to the Spanish border. Swinburne had visited the area and swum in the lake in 1862—many years before the composition of the poem.

Roundel

For the form, see notes (above) for *A Century of Roundels.*

[Subtitle]. *From the French of Villon.* The original French 'lay' or *rondeau* is found in Villon's *Testament* (§ 102); the form is quite different.

Further Reading

Early editions of Swinburne's individual works are, on the whole, not too scarce; the best known works are common in secondhand bookshops. The 1904 complete edition of the *Poems* in six volumes, edited by Swinburne himself, can be found without much difficulty, and sets are rarely expensive. The later, larger 'Bonchurch' edition of the *Complete Works* (20 vols, 1925–27, ed. Gosse and Wise) is much less reliable, but is, at least, not limited to the 'poetry'. There was a six-volume edition of the *Tragedies* (London, 1905), and also a later, single-volume American edition; but both are far less common than the *Poems*. Of critical selections currently in print, there is a Yale edition of *Major Poems and Selected Prose*, with ample notes, edited by Jerome McGann and Charles L. Sligh (2004), and a Penguin paperback edition of *Poems and Ballads and Atalanta in Calydon*, edited by Kenneth Haynes, also with notes (2000). An Oxford World's Classics edition by Francis O'Gorman, which will include prose and drama as well as verse, is forthcoming at the time of writing. Some of Swinburne's critical work is conveniently collected in *Swinburne as Critic*, edited by Clyde K. Hyder (1972). Hyder also edited *Swinburne: The Critical Heritage* (1970), which collects important reviews and early critical responses. Swinburne's correspondence was edited by Cecil Y. Lang, *The Swinburne Letters*, 6 vols (Yale, 1959–62), and this has been supplemented by Terry L. Meyers (ed.), *The Uncollected Letters of Algernon Charles Swinburne* (London, 2005).

Important monographs on Swinburne, biographical and critical, include those by Humphry Hare (1949), John A. Cassidy (1964), Jean Overton Fuller (1968), Jerome McGann (1971), Philip Henderson (1974), David G. Riede (1978), Donald Thomas (1979), Margot K. Louis (1990), Rikky Rooksby (1997), and Catherine Maxwell (2006). Critically, McGann's peculiar book (composed in dialogue form) is among the most important studies, and Maxwell is currently the standard introduction; from a biographical point of view, Rooksby may be the best place to start. Some of the most recent academic work on Swinburne is found in the volume *Algernon Charles Swinburne: Unofficial Laureate*, edited by Catherine Maxwell and Stefano Evangelista (2013). Earlier biographical studies include the *Life* by Gosse (1917); Mary Disney Leith's *Boyhood of Algernon Charles Swinburne* (1917); Clara Watts-Dunton's *The Home Life of Swinburne* (1922); T. Erle Welby's *Study of Swinburne* (1926); and Georges Lafourcade's *La Jeunesse de Swinburne* (1928).

Index of Titles and First Lines

Titles are set in italic type, first lines in roman.